John Wesley

The works of the Rev. John Wesley

late fellow of Lincoln-College, Oxford

John Wesley

The works of the Rev. John Wesley
late fellow of Lincoln-College, Oxford

ISBN/EAN: 9783743322080

Manufactured in Europe, USA, Canada, Australia, Japa

Cover: Foto ©Thomas Meinert / pixelio.de

Manufactured and distributed by brebook publishing software
(www.brebook.com)

John Wesley

The works of the Rev. John Wesley

WORKS

OF THE

Rev. JOHN WESLEY, M. A.

Late Fellow of *Lincoln-College*, OXFORD.

VOLUME XXIV.

BRISTOL:

Printed by WILLIAM PINE, in *Wine-Street*.
MDCCLXXIII.

A

PLAIN ACCOUNT

OF

CHRISTIAN PERFECTION,

AS BELIEVED AND TAUGHT

By the Rev. Mr. JOHN WESLEY,

From the Year 1725, to the Year 1773.

---

1. WHAT I purpose in the following pages
is, to give a plain and distinct account
of the steps by which I was led, during a course
of many years, to embrace the doctrine of Christian Perfection. This I owe to the serious part
of mankind, those who desire to know all *the
truth as it is in Jesus*. And these only are concerned in questions of this kind. To these I

A 2 would

would nakedly declare the thing as it is: endeavouring all along to shew from one period to another, both *what I thought, and why I thought so.*

2. In the year 1725, being in the twenty-third year of my age, I met with Bp. Taylor's " Rule and exercises of holy living and dying." In reading several parts of this book, I was exceedingly affected: that part in particular which relates to *Purity of Intention.* Instantly I resolved, to dedicate *all my life* to God; *all* my thoughts, and words, and actions; being throughly convinced, there was no medium; but that *every part* of my life, (not *some* only) must either be a sacrifice to God, or myself, that is in effect, to the devil.

Can any serious person doubt of this? or find a medium between serving God and serving the devil?

3. In the year 1726, I met with *Kempis's Christian Pattern.* The nature and extent of *Inward Religion,* the religion of the heart, now appeared to me in a stronger light than ever it had done before. I saw, that giving even *all my life* to God, (supposing it possible to do this and go no farther) would profit me nothing, unless I gave *my heart,* yea, *all my heart,* to him. I saw, that " Simplicity of Intention and Purity of Affection," *one design* in *all* we speak or do, and *one desire* ruling all our tempers, are indeed " the

wings

wings of the foul," without which fhe can never afcend to the mount of God.

4. A year or two after, Mr. Law's " Chriftian Perfection", and " Serious Call" were put into my hands. Thefe convinced me more than ever, of the abfolute impoffibility of being *half a Chriftian*. And I determined, through his grace, (the abfolutely neceffity of which I was deeply fenfible of) to be *all-devoted* to God, to give him *all* my foul, my body, and my fubftance.

Will any confiderate man fay, that this is carrying matters *too far*? Or that any thing *lefs* is due to him, who has given himfelf for us, than to give him ourfelves, *all* we have and *all* we are?

5. In the year 1729, I began not only to read, but to *ftudy* the bible, as the one, the only ftandard of truth, and the only model of pure religion. Hence I faw, in a clearer and clearer light, the indifpenfable neceffity of having *the mind which was in Chrift*, and of *walking as Chrift alfo walked*: even of having, not *fome part* only, but all the mind which was in him, and of walking as he walked, not only in *many* or in *moft* refpects, but in *all* things. And this was the light wherein at this time, I generally confidered religion, as an *uniform* following of Chrift, an *entire* inward and outward conformity to our Mafter. Nor was I afraid of any thing more, than of *bending* this rule to the experience of myfelf, or of other men: of allowing myfelf

in

in any *the least* difconformity to our grand Ex-
ampler.

6. On January 1, 1733, I preached before the
Univerfity, in St. Mary's church, on *the circumcifion of the heart,* an account of which I gave in
thofe words, " It is that habitual difpofition of
foul, which in the facred writings is termed holinefs, and which directly implies, the being
cleanfed from fin, from all filthinefs both of flefh
and fpirit, and by confequence, the being endued
with thofe virtues which were in Chrift Jefus,
the being fo *renewed in the image of our mind,* as
to be *perfect as our Father in heaven is † perfect.*"

In the fame fermon I obferved, " *Love is the
fulfilling of the law, the end of the commandment.*
It is not only *the firft and great command,* but all
the commandments in one. *Whatfoever things
are juft, whatfoever things are pure, if there be any
virtue, if there be any praife,* they are all com-
prized in this one word, Love. In this is perfection, and glory, and happinefs : the royal law
of heaven and earth is this, *Thou fhalt love the
Lord thy God with all thy heart, and with all thy
foul, and with all thy mind, and with all thy
ftrength.* The one perfect good fhall be your
one ultimate end. One thing fhall ye defire for
its own fake, the fruition of him who is all in all.
One happinefs fhall ye propofe to your fouls,
even an union with him that made them : the
having *fellowfhip with the Father and the Son,* the
being

being *joined to the Lord in one spirit*. One defign ye are to purfue to the end of time, the enjoyment of God in time and in eternity. Defire other things fo far, as they tend to this: love the creature, as it leads to the Creator. But in *every ftep* you take, be this the glorious point tha terminates your view. Let every affection, and thought, and word, and action, be fubordinate to this. Whatever ye defire or fear, whatever ye feek or fhun, whatever ye think, fpeak, or do, be it in order to your happinefs in God, the fole end, as well as fource ‡ of your being."

I concluded in thefe words : " Here is the fum of *the perfect law*, the circumcifion of the heart. Let the fpirit return to God that gave it, with the whole train of its affections. —Other facrifices from us he would not, but the living facrifice of the heart hath he chofen. Let it be *continually* offered up to God through Chrift, in flames of holy love. And let no creature be fuffered to fhare with him : for he is a jealous God. His throne will he not divide with another : he will reign without a rival. Be no defign, no defire admitted there, but what has him for its ultimate object. This is the way wherein thofe children of God once walked, who being dead ftill fpeak to us. " Defire not to live but to praife his name : let *all* your thoughts, words, and works tend to his glory." " Let your foul be filled with fo entire a love to him, that you may love nothing

A 4 but

but for his fake." " Have a *pure intention* of heart, a ftedfaft regard to his glory in *all* your actions." For then, and not till then, is that mind in us, which was alfo in Chrift Jefus, when in *every* motion of our heart, in *every* word of our tongue, in *every* work of our hands, we " purfue nothing but in relation to him, and in fubordination to his pleafure:" when we too neither think, nor fpeak, nor act, to fulfil *our own will, but the will of him that fent us :* when, *whether* we *eat, or drink, or whatever* we *do,* we *do it all to the glory* † *of God."*

It may be obferved, this fermon was compofed the firft of all my writings which have been publifhed. This was the view of religion I then had, which even then I fcrupled not to term *perfection.* This is the view I have of it now, without any material addition or dimunition. And what is there here, which any man of underftanding, who believes the bible, can object to? What can he deny, without flatly contradicting the fcripture? What retrench, without taking from the word of God?

7. In the fame fentiment did my brother and I remain, (with all thofe young gentlemen in derifion termed *Methodifts)* till we embarked for America, in the latter end of 1735. It was the next year, while I was at Savannah, that I wrote the following lines :

Is

Is there a thing beneath the fun,
 That ftrives with thee my heart to fhare?
Ah tear it thence, and *reign alone!*
 The Lord of *every motion* there!

In the beginning of the year 1738, as I was returning from thence, the cry of my heart was,

O grant that nothing in my foul
 May dwell, but thy *pure love alone!*
O may thy love *poffefs me whole,*
 My joy, my treafure, and my crown!
Strange fires far from my heart remove:
My *every act, word, thought, be love!*

I never heard that any one objected to this. And indeed who can object? Is not this the language, not only of every believer, but of every one that is truly awakened? But what have I wrote to this day, which is either ftronger or plainer?

8. In Auguft following I had a long converfation with Arvin Gradin, in Germany. After he had given me an account of his experience, I defired him to give me in writing a definition of *the full affurance of faith,* which he did in the following words:

· " Requies in fanguine Chrifti; firma fiducia in Deum & perfuafio de gratia divina; tranquillitas mentis fumma, atque ferenitas & pax, cum abfentia omnis defiderii carnalis, & ceffatione peccatorum etiam internorum."

" Repofe in the blood of Chrift ; a firm confidence in God and perfuafion of his favour; the higheft tranquility, ferenity, and peace of mind, with a deliverance from *every flefhly defire*, and a *ceffation of all, even inward fins*."

This was the firft account I ever heard from any living man, of what I had before learned myfelf from the oracles of God, and had been praying for (with the little company of my friends) and expecting for feveral years.

9. In 1739, my brother and I publifhed a volume of " hymns and facred poems." In many of thefe we declared our fentiments ftrongly and explicitly.

So p. 24. Turn the full ftream of nature's tide :
　　　Let *all* our actions tend
　　To thee, their fource; thy love the guide,
　　　Thy glory be the end.
　　Earth then a fcale to heaven fhall be :
　　　Senfe fhall point out the road :
　　The creatures *all* fhall lead to thee,
　　　And all we tafte be God.

Again. Lord, arm me with thy Spirit's might,
　　　Since I am call'd by thy great name :
　　In thee my wand'ring thoughts unite,
　　　Of *all* my works be thou the aim :
　　　　　　　　　　　　　　Thy

Thy love attend me all my days,
And my *fole bufinefs* be thy praife.

p. 122.

Again.   Eager for thee, I afk and pant,
So ftrong the principle divine.
Carries me out with fweet conftraint,
Till *all my hallow'd foul* be thine:
Plung'd in the Godhead's deepeft fea,
And loft in thine immenfity!   p. 125.

Once more. Heavenly Adam, life divine,
Change my nature into thine:
Move and fpread throughout my foul,
Actuate and *fill the whole.*   p. 153.

It would be eafy to cite many more paffages to
the fame effect. But thefe are fufficient to fhew
beyond contradiction, what our fentiments then
were.

10. The firft tract I ever wrote exprefly on this
fubject, was publifhed in the latter end of this
year. That none might be prejudiced before
they read it, I gave it the indifferent title of
" The Character of a Methodift." In this I defcribed a *perfect Chriftian,* placing in the front,
Not as though I had already obtained. Part of it
I fubjoin without any alteration.

" A *Methodift* is one who loves the Lord his
God with all his heart, with all his foul, with all
his mind, and with all his ftrength. God is the
joy of his heart and the defire of his foul, which

A 6

is continually crying out, " *Whom have I in heaven but thee, and there is none upon earth whom I desire besides thee.* My God and my all ! Thou art the strength of my heart, and my portion for ever." He is therefore happy in God, yea always happy, as having in him a well of water, springing up into everlasting life, and overflowing his soul with peace and joy. *Perfect love having now cast out fear,* he *rejoices evermore.* Yea, his joy is full, and all his bones cry out, *Blessed be the God and Father of our Lord Jesus Christ, who according to his abundant mercy hath begotten me again, unto a living hope of an inheritance incorruptible and undefiled, reserved in heaven for me.*

" And he who has this *hope, thus full of immortality, in every thing giveth thanks,* as knowing that this (whatsoever it is,) *is the will of God in Christ Jesus concerning him.* From him therefore he chearfully receives all, saying. *Good is the will of the Lord*; and whether he giveth or taketh away, equally *blessing the name of the Lord.* Whether in ease or pain, whether in sickness or health, whether in life or death, he giveth thanks from the ground of the heart, to him who orders it for good ; into whose hands he hath wholly committed his body and soul, *as into the hands of a faithful Creator.* He is therefore anxiously careful for nothing, as having *cast all his care on him that careth for him,* and *in all things* resting on
him

him after *making his requeſt known to him with thankſgiving.*

" For indeed he *prays without ceaſing* : At all times the language of his heart is this, " Unto thee is my mouth, though without a voice, and my ſilence ſpeaketh unto thee." His heart is lifted up to God at all times and in all places. In this he is never hindered, much leſs interrupted by any perſon or thing. In retirement or company, in leiſure, buſineſs, or converſation, his heart is ever with the Lord. Whether he lie down or riſe up, *God is in all his thoughts : He walks with God* continually, having the loving eye of his ſoul fixt on him, and every where *ſeeing him that is inviſible.*

" And loving God, he *loves his neighbour as himſelf* ; he loves every man as his own ſoul. He loves his enemies, yea, and the enemies of God. And if it be not in his power, to *do good to them that hate* him, yet he ceaſes not to *pray for them,* though they ſpurn his love and ſtill *deſpitefully uſe him and perſecute him.*

" For he is *pure in heart.* Love has purified his heart from envy, malice, wrath, and every unkind temper. It has cleanſed him from pride, whereof *only cometh contention :* and he hath now *put on bowels of mercies, kindneſs, humbleneſs of mind, meekneſs, long-ſuffering.* And indeed all poſſible ground for contention, on his part is cut off. For none can take from him what he deſires : Seeing he *loves not the world nor any of the things*

of

of the world : But all his desire is unto God, and to the remembrance of his name.

" Agreeable to this his one desire, is the one design of his life, namely, *To do not his own will, but the will of him that sent him.* His one intention at all times and in all places is, not to please himself, but him whom his soul loveth. He hath a single eye. And because his *eye is single, his whole body is full of light. The whole is light, as when the bright shining of a candle doth inlighten the house.* God reigns alone ; all that is in the soul is *holiness to the Lord.* There is not a motion in his heart, but is according to his will. Every thought that arises points to him, and is in *obedience to the law of Christ.*

" And the tree is known by its fruits. For as he loves God, so he *keeps his commandments :* not only *some* or *most* of them, but *all,* from the least to the greatest. He is not content to *keep the whole law, and offend in one point,* but has in all points *a conscience void of offence, toward God and toward man.* Whatever God has forbidden he avoids, whatever God has enjoined he does. *He runs the way of God's commandments, now he hath set his heart at liberty.* It is his glory and joy so to do ; it is his daily crown of rejoicing, to *do the will of God on earth, as it is done in heaven.*

" All the commandments of God he accordingly keeps, and that with all his might. For his obedience is in proportion to his love, the source from whence it flows. And therefore,

therefore, loving God with all his heart, he
serves him with all his ftrength. He continually *prefents* his foul and *body a living facrifice,.
holy acceptable to God :* entirely and without
referve, devoting himfelf, all he has, all he is to
his glory. All the talents he has, he conftantly
employs according to his mafter's will: every
power and faculty of his foul, every member of
his body.

: "By confequence, *whatfoever he doth it is all to
the glory of God.* In all his employments of every
kind, he not only aims at this (which is implied
in having a fingle eye) but actually *attains* it. His
bufinefs and his refrefhments, as well as his prayers, all ferve to this great end. Whether he
fit in the houfe or walk by the way, whether he
lie down or rife up, he is promoting in all he
fpeaks or does, the one bufinefs of his life.
Whether he put on his apparel, or labour, or
eat and drink, or divert himfelf from too wafting
labour, it all tends to advance the glory of God,
by peace and good-will among men. His one invariable rule is this, *Whatfoever ye do in word or
deed, do it all in the name of the Lord Jefus, giving
thanks to God even the father through him.*

" Nor do the cuftoms of the world at all hinder
his *running the race which is fet before him.* He
cannot therefore *lay up treafures upon earth,* no
more than he can take fire into his bofom. He
cannot *fpeak evil* of his neighbour, any more
than he can lie either for God or man. He cannot

not utter an unkind word of any one : for love keeps the door of his lips. He cannot *speak idle words: no corrupt conversation ever comes out of his mouth*; as is all that is not *good to the use of edifying*, not fit to *minister grace to the hearers. But whatsoever things are pure, whatsoever things are lovely, whatsoever things are justly of good report*, he thinks, speaks, and acts, *adorning the doctrine of God our Saviour in all things."*

These are the very words, wherein I largely declared, for the first time, my sentiments of Christian Perfection. And is it not easy to see, 1. That this is the very point at which I aimed all along from the year 1725 ? And more determinately from the year 1730, when I began to be *homo unius libri*, a man of one book, regarding none (comparatively) but the bible? Is it not easy to see, 2. That this is the very same doctrine, which I believe and teach at this day ? Not adding one point either to that inward or outward holiness, which I maintained six and twenty years ago? And it is the same, which by the grace of God, I have continued to teach from that time till now ; as will appear to every impartial person, from the extracts subjoined below.

11. I do not know that any writer has made any objection against that tract, to this day. And for some time I did not find much opposition upon the head, at least, not from serious persons. But after a time, a cry arose, and (what a little surprized

furprized me) among religious men, who affirmed, not that I ftated perfection wrong, but that
" there is *no perfection* on earth :" nay, and fell
vehemently on my brother and me, for affirming
the contrary. We fcarce expected fo rough an
attack from thefe: efpecially as we were clear
on juftification by faith, and careful to afcribe
the whole of falvation to the mere grace of God.
But what moft furprized us was, that we were
faid to " difhonour Chrift," by afferting that *he
faveth to the uttermoft* ; by maintaining, he will
reign in our hearts alone, and fubdue *all things*
to himfelf !

12. I think it was in the latter end of the year
1740, that I had a converfation with Dr. Gibfon,
then bifhop of London, at Whitehall. He afked
me, What I meant by perfection ? I told him
without any difguife or referve. When I ceafed
fpeaking, he faid, " Mr. Wefley, if this be all
you mean, publifh it to all the world. If any
one then can confute what you fay, he may have
free leave." I anfwered, " My Lord, I will,"
and accordingly wrote and publifhed the fermon
on *Chriftian perfection.*

In this " I endeavoured to fhew, 1. In what
fenfe Chriftians *are not,* 2. In what fenfe they *are
perfect.*

I. In what fenfe they are not : they *are not
perfect* in *knowledge.* They are not free from
ignorance, no nor from *miftake.* We are no more
to expect any living man to be *infallible* than to

be

be omnifcient. They are not free from *infirmi-ties*; fuch as weaknefs or flownefs of underftand-ing, irregular quicknefs or heavinefs of imagina-tion. Such in another kind are, impropriety of language, ungracefulnefs of pronunciation to which one might add a thoufand namelefs defects either in converfation or behaviour. From fuch infirmities as thefe none are perfectly freed, till their fpirit returns to God. Neither can we expect till then to be wholly freed from *temptation*; *for the fervant is not above his mafter*. But neither is there any *abfolute perfection* on earth. There is no *perfection of degrees*, none which does not admit of a continual increafe.

· II. In what fenfe then are they *perfect?* Obferve we are not now fpeaking of babes in Chrift but adult Chriftians. But even babes in Chrift are fo far perfect as not to commit fin. This St. John affirms exprefsly; and it cannot be difproved by the examples of the Old Teftament. For what if the holieft of the antient Jews did *fometimes com-mit fin?* We cannot infer from hence, that "all Chriftians do and muft commit fin as long as they live."

But does not the fcripture fay, *A juft man fin-neth feven times a day?* It does not. Indeed it fays, *A juft man falleth feven times.* But this is quite another thing. For, firft, the words *a day* are not in the text. Secondly, here is no men-tion of *falling into fin* at all. What is here men-tioned is, *falling into temporal affliction*.

"But

" But elsewhere Solomon says, *There is no man that sinneth not.*" Doubtless thus it was in the days of Solomon : yea, " and from Solomon to Christ there was *then* no man that sinned not." But whatever was the case of those under the law, we may safely affirm with St. John, that since the gospel was given, *he that is born of God sinneth not.*

The privileges of Christians are in no wise to be measured, by what the Old Testament records concerning those who were under the Jewish dispensation : seeing *the fulness of time is* now *come; the Holy Ghost is* now *given;* the great *salvation* of God is now *brought* to men *by the revelation of Jesus Christ.* The kingdom of heaven is now set up on earth, concerning which the Spirit of God declared of old time, (so far is David from being the pattern or standard of Christian perfection) *He that is feeble among them at that day shall be as David, and the house of David shall be as the angel of the Lord before them,* Zech. xii. 8. " But the apostles themselves committed sin, Peter by *dissembling,* Paul by his *sharp contention* with Barnabas." Suppose they did, will you argue thus : if two of the apostles once committed sin, then *all other Christians* in *all ages*, do and must commit sin *as long as they live ?* Nay, God forbid we should thus speak. No necessity of sin was laid upon *them :* the grace of God was surely sufficient for them. And it is sufficient for *us* at this day.

But

But St. James says, "*In many things we offend all.*" True: but who are the persons here spoken of? Why, those *many masters* or teachers whom God had not sent: not the apostle himself, nor any real Christian. In the word *we* (used by a figure of speech, common in all other, as well as the inspired writings) the apostle could not possibly include himself, or any other true believer, appears, first from the ninth verse, *Therewith bless we God, and therewith curse we men.* Surely not *we apostles!* Not *we believers!* Secondly, from the words preceding the text: *My brethren, be not many masters or teachers, knowing that we shall receive the greater condemnation. For in many things we offend all.* We! Who? Not the apostles nor true believers, but they who were to *receive the greater condemnation*, because of those many offences. Nay, thirdly, the verse itself proves, that *we offend* all, cannot be spoken either of all men, or of all Christians. For in it immediately follows the mention of a man who *offends not,* as the *we* first mentioned did: from whom therefore he is professedly contradistinguished, and pronounced *a perfect man.*

" But St. John himself says, *If we say that we have no sin, we deceive ourselves.* And, *if we say we have not sinned, we make him a liar, and his word is not in us.*"

I answer, 1. The tenth verse fixes the sense of the eighth. *If we say we have no sin,* in the former,

being

being explained by *If we say we have not sinned*, in the latter verse: 2. The point under considera-tion is not, whether we have or have not sinned *heretofore:* and neither of these verses asserts, that we do sin or commit sin *now:* 3. The ninth verse explains both the eighth and tenth, *If we confess our sins, he is faithful and just, to forgive our sins, and to cleanse us from all unrighteousness.* As if he had said, I have before affirmed, *The blood of Christ cleanseth from all sin.* And no man can say, I need it not: I have no sin to be cleans-ed from. *If we say we have no sin, that we have not sinned, we deceive ourselves,* and *make* God a liar. But *if we confess our sins, he is faithful and just,* not only *to forgive us our sins,* but also to *cleanse us from all unrighteousness,* that we may *go and sin no more.* In conformity therefore both to the doctrine of St. John, and the whole tenor of the New Testament, we fix this conclu-sion, A Christian is so far perfect, as not to com-mit sin.

This is the glorious privilege of every Chris-tian, yea, though he be but a babe in Christ. But it is only of grown Christians it can be af-firmed, they are in such a sense perfect, as second-ly, to be freed from evil thoughts and evil tem-pers. First, from evil or sinful thoughts. Indeed whence should they spring? *Out of the heart of man,* if at all, *proceed evil thoughts.* If therefore the heart be no longer evil, then evil thoughts no longer proceed out of it. For *a good tree cannot bring forth evil fruit.*

And

And as they are freed from evil thoughts, so
likewise from evil tempers. Every one of these
can say with St. Paul, *I am crucified with Christ:
nevertheless I live: yet not I, but Christ liveth in
me:* words that manifestly describe a deliverance
from inward, as well as from outward sin. This
is expreſſ both negatively, *I live not;* my evil
nature, the body of sin is deſtroyed: and poſi-
tively, *Christ liveth in me*, and therefore all that
is holy, and juſt, and good. Indeed, both theſe,
Christ liveth in me, and *I live not*, are inſeparably
connected. For what communion hath light
with darkneſs, or Christ with Belial?

He therefore who liveth in theſe Christians,
hath *purified their hearts by faith:* inſomuch that
every one that has Christ in him, *the hope of
glory, purifieth himſelf even as he is pure.* He is
purified from pride: for Christ was lowly in
heart. He is pure from desire and ſelf-will : for
Christ desired only to do the will of his Father.
And he is pure from anger, in the common
ſenſe of the word ; for Christ was meek and
gentle. I ſay, in the comon ſenſe of the word;
for he is angry at sin, while he is grieved for
the sinner. He feels a diſplicency at every
offence againſt God, but only tender compaſſion
to the offender.

Thus doth Jeſus ſave his people from their sins,
not only from outward sins, but from the sins of
their hearts. " True, ſay ſome, but not till death;
not in this world." Nay, St. John ſays, *Herein*

*is our love made perfect, that we may have boldness.
in the day of judgment, because as he is so are we
in this world.* The apostle here, beyond all contradiction, speaks of himself and other living Christians, of whom he flatly affirms, that not only at,
or after death, but *in this world* they are *as their
master.*

Exactly agreeable to this are his words in the
first chapter ; *God is light, and in him is no darkness at all. If we walk in the light, as he is in the
light, we have fellowship one with another, and the
blood of Jesus Christ his Son cleanseth us from all
sin.* And again : *If we confess our sins, he is faithful and just to forgive us our sins and to cleanse us.
from all unrighteousness.* Now it is evident the a-
postle here speaks of a deliverance wrought in this
world. For he saith not the blood of Christ *will
cleanse,* (at the hour death, or in the day of judgment) but it *cleanseth* at the time present, us living Christians, *from all* sin. And it is equally
evident, that if *any* sin remain, we are not
cleansed from all sin. If any unrighteousness
remain in the soul, it is not cleansed from all
unrighteousness. Neither let any say, that
this relates to justification only, or the cleansing us from the guilt of sin : first, because this is
confounding together what the apostle clearly dis-
tinguishes, who mentions first, *to forgive us our sins,*
and then, *to cleanse us from all unrighteousness :*
secondly, because this is asserting justification by
works

works in the ftrongeft fenfe poffible ; it is making all inward, as well as all outward holinefs, neceffarily previous to juftification. For if the cleanfing here fpoken of, is no other than the cleanfing
us from the guilt of fin, then we are not cleanfed from guilt, that is, not juftified, unlefs on condition of walking in the light as he is in the light.
It remains then, that Chriftians are faved in this
world from all fin, from all unrighteoufnefs : that
they are now in fuch a fenfe perfect as not to
commit fin, and to be freed from evil thoughts
and evil tempers."

It could not be but that a difcourfe of this kind,
which directly contradicted the favourite opinion
of many who were efteemed by others, and poffibly efteemed themfelves fome of the beft of
Chriftians, (whereas if thefe things were fo,
they were not Chriftians at all) fhould give no
fmall offence. Many anfwers or animadverfions
therefore were expected ; but I was agreeably dif-
appointed. I do not know that any appeared ; fo
I wen quietly on my way.

13. Not long after, I think in the fpring, 1741,
we publifhed a fecond volume of hymns. As the
doctrine was ftill much mifunderftood, and confequently mifreprefented, I judged it needful to explain yet farther upon the head, which was done
in the preface to it as follows :

" This great gift of God, the falvation of our
fouls, is no other, than the image of God, frefh
ftamped on our hearts. It is a *renewal of believers,
in the fpirit of their minds, after the likenefs of him*
that

that created, God hath now laid *the ax unto the root of the tree, purifying their hearts by faith,* and " cleanfing all the thoughts of their hearts by the infpiration of his holy Spirit." Having this hope, that they fhall fee God as he is, they *purify themfelves even as he is pure,* and are *holy, as he that hath called them is holy, in all manner of converfation.* Not that they have already *attained* all that they fhall attain, *either are* already (in this fenfe) *perfect.* But they daily go *on from ftrength to ftrength;* beholding now, as in *a glafs the glory of the Lord, they are changed into the fame image, from glory to glory, by the fpirit of the Lord.*

" And *where the fpirit of the Lord is, there is liberty,* fuch liberty, *from the law of fin and death,* as the children of this world will not believe, tho' a man declare it unto them. *The Son hath made them free* who are thus born of God, from that great root of fin and bitternefs *pride.* They feel that *all* their *fufficiency is of God,* that it is he alone who *is in all their thoughts, and worketh in them both to will and to do, of his good pleafure.* They feel, that *it is not they that fpeak but the fpirit of* their *Father who fpeaketh* in them, and that whatfoever is done by their hands, the *Father who is in them, he doth the works.* So that God is to them all in all, and they are nothing in his fight. They are freed from felf-will, as defiring nothing but the holy, and perfect will of

God : not supplies in want, not † ease in pain, not life, or death, or any creature, but continually crying in their inmost soul, " Father, thy will he done." They are freed from *evil thoughts*, so that they cannot enter into them, no not for a moment. Aforetime when an evil thought came in, they looked up and it vanished away. But now it does not come in, there being no room for this, in a soul which is full of God. They are freed from *wandrings* in prayer. Whensoever they pour out their hearts in a more immediate manner before God, they have ‡ *no thought* of any thing past, or absent, or to come, but of God alone. In times past, they had wandring thoughts darted in, which yet fled away like smoke : but now that smoke does not rise at all. They have no fear or doubt, either as to their state in general or as to any § particular action. The *unction from the Holy One* teacheth ‖ them every hour, what they shall do and what they shall speak. Nor therefore have they any † need to *reason* concerning it. They are *in one sense* freed from *temptations* : for tho' numberless temptations *fly about them*, yet they ‡ trouble them not. At all times their souls are even and calm, their hearts are stedfast

and·

---

† This is too strong. Our Lord himself desired ease in pain. He asked for it, only with resignation: *Not as I will, I desire, but as thou wilt*.

‡ This is far too strong. See the sermon on *Wandring Thoughts*.

§ Frequently this is the case : but only *for a time*.

‖ For a time it may be so : but not always.

† Sometimes they have no need : at other times they have.

‡ Sometimes they do not ; at other times they do, and that grievously.

end unmoveable. Their peace, flowing as a river, *passeth all understanding*, and they *rejoice with joy unspeakable and full of glory*. For § *they are sealed by the Spirit unto the day of redemption*, having the witness in themselves, that *there is laid up for* them *a crown of righteousness, which the Lord will give* them *in that day*.

" Not that every one is a child of the devil, till he is thus renewed in love. On the contrary, whoever has " a sure confidence in God, that through the merits of Christ, his sins are forgiven," he is a child of God; and if he abide in him, an heir of all the promises. Neither ought he in any wise to *cast away* his *confidence* or to deny the faith he has received, because it is weak, or because it is *tried with fire*, so that his soul is *in heaviness through manifold temptations*.

" Neither dare we affirm, as some have done, that *all this salvation* is given *at once*. There is indeed an *instantaneous* (as well as a *gradual*) work of God in his children : and there wants not, we know, a cloud of witnesses, who have received, in one moment, either a clear sense of the forgiveness of their sins, or the abiding witness of the Holy Spirit. But we do not know a single instance, in any place, of a person's receiving *in one and the same moment*, remission of sins, the abiding witness of the spirit, and a new, a clean heart.

B 2

Indeed

§ Not all who are saved from sin; many of them have not attained it yet.

Indeed how God *may* work, we cannot tell : but the general manner wherein he *does* work is this : those who once trusted in themselves, that they were righteous, that they were *rich, and increased in goods, and had need of nothing*, are by the Spirit of God applying his word, convinced that they are poor and naked. All the things that they have done are brought to their remembrance, and set in array before them, so that they see the wrath of God hanging over their heads, and feel that they deserve the damnation of hell. In their trouble they cry unto the Lord, and he shews them that he hath taken away their sins, and opens the kingdom of heaven in their hearts; *righteousness, and peace, and joy in the Holy Ghost.* Sorrow and pain are fled away, and *sin has no more dominion* over them. Knowing they are *justified freely* through faith in his blood, they *have peace with God through Jesus Christ*; they *rejoice in hope of the glory of God*, and *the love of God is shed abroad in their hearts.*

" In this peace they remain for days, or weeks, or months, and commonly suppose, they shall not know war any more: till some of their old enemies, their bosom sins, or the sin which *did* most easily beset them, (perhaps anger or desire) assault them again, and thrust sore at them that they may fall. Then arises fear, that they shall not endure to the end, and often doubt, whether God has not forgotten them, or whether they did not deceive themselves, in think-

ing

ing their fins were forgiven. Under thefe clouds, efpecially if they reafon with the devil, they go *mourning* all the day long. But it is feldom long before their Lord anfwers for himfelf, fending them the Holy Ghoft to *comfort* them, to bear witnefs continually with their fpirits, that they are the children of God. Then they are indeed *meek* and gentle and teachable, even as a little child. And now † firft do they fee the ground of their heart, which God before would not dif-clofe unto them, left the foul fhould fail before him, and the fpirit which he had made. Now they fee all the hidden abominations there, the depths of pride, felf-will and hell : yet having the witnefs in themfelves, Thou art an heir of God, a joint-heir with Chrift, even in the midft of this fiery trial, which continually heightens both the ftrong fenfe they then have, of their inability to help themfelves, and the inexpref-fible *hunger* they feel *after* a full renewal in his image, in *righteoufnefs and true holinefs*. Then God is mindful of the defire of them that fear him, and gives them a fingle eye, and a pure heart : he ftamps upon them his own image and fuperfcription : he createth them anew in Chrift Jefus : he *cometh unto* them with his Son and Bleffed Spirit, and fixing his abode in their fouls,

B 3   bringeth

† Is it not aftonifhing, that while this book is extant, which was publifhed four and twenty years ago, any one fhould face *me* down, That this is a *new* doctrine, and what I never taught be-fore,

bringeth them into the *reſt* which *remaineth for the people of God."*

Here I cannot but remark, 1. That this is the ſtrongeſt account we ever gave of Chriſtian perfection; indeed too ſtrong in more than one particular, as is obſerved in the notes annexed ; 2. That there is nothing which we have ſince advanced upon the ſubject, either in verſe or proſe, which is not either directly or indirectly contained in this preface. So that whether our preſent doctrine be right or wrong, it is however the ſame which we taught from the beginning.

14. I need not give additional proofs of this, by multiplying quotations from the volume itſelf. It may ſuffice, to cite part of one hymn only, the laſt in that volume.

> Lord, I believe a reſt remains
> To all thy people known,
> A reſt, where *pure enjoyment* reigns,
> And thou art *lov'd alone:*
> A reſt where *all our* ſoul's *deſire*
> Is fixt on things above :
> Where doubt, and pain, and fear expire,
> Caſt out by *perfect love.*
> From *every evil motion* freed
> (The Son hath made us free)
> On all the powers of hell we tread
> In glorious liberty.

Safe

Safe in the way of life, above
  Death, earth, and hell we rife:
We find, when *perfected in love*,
  Our long-fought paradife.
O that I now the reft might know,
  Believe and enter in !
Now, Saviour *now*, the power beftow,
  And let me ceafe from fin !
Remove this hardnefs from my heart,
  This *unbelief* remove :
To me the reft of *faith* impart,
  The fabbath of thy love.
Come, O my Saviour, come away !
  Into my foul defcend !
No longer from thy creature ftay,
  My author and my end.
The blifs thou haft for me prepar'd
  No longer be delay'd :
Come, my exceeding great reward,
  For whom I firft was made.
Come Father, Son, and Holy Ghoft,
  And feal me thine abode !
Let all I am in thee be loft :
  Let all be loft in God !

Can any thing be more clear, than 1. That
here alfo is as *full* and *high* a *falvation* as we have
ever fpoken of ? 2. That this is fpoken of, as
receivable by mere *faith*, and as hindred only by
unbelief ? 3. That this faith, and confequently
the falvation which it brings, is fpoken of as

given

given *in an inftant?* 4. That it is fuppofed that inftant may be *now :* that we need not ftay ano-ther moment; that *now,* the very *now is the ac-cepted time! Now is the day of* this full *falvation!* And, laftly, that, if any fpeak otherwife, he is the perfon that brings *new* doctrine among us?

15. About a year after, namely in the year 1742, we publifhed another volume of hymns. The difpute being now at the height, we fpoke upon the head more largely than ever before. Accordingly abundance of the hymns in this vo-lume treat exprefsly on the fubject. And fo does the preface, which as it is fhort, it may not be amifs to infert entire.

" 1. Perhaps the general prejudice againft Chriftian perfection, may chiefly arife from a mifapprehenfion of the nature of it. We wil-lingly allow, and continually declare, there is *no fuch perfection* in this life, as implies either a difpenfation from doing good, and attending all the ordinances of God, or a feedom from ignor-ance, miftake, temptation, and a thoufand in-firmities neceffarily connected with flefh and blood.

" 2. Firft, we not only allow, but earneftly contend, that there is no perfection in this life, which implies any difpenfation from attending all the ordinances of God, or from *doing good unto all men, while we have time,* though *fpecial-ly unto the houfhold of faith.* We believe, that not only the babes in Chrift, who have newly found

found redemption in his blood, but thofe alſo
who are *grown up into perfect men*, are indifpen-
fably obliged, as often as they have opportunity,
to eat bread and drink wine in remembrance of him,
and to *fearch the fcriptures :* by *fafting*, as well as
temperance; to *keep their bodies under, and bring
them into fubjection :* and above all, to pour out
their fouls in *prayer*, both ſecretly, and in the
great congregation.

"3. We ſecondly believe, that there is no
fuch perfection in this life, as implies an entire
deliverance, either from ignorance, or miſtake,
in things not eſſential to falvation, or from manifold temptations, or from numberlefs infirmities, wherewith the corruptible body more or
lefs preſſes down the foul. We cannot find any
ground in fcripture to fuppofe, that any inhabi-
tant of an houfe of clay, is wholly exempt, either from bodily infirmities, or from ignorance
of many things; or to imagine any is incapable
of miſtake, or falling into divers temptations.

4. "But whom then do you mean by *one that
is perfect?* We mean one in whom *is the mind
which was in Chrift*, and who fo *walketh as Chrift
walked :* a *man that hath clean hands and a pure
heart*, or that is *cleanfed from all filthinefs of
flefh and fpirit :* one in whom *is no occafion of
ftumbling*, and who accordingly *doth not commit
fin.* To declare this a little more particularly :
we underſtand by that fcriptural expreſſion, *a
perfect man*, one in whom God hath fulſilled his

faithful

faithful word, *From all your filthiness and from all your idols I will cleanse you: I will also save you from all your uncleannesses.* We understand hereby one whom God hath *sanctified throughout, in body, soul, and spirit:* one who *walketh in the light as he is in the light, in whom is no darkness at all*; *the blood of Jesus Christ his Son, having cleansed him from all sin.*

" 5. This man can now testify to all mankind, *I am crucified with Christ: nevertheless I live; yet not I, but Christ liveth in me.* He is *holy*, *as God who called* him *is holy*, both in heart and *in all manner of conversation.* He *loveth the Lord his God with all his heart*, and serveth him *with all his strength.* He *loveth his neighbour*, every man, *as himself*; yea, *as Christ loveth us :* them in particular, that *despitefully use him and persecute him, because they know not the Son neither the* **Father.** Indeed his soul is all love, filled with *bowels of mercies, kindness, meekness, gentleness, long-suffering.* And his life agreeth thereto, full of *the work of faith, the patience of hope, the labour of love.* And *whatsoever* he *doth either in word or deed*, he *doth it all in the name*, in the love and power *of the Lord Jesus.* In a word, he doth *the will of God on earth, as it is done in heaven.*

" 6. This it is to be a perfect man, to be *sanctified throughout :* even " to have a heart so all-flaming with the love of God, (to use archbishop Usher's words) as continually to offer up every thought,

thought, word and work, as a spiritual sacrifice, acceptable to God through Christ." In every thought of our hearts, in every word of our tongues, in every work of our hands, to *shew forth his praise, who hath called us out of darkness into his marvellous light.* O that both we, and all who seek the Lord Jesus in sincerity, may thus *be made perfect in one!*

This is the doctrine which we preached from the beginning, and which we preach at this day. Indeed by viewing it in every point of light, and comparing it again and again, with the word of God on the one hand, and the experience of the children of God on the other, we saw farther into the nature and properties of Christian perfection. But still there is no contrariety at all, between our first and our last sentiments. Our first conception of it was, it is to have *the mind which was in Christ,* and to *walk as he walked:* to have *all* the mind that was in him, and *always* to walk as he walked. In other words, to be inwardly and outwardly devoted to God; *all devoted* in heart and life. And we have the same conception of it now, without either addition or diminution.

16. The hymns concerning it in this volume are too numerous to transcribe. I shall only cite a part of three.

P. 80. Saviour from sin, I wait to prove
That Jesus is thy healing name:

To

To lofe, when perfected in love,
  Whate'er I have, or can, or am :
I ftay me on thy faithful word,
The fervant fhall be as his Lord.

Anfwer that gracious end in me
  For which thy precious life was given :
Redeem from *all iniquity*,
  Reftore and make me meet for heaven :
Unlefs thou purge my *every ftain*,
Thy fuffering and my faith is vain.

Didft thou not die, that I might live
  No longer to myfelf, but thee ?
Might body, foul, and fpirit give
  To him who gave himfelf for me ?
Come then, my Mafter and my God,
Take the dear purchafe of thy blood.

Thy own peculiar fervant claim,
  For thy own truth and mercy's fake :
Hallow in me thy glorious name :
  Me for thine own *this moment* take :
And change and *throughly purify* :
Thine only may I live and die.

P. 258. Chofe from the world if now I ftand,
  Adorn'd with righteoufnefs divine ;
If brought into the promis'd land
  I juftly call the Saviour mine :
                                        Thy

Thy fanctifying fpirit pour
 To quench my thirft and wafh me elean:
Now, Saviour, let the gracious fhower
 Defcend, and make me *pure from fin.*
Purge me from *every finful blot* ;
 My idols all be caft afide :
Cleanfe me from *every evil thought*,
 From *all* the filth of felf and pride.
The hatred of the carnal mind
 Out of my flefh *at once* remove :
Give me a tender heart, refign'd,
 And pure, and full of faith and love.
O that I *now* from fin releas'd
 Thy word might to the utmoft prove :
Enter into thy promis'd reft !
 The *Canaan* of thy *perfect love !*
Now let me gain Perfection's height !
 Now let me into nothing fall ;
Be lefs than nothing in my fight,
 And feel that Chrift is all in all.

P. 298. Lord, I believe, thy work of grace
 Is perfect in the foul :
His heart is pure who fees thy face,
 His fpirit is made whole:
From *every ficknefs* by thy word,
 From *every foul-difeafe*
Sav'd, and to *perfect health* reftor'd,
 To *perfect holinefs.*
He walks in glorious liberty,
 To fin *entirely dead* ;

The

The Truth, the Son hath made him free,
  And he is free indeed.
Throughout his foul thy glories fhine,
  His foul is *all renewed*,
And decked in righteoufnefs divine,
  And cloath'd and *fill'd with* God.
This is the reft, the life, the peace,
  Which all thy people prove !
Love is the bond of perfectnefs,
  And all their foul is love.
O joyful found of gofpel-grace !
  Chrift fhall in me appear :
I, even I fhall fee his face :
  I fhall be holy *here !*
He vifits now the houfe of clay :
  He fhakes his future home,
O wouldft thou, Lord, on *this glad day*
  Into thy temple come !
Come, O my God, thyfelf reveal,
  Fill all this mighty void !
Thou only canft my fpirit fill ;
  Come, O my God, my God !
Fulfil, fulfil my large defires,
  Large as infinity !
Give, give me all my foul requires,
  All, all that is in thee !

17. On Monday, *June 25,* 1744, our firft conference began, fix clergymen, and all our preachers being prefent. The next morning we ferioufly confidered the doctrine of fanctification

tion or perfection. The questions asked concerning it, and the substance of the answers given were as follows:

Q. What is it to be *sanctified?*

A. To be renewed in the image of God, *in righteousness and true holiness.*

Q. What is implied in being a *perfect Christian?*

A. The loving God with all our heart, and mind, and soul, Deut. vi. 5.

Q. Does this imply, that *all inward sin* is taken away?

A. Undoubtedly: or how can we be said to be *saved from all our uncleannesses?* Ezek. xxxvi. 29.

Our second conference began Aug. 1, 1745. The next morning we spoke of sanctification, as follows:

Q. When does inward sanctification begin?

A. In the moment a man is justified. (Yet sin remains in him, yea the seed of all sin, till he is *sanctified throughout.*) From that time a believer gradually dies to sin, and grows in grace.

Q. Is this ordinarily given till a little before death?

A. It is not, to those who expect it no sooner.

Q. But may we expect it sooner?

A. Why not? For although we grant, 1. That the generality of believers whom we have hitherto known, were not so sanctified till near death: 2. That few of those to whom St. Paul wrote his
epistles,

epistles, were so at that time: nor 3. He himself at the time of writing his former epistles: yet
all this does not prove, that we may not be so
to-day.

Q. In what manner should we preach sanctification?

A. Scarce at all to those who are not pressing
forward: to those who are, always by way of
promise; always *drawing*, rather than *driving*.

Our third conference began Tuesday, May 26,
1746.

In this we carefully read over the minutes of
the two preceding conferences, to observe whether any thing contained therein might be re-
trenched or altered on more mature consideration.
But we did not see cause to alter in any respect
what we had agreed upon before.

Our fourth conference began on Tuesday, June
the 16th. 1747. As several persons were present, who did not believe the doctrine of perfection, we agreed to examine it from the foundation.

In order to this, it was asked,

" How much is allowed by our brethren who
differ from us, with regard to entire sanctification?"

A. They grant, 1. That every one must be entirely sanctified in the article of death: 2. That
till then a believer daily grows in grace, comes
nearer and nearer to perfection: 3. That we
ought

ought to be continually preffing after it, and to exhort all others fo to do.

Q. What do we allow them?

A. We grant, 1. That many of thofe who have died in the faith, yea, the greater part of thofe we have known, were not *perfected in love*, till a little before their death: 2. That the term *fanctified*, is continually applied by St. Paul, to all that were juftified. 3. That by this term alone, he rarely, if ever, means " Saved from all fin :" 4. That confequently it is not proper to ufe it in that fenfe, without adding the word *wholly*, *entirely*, or the like: 5. That the infpired writers almoft continually fpeak of or to thofe who were juftified, but very rarely of or to thofe who were wholly fanctified :† 6. That confequently it behoves us to fpeak almoft continually of the ftate of juftification; but more rarely, " at leaft ‡ in full and explicit terms, concerning entire fanctification."

Q. What then is the point where we divide?

A. It is this: fhould we expect to be faved from *all fin* before the article of death?

Q. Is there any clear fcripture-*promife* of this, that God will fave us from *all fin?*

A. There is. Pfal. cxxx. 8. *He fhall redeem Ifrael from* all his fins.

This

---

† That is, unto thofe alone, exclufive of others: but they fpeak to them, jointly with others almoft continually.

‡ More rarely I allow; but yet in fome places very frequently, ftrongly, and explicitly.

This is more largely expreſt in the prophecy of Ezekiel; *Then will I ſprinkle clean water upon you, and ye ſhall be clean: from* all *your filthineſs and from all your idols will I cleanſe you—I will alſo ſave you from* all your uncleanneſſes, chap. xxxvi. ver. 25. 29. No promiſe can be more clear. And to this the apoſtle plainly refers in that exhortation, *Having theſe promiſes, let us cleanſe ourſelves from all filthineſs of fleſh and ſpirit, perfecting holineſs in the fear of God,* 2 Cor. vii. 1. Equally clear and expreſs is that antient promiſe, *The Lord thy God will circumciſe thy heart, and the heart of thy ſeed, to love the Lord thy God with all thy heart and with all thy ſoul.* Deut. xxx. 6.

Q. But does any *aſſertion* anſwerable to this, occur in the New Teſtament?

A. There does, and that laid down in the plaineſt terms. So 1 John iii. 8. *For this purpoſe, the Son of God was manifeſted, that he might deſtroy the works of the devil,* without any limitation or reſtriction; but all ſin is *the work of the devil.* Parallel to which is the aſſertion of St. Paul, Eph. v. 25, 27. *Chriſt loved the church and gave himſelf for it,—that he might preſent it to himſelf a glorious church, not having ſpot or wrinkle, or any ſuch thing, but that it might be holy and without blemiſh.*

And to the ſame effect is his aſſertion in the eighth of the Romans, ver. 3, 4. *God ſent his Son—that the righteouſneſs of the law might be ful-*
filled

filled *in us, who walk not after the flesh, but after the spirit.*

Q. Does the New Testament afford any farther ground for expecting to be saved from *all sin ?*

A. Undoubtedly it does, both in those *prayers* and *commands,* which are equivalent to the strongest assertions.

Q. What *prayers* do you mean ?

A. Prayers for entire sanctification, which, were there no such thing, would be mere mockery of God. Such in particular are, 1. *Deliver us from evil.* Now when this is done, when we are delivered from all evil, there can be no sin remaining. 2. *Neither pray I for these alone, but for them also who shall believe on me through their word : that they all may be one, as thou, Father, art in me and I in thee, that they also may be one in us : I in them, and thou in me, that they may be made perfect in one,* John xvii. ver. 20, 21, 23. 3. *I bow my knees unto the God and Father of our Lord Jesus Christ,—that he would grant you—that ye being rooted and grounded in love, may be able to comprehend with all saints, what is the breadth, and length, and depth, and height, and to know the love of Christ which passeth knowledge. That ye may be filled with all the fulness of God,* Eph. iii. 14, &c. 4. *The very God of peace sanctify you wholly. And I pray God, your whole spirit, soul and body, may be preserved blameless, unto the coming of our Lord Jesus Christ,* 1 Thes. v. 23.

Q. What

Q. What *command* is there to the fame effect?

A. 1. *Be ye perfect, as your Father who is in heaven is perfect,* Matt. v. 48. 2. *Thou sha't love the Lord thy God with all thy heart, and with all thy foul, and with all thy mind,* Matt. xxii. 37. But if the love of God fill *all the heart,* there can be no fin there.

Q. But how does it appear, that this is to be done before the article of death?

A. 1. From the very nature of a command, which is not given to the dead, but to the living. Therefore *thou shalt love God with all thy heart,* cannot mean, thou shalt do this, when thou dieſt, but while thou liveſt.

2. From expreſs texts of fcripture. 1. *The grace of God that bringeth falvation hath appeared to all men ; teaching us, that having renounced ungodly and worldly luſts, we ſhould live foberly, righteouſly, and godly in this preſent world : looking for the glorious appearing of our Lord Jeſus Chriſt, who gave himſelf for us, that he might redeem us from all iniquity, and purify unto himſe'f a peculiar people, zealous of good works,* Tit. ii. 11—14. 2. *He hath raiſed up an horn of falvation for us—to perform the mercy promiſed to our fathers ; the oath which he ſwore to our father Abraham, that he would grant unto us, that we being delivered out of the hands of our enemies, ſhould ſerve him without fear, in holineſs and righteouſneſs before him, all the days of our life,* Luke i. ver. 69, &c.

Q. Is

Q. Is there any *example* in fcripture of perfons who had attained to this ?

A. Yes, St. John, and all thofe of whom he fays, *Herein is our love made perfect, that we may have boldnefs in the day of judgment, becaufe as he is, fo are we in this world,* 1 John iv. 17.

Q. Can you fhew one fuch example now ? Where is he that is thus perfect?

A. To fome that make this enquiry one might anfwer, If I knew one here, I would not tell *you:* for you do not enquire out of love. You are like Herod. You only feek the young child to flay it.

But more directly we anfwer. There are many reafons, why there fhould be few, if any, *indifputable* examples. What inconveniencies would this bring on the perfon himfelf, fet as a mark for all to fhoot at ? And how unprofitable would it be to gainfayers ? *For if they hear not Mofes and the prophets,* Chrift and his apoftles, *neither would they be perfuaded though one rofe from the dead.*

Q. Are we not apt to have a fecret diftafte to any who fay they are faved from all fin ?

A. 'Tis very poffible we may, and that upon feveral grounds : partly from a concern for the good of fouls, who may be hurt, if thefe are not what they profefs : partly from a kind of implicit envy at thofe who fpeak of higher attainments than our own: and partly from our natural flownefs and unreadinefs of heart, to believe the works of God.

Q. Why

Q. Why may we not continue in the joy of faith, till we are *perfected in love?*

A. Why indeed? Since holy grief does not quench this joy: since even while we are under the cross, while we deeply partake of the sufferings of Christ, we may rejoice with joy unspeakable."

From these extracts it undeniably appears, not only what was mine and my brother's judgment, but what was the judgment of all the preachers in connexion with us, in the years 44, 45, 46, and 47. Nor do I remember, that in any one of these conferences we had one dissenting voice: but whatever doubts any one had when we met, they were all removed before we parted.

·18. In the year 1749, my brother printed two volumes of " Hymns and sacred Poems." As I did not see these before they were published, there were some things in them which I did not approve of. But I quite approved of the main of the hymns on this head; a few verses of which are subjoined.

Come, Lord, be manifested here,
　And *all the devil's works* destroy !
Now, without sin in me appear,
　And fill with everlasting joy :
Thy beatific face display :
Thy presence is the perfect day. *Vol.* I. *p.* 203.

Swift

Swift to my refcure come,
Thy own *this moment* feize !
Gather my wandering fpirit home,
And keep in perfect peace.

Suffer'd no more to rove
O'er all the earth abroad,
Arreft the prifoner of thy love,
And fhut me up in God.   *p.* 247.

Thy prifoners releafe, vouchfafe us thy peace ;
And our forrows and fins *in a moment* fhall ceafe.
That moment be now ! Our petition allow,
Our *prefent* Redeemer and Comforter thou.*Vol.*II.

(*p.* 124.

From this inbred fin deliver :
Let the yoke *Now* be broke :
Make me thine for ever.

Partner of thy perfect nature,
Let me be *Now* in thee
A new finlefs creature.   *p.* 156.

Turn me, Lord, and turn me now,
To thy yoke my fpirit bow ; ,
Grant me now the pearl to find
Of a meek and quiet mind.
Calm, O calm my troubled breaft ;
Let me gain that fecond reft ;
From my works for ever ceafe,
Perfected in holinefs.   *p.* 162.

Come

Come in *this* accepted *hour*,
　　Bring thy heavenly kingdom in !
Fill us with the glorious power
　　Rooting out the seeds of sin.　　*p.* 168.

Come, thou dear Lamb for sinners slain,
　　Bring in the cleansing flood;
Apply, to wash out every stain,
　　Thine efficacious blood.

'O let it sink into our soul
　　Deep as the in-bred sin :
Make every wounded spirit whole
　　And every leper clean !　　*p.* 171.

Prisoners of hope arise
　　And see your Lord appear !
Lo ! On the wings of love he flies,
　　And brings redemption near.
Redemption in his blood
He calls you to receive:
Come unto me, the pard'ning God :
　　Believe, he cries, believe !
Jesus to thee we look,
　　'Till saved from sin's remains,
Reject the inbred tyrant's yoke,
　　And cast away his chains.
Our nature shall no more
O'r us dominion have :
By faith we apprehend the power,
　　Which shall for ever save.　　*p.* 188.

　　　　　　　　　　　　Jesu,

Jefu, our life, in us appear,
 Who daily die thy death !
Reveal thyfelf the finifher :
 Thy quick'ning Spirit breathe !
Unfold the hidden myftery !
 The fecond gift impart !
Reveal thy glorious felf in me :
 In every waiting heart.   *p.* 195.

In Him we have peace, In him we have power !
Preferved by his grace throughout the dark hour.
In all our temptations, he keeps us to prove
His utmoft falvation, His fullnefs of love.
Pronounce the glad word, and bid us be free ;
Ah, haft thou not, Lord, A blefling for me ?
The peace thou haft given, *this moment* impart,
And open thy heaven, O Love in my heart! *p.*324.

A fecond edition of thefe hymns was publifhed in the year 1752 ; and that without any
other alteration, than that of a few literal miftakes.

I have been the more large in thefe extracts,
becaufe hence it appears, beyond all poffibility
of exception, that to this day, both my brother
and I maintained, 1. That Chriftian Perfection is
that love of God and our neighbour, which implies deliverance from *all fin* ; 2. That this is received merely *by faith* ; 3. That it is given
inftantaneoufly, in one moment ; 4. That we are
to expect it (not at death but) *every moment* :

VOL. XXIV.   C   That

That now is the accepted time, now is the day of this salvation.

19. At the conference in the year 1759, perceiving some danger that a diversity of sentiments, should insensibly steal in among us, we again largely considered this doctrine. And soon after I published " Thoughts on Christian perfection," prefaced with the following advertisement :

" The following tract is by no means designed to gratify the curiosity of any man. It is not intended to prove the doctrine at large, in opposition to those who explode and ridicule it : no nor to answer the numerous objections against it, which may be raised even by serious men. All I intend here, is simply to declare, what are my sentiments on this head : what Christian perfection does, according to my apprehension include, and what it does not ; and to add a few practical observations and directions relative to the subject.

" As these thoughts were at first thrown together by way of question and answer, I let them continue in the same form—They are just the same that I have entertained for above twenty years."

" Q. What is Christian perfection ?

A. The loving God with all our heart, mind, soul and strength. This implies that no wrong temper, none contrary to love, remains in the soul :

foul: and that all the thoughts, words and actions are governed by pure love.

Q. Do you affirm, that this perfection excludes all infirmities, ignorance and miftake ?

A. I continually affirm quite the contrary, and always have done fo.

Q. But how can every thought, word and work be governed by pure love, and the man be fubject at the fame time to ignorance and miftake ?

A. I fee no contradiction here. " A man may be filled with pure love, and ftill be liable to miftake." Indeed I do not expect to be freed from actual miftakes, till this mortal puts on immortality. I believe this to be a natural confequence of the foul's dwelling in flefh and blood. For we cannot now think at all, but by the mediation of thofe bodily organs, which have fuffered equally with the reft of our frame. And hence we cannot avoid fometimes *thinking wrong*, till this corruptible fhall have put on incorruption.

But we may carry this thought farther yet. A miftake in judgment may poffibly occafion, a miftake in practice. For inftance Mr. de *Renty's* miftake touching the nature of mortification, arifing from prejudice of education, occafioned that practical miftake, his wearing an iron girdle. And a thoufand fuch inftances there may be, even in thofe who are in the higheft ftate of grace. Yet where every word and action fprings

from

from love, such a mistake is not properly a *sin*. However it cannot bear the rigor of God's justice, but needs the atoning blood.

Q. What was the judgment of all our brethern, who met at Bristol in August 1758, on this head?

A. It was expressed in these words; 1. Every one may mistake as long as he lives ; 2. A mistake in *opinion* may occasion a mistake in *practice:* 3. Every such mistake is a transgression of the perfect law. Therefore, 4. Every such mistake, were it not for the blood of atonement, would expose to eternal damnation. 5. It follows, that the most perfect have continual need of the merits of Christ, even for their actual transgressions, and may say for themselves, as well as for their brethern, *Forgive us our trespasses.*

This easily accounts for what might otherwise seem to be utterly unaccountable : namely, that those who are not offended when we speak of the highest degree of love, yet will not hear of living *without sin.* The reason is, they know all men are liable to mistake, and that in practice as well as in judgment. But they do not know, or do not observe, that this is not sin, if love is the sole principle of action.

Q. But still if they live without sin, does not this exclude the necessity of a mediator? At least, is it not plain, that they stand no longer in need of Christ in his priestly office?

A. Far from it. None feel their need of Christ like

like thefe : none fo entirely depend upon him.
For Chrift does not give life to the foul feparate from, but in and with himfelf. Hence his
words are equally true of all men, in whatfoever
ftate of grace they are, *As the branch cannot bear
fruit of itfelf, except it abide in the vine, no more
can ye, except ye abide in me : without* (or feparate from) *me, ye can do nothing.*

* In every ftate we need Chrift in the following
refpects : 1. Whatever grace we receive, it is a
free gift from him : 2. We receive it as his purchafe, merely in confideration of the price he
paid : 3. We have this grace not only from
Chrift, but in him. For our prefection is not
like that of a tree, which flourifhes by the fap
derived from its own root, but, as was faid before, like that of a branch, which united to the
vine, bears fruit, but fevered from it, *is dried up
and withered*: 4. All our bleffings, temporal,
fpiritual, and eternal, depend on his interceffion
for us, which is one branch of his prieftly office,
whereof therefore we have always equal need :
5. The beft of men ftill need Chrift in his prieftly office, to atone for their omiffions, their fhort-
comings. (as fome not improperly fpeak) their miftakes in judgment and practice, and their defects
of various kinds. For thefe are all deviations
from the perfect law, and confequently need an
atonement. Yet that they are not properly fins,
we apprehend may appear from the words of
of St. Paul, *He that loveth hath fulfilled the law ; for*

love

love is the fulfilling of the law.† Now miſtakes, and whatever infirmities neceſſarily flow from the corruptible ſtate of the body, are no way contrary to love, nor therefore in the ſcripture-ſenſe, ſin.

To explain myſelf a little farther on this head: 1. Not only *ſin properly ſo called,* that is a voluntary tranſgreſſion of a known law, but ſin, improperly ſo called, that is, an involuntary tranſgreſſion of a divine law, known or unknown, needs the atoning blood. 2. I believe, there is no ſuch perfection in this life, as excludes theſe involuntary tranſgreſſions, which I apprehend to be naturally conſequent on the ignorance and miſtakes inſeparable from mortality. 3. Therefore *ſinleſs perfection* is a phraſe I never uſe, left I ſhould ſeem to contradict myſelf: 4. I believe a perſon filled with the love of God, is ſtill liable to theſe involuntary tranſgreſſions: 5. Such tranſgreſſions you may call ſins, if you pleaſe: I do not, for the reaſons above-mentioned.

Q. What advice would you give to thoſe that do, and thoſe that do not call them ſo?

A. Let thoſe that do not call them *ſins,* never think that themſelves, or any other perſons, are in ſuch a ſtate, as that they can ſtand before infinite juſtice without a mediator. This muſt argue, either the deepeſt ignorance, or the higheſt arrogance and preſumption.

Let thoſe who do call them ſo, beware how they confound theſe *defects* with *ſins,* properly ſo called.

† Rom. xiii. 10, 12.

called. But how will they avoid it? How will these be diftinguifhed from thofe, if they are all promifcuoufly called *fins*? I am much afraid, if we fhould allow any fins to be confiftent with perfection, few would confine the idea to thofe *defects*, concerning which only the affertion could be true.

Q. But how can a liablenefs to miftake confift with perfect love? Is not a perfon who is perfected in love, every moment under its influence? And can any miftake flow from pure love?

A. I anfwer, 1. Many miftakes may confift with pure love: 2. Some may accidentally flow from it. I mean, love itfelf may incline us to miftake. The pure love of our neighbour fpringing from the love of God, *thinketh no evil, believeth and hopeth all thing.* Now this very temper, unfufpicious, ready to believe, and hope the beft of all men may occafion our thinking fome men better than they really are. Here then is a manifeft miftake, accidentally flowing from pure love.

Q. How fhall we avoid fetting perfection too high or too low?

A. By keeping to the bible, and fetting it juft as high as the fcripture does. It is nothing higher, and nothing lower than this. The pure love of God and man; the loving God with all our heart and foul, and our neighbour as ourfelves. It is love governing the heart and life,

running

running though all our tempers words and actions.

Q. Suppofe one had attained to this, would you advife him to fpeak of it?

A. At firft perhaps he would fcarce be able to refrain, the fire would be fo hot within him : his defire to declare the loving-kindnefs of the Lord, carrying him away like a torrent. But afterwards he might : and then it would be advifeable, not to fpeak of it to them that know not God. 'Tis moft likely it would only provoke them to contradict and blafpheme : nor to others without fome particular reafon, without fome good in view. And then he fhould have efpecial care, to avoid all appearance of boafting ; to fpeak with the deepeft humility and reverence giving all the glory to God.

Q. But would it not be better, to be intirely filent? Not to fpeak of it at all?

A. By filence he might avoid many croffes, which will naturally and neceffarily enfue, if he fimply declare even among believers, what **God** has wrought in his foul. If therefore fuch an one were to confer with flefh and blood, he would be intirely filent. But this could not be done with a clear confcience : for undoubtedly he ought to fpeak. Men do not light a candle to put it under a bufhel ; much lefs does the all-wife God. He does not raife fuch a monument of his power and love, to hide it from all mankind. Rather he intends it as a general bleffing, to

thofe

thofe who are fimple of heart. He defigns thereby not barely the happinefs of that individual
perfon, but the animating and encouraging
others, to follow after the fame blefling. His
will is, *that many fhall fee it* and rejoice, *and
put their trust in the Lord.* Nor does any thing
under heaven more quicken the defires of thofe
who are juftified, than to converfe with thofe
whom they believe to have experienced a ftill
higher falvation. This places that falvation full in
their view, and increafes their hunger and thirft
after it : an advantage which muft have been
entirely loft, had the perfon fo faved buried himfelf in filence.

Q. But is there no way to prevent thefe crofſes
which ufually fall on thofe who fpeak of being
thus faved ?

A. It feems they cannot be prevented altogether, while fo much of nature remains even in
believers. But fomething might be done if the
preacher in every place would 1. Talk freely
with all who fpeak thus, and 2. Labour to prevent the unjuft or unkind treatment of thofe, in
favour of whom there is reafonable proof.

Q. What is reafonable proof? How may we
certainly know one that is faved from all fin ?

A. We cannot infallibly know one that is
thus faved (no, nor even one that is juftified) unlefs it fhould pleafe God to endow us with the
miraculous difcernment of fpirits. But we apprehend thofe would be fufficient proofs to any

reafonable

reasonable man, and such as would leave little
room to doubt, either the truth or depth of the
work: 1. If we had clear evidence of his exemplary behaviour, for some time before this
supposed change. This would give us reason to
believe, he would not *lie for God*, but speak neither more nor less then he felt: 2. If he gave
a distinct account of the time and manner wherein the change was wrought, with sound speech
which could not be reproved: and 3. If it appeared that all his subsequent words and actions were
holy and unblameable.

* The short of the matter is this: 1. I have
abundant reason to believe, this person will not
lie: 2. He testifies before God, "I feel no sin,
but all love; I pray, rejoice, and give thanks,
without ceasing: and I have as clear an inward
witness, that I am fully renewed, as that I am
justified." Now if I have nothing to oppose to
this plain testimony, I ought in reason to believe it.

It avails nothing to object, " But I know several things wherein he is quite mistaken." For
it has been allowed, that all who are in the body
are liable to mistake: and that a mistake in judgment may sometimes occasion a mistake in practice: (tho' great care is to be taken that no ill
use be made of this concession.) For instance ;
even one that is perfected in love may mistake
with regard to another person, and may think
him in a particular case, to be more or less faul-
ty

ty than he really is, and hence he may fpeak to him with more or lefs feverity than the truth requires. And in this fenfe (tho' that be not the primary meaning of St. James *in many things we offend all.* This therefore is no proof at all that the perfon fo fpeaking is not perfect.

Q. But is it not a proof, if he is *furprized or fluttered* by a noife, a fall, or fome fudden danger ?

A. * It is not : for one may flart, tremble, change colour or be otherwife difordered in body, while the foul is calmly ftayed on God, and remains in perfect peace. Nay, the mind itfelf may be deeply diftreft, may be exceeding forrowful, may be perplext and preffed down by heavinefs and anguifh, even to agony, while the heart cleaves to God by perfect love, and the will is wholly refigned to him. Was it not fo with the fon of God himfelf ? Does any child of man endure the diftrefs, the anguifh, the agony, which he fuftained ? And yet he *knew on fin.*

Q. But can any one who has a pure heart prefer pleafing to unpleafing food ? Or ufe any pleafure of fenfe which is not ftrictly neceffary ? If fo how do they differ from others ?

A. The difference between thefe and others in taking pleafant food, is, 1. They need none of thefe things to make them happy ; for they have a fpring of happinefs within. They fee and love God. Hence they *rejoice evermore,* and *in every thing give thanks.* 2. They may ufe them, but

C 6

they

they do not feek them : 3. They ufe them fparingly, and not for the fake of the thing itfelf. This being premifed, we anfwer directly, fuch an one may ufe pleafing food, without the danger which attends thofe who are not faved from fin. He may prefer it to unpleafing, though equally wholefome food, as a means of increafing thankfulnefs, with a fingle eye to God, *who giveth us all things richly to enjoy:* on the fame principle, he may fmell to a flower, or eat a bunch of grapes, or take any other pleafure which does not leffen but increafe his delight in God. Therefore neither can we fay, that one perfected in love would be incapable of marriage, and of worldly bufinefs ; if he were called thereto, he would be more capable than ever ; as being able to do all things without hurry or carefulnefs, without any diftraction of fpirit.

Q. But if two perfect Chriftians had children, how could they be born in fin, fince there was none in the parents?

A. It is a poffible, but not a probable cafe; I doubt whether it ever was or ever will be. But waving this, I anfwer, fin is entailed upon me, not by my immediate, but by my firft parent. *In* Adam *all died : by the difobedience of one all men were made finners :* all men without exception who were in his loins when he ate the forbidden fruit.

We have a remarkable illuftration of this in gardening

gardening. Grafts on a crab-stock bear excellent fruit. But sow the kernels of this fruit and what will be the event? They produce as mere crabs as ever were eaten.

Q. But what does the perfect one do more than others? More than common believers?

A. Perhaps nothing: so may the providence of God have hedged him in, by outward circumstances. Perhaps not so much; (tho' he desires and longs to *spend and be spent* for God;) at least not externally: he neither speaks so many words, nor does so many works. As neither did our Lord himself speak so many words, or do so many, no nor so great works, as some of his apostles, (John xiv. 12.) But what then? This is no proof that he has not more grace: and by this God measures the outward work. Hear ye him. *Verily I say unto you, this poor widow has cast in more than them all.* Verily this poor man, with his few broken words, hath spoke more than them all. Verily this poor woman, that hath given a cup of cold water, hath done more than them all! O cease to *judge according to appearance,* and learn to *judge righteous judgment!*

Q. But is not this a proof against him? I feel no power either in his words or prayer?

A. It is not: for perhaps that is your own fault. You are not likely to feel any power therein, if any of these hindrances lie in the way: 1. Your own deadness of soul. The dead Pharisees felt no

power

power even in his words, who *fpake as never man fpake*; 2. The guilt of fome unrepented fin lying upon the confcience ; 3. *Prejudice* toward him of any kind : 4. Your *not believing* that ftate to be attainable, wherein he profeffes to be : 5. *Unreadinefs* to think or own he has attained it : 6. *Over-valuing* or *idolizing* him ; 7. *Over-valuing yourfelf* and your own judgment. If any of thefe is the cafe, what wonder is it, that you feel no power in any thing he fays ? But do not others feel it ? If they do, your argument falls to the ground. And if they do not, do none of thefe hindrances lie in their way too ? You muft be certain of this before you can build any argument thereon. And even then your argument will prove no more, than that grace and gifts do not always go together.

" But he does not come up to my *Idea* of a perfect Chriftian." And perhaps no one ever did or ever will. For *your idea* may go *beyond*, or at leaft *befide* the fcriptural account. It may in-clude *more* than the bible includes therein, or however *fomething* which that does not include. Scripture perfection is, pure love filling the heart and governing all the words and actions. If your idea includes any thing more or any thing elfe, it is not fcriptural : and then no wonder, that a fcripturally-perfect Chriftian does come up to it.

I fear many ftumble on this ftumbling-block. They include as many ingredients as they pleafe, not according to fcripture, but their own

imagination,

imagination, in their idea of one that is perfect: and then readily deny any one to be such, who does not anfwer that imaginary idea.

The more care fhould we take, to keep the fimple, fcriptural account continually in our eye. Pure love reigning alone in the heart and life, this is the whole of fcriptural perfection.

Q. When may a perfon judge himfelf to have attained this?

A. When after having been fully convinced of inbred fin, by a far deeper and clearer conviction, than that he experienced before juftification, and after having experienced a gradual mortification of it, he experiences a total death to fin, and an entire renewal in the love, and image of God, fo as to *rejoice evermore, to pray without ceafing, and in every thing to give thanks.* Not that " to feel all love and no fin," is a fufficient proof; feveral have experienced this for a time, before their fouls were fully renewed. None therefore ought to believe, that the work is done, till there is added the teftimony of the Spirit, witneffing his entire fanctification, as clearly as his juftification.

Q. But whence is it, that fome imagine they are thus fanctified, when in reality they are not?

A. It is hence : they do not judge by all the preceding marks, but either by part of them, or by others, that are ambiguous. But I know no inftance of a perfon attending to them all, and

yet

yet deceived in this matter. I believe, there can be none in the world. If a man be deeply and fully convinced, after justification, of imbred sin; if he then experience a gradual mortification of sin, and afterwards an entire renewal in the image of God : if to this change, immensely greater than that wrought when he was justified, be added a clear, direct witness of the renewal : I judge it as impossible this man should be deceived herein, as that God should lie. And if one whom I know to be a man of veracity testify these things to me, I ought not, without some sufficient reason, to reject his testimony.

Q. Is this death to sin and renewal in love, gradual or instantaneous ?

A. A man may be dying for some time ; yet he does not, properly speaking, die, 'till the instant the soul is separated from the body : and in that instant he lives the life of eternity. In like manner, he may be dying *to sin,* for some time ; yet he is not dead to sin till sin is separated from his soul. And in that instant he lives the full life of love. And as the change undergone when the body dies, is of a different kind, and infinitely greater than any we had known before, yea such as till then it is impossible to conceive : so the change wrought when the soul dies to sin, is of a different kind, and infinitely greater than any before, and than any can conceive 'till he experiences it. Yet he still grows in grace, in the knowledge of Christ, in the love and image

of

of God: and will do fo, not only 'till death, but to all eternity.

Q. How are we to wait for this change?

A. Not in carelefs indifference or indolent inactivity; but in vigorous, univerfal obedience, in a zealous keeping of all the commandments, in watchfulnefs and painfulnefs, in denying ourfelves and taking up our crofs daily; as well as in earneft prayer and fafting, and a clofe attendance on all the ordinances of God. And if any man dream of attaining it any other way, (yea or of keeping it, when it is attained, when he has received it even in the largeft meafure) he deceiveth his own foul. 'Tis true we receive it by fimple faith. But God does not, will not give that faith, unlefs we feek it with all diligence, in the way which he hath ordained.

This confideration may fatisfy thofe who enquire, Why fo few have received the blefling? Enquire, how many are feeking it in this way? And you have a fufficient anfwer.

* Prayer efpecially is wanting. Who *continues inftant* therein? Who *wreftles with God* for this very thing? So *ye have not becaufe ye afk not* : or becaufe *ye afk amifs*, namely, " That you may be renewed *before you die.*" Before you die! Will that content you? Nay but afk that it may be done now! To day! While it is called to-day! Do not call this " fetting God a time." Certainly *to day is his time* as well as to morrow. Make hafte man, make hafte! Let

Thy

Thy foul break out in ftrong defire
  The perfeΩ blifs to prove !
Thy longing heart be all on fire
  To be diffolv'd in love !

Q. But may we continue in peace and joy,
'till we are perfeΩ in love ?

A. Certainly we may : for the kingdom of
God is not divided againft itfelf. Therefore let
not believers be difcouraged, from *rejoicing in the
Lord always.* And yet we may be fenfibly pained at the finful nature that ftill remains in us.
It is good for us to have a piercing fenfe of this,
and a vehement to defire to be delivered from
it. But this fhould only incite us, the more zeal-
oufly to fly every moment to our ftrong helper,
the more earneftly to *prefs forward to the mark,
the prize of our high calling in Chrift Jefus.* And
when the fenfe of our fin moft abounds, the fenfe
of his love fhould much more abound.

Q. How fhould we treat thofe who think
they have attained ?

A. Examine them candidly, and exhort them
to pray fervently, that God would fhew them
all that is in their hearts. The moft earneft ex-
hortations to abound in every grace, and the
ftrongeft cautions to avoid all evil, are given
throughout the New Teftament, to thofe who are
in the higheft ftate of grace. But this fhould
be done with the utmoft tendernefs, and without any harfhnefs, fternnefs or fournefs. We
                                   fhould

fhould carefully avoid the very appearance of anger, unkindnefs, or contempt. Leave it to Satan
thus to tempt, and to his children to cry out,
Let us examine him with defpitefulnefs and torture,
that we may know his meeknefs and prove his
patience. If they are faithful to the grace given,
they are in no danger of perifhing thereby ; no
not if they remain in that miftake, till their
fpirit is returning to God.

Q. * But what hurt can it do to deal harfhly
with them ?

A. Either they are miftaken, or they are not. If
they are, it may deftroy their fouls. This is
nothing impoffible, no nor improbable. It may
fo enrage or fo difcourage them, that they will
fink, and rife no more. If they are not miftaken,
it may grieve thofe whom God has not grieved,
and do much hurt unto our own fouls. For undoubtedly he that toucheth them, toucheth as it
were the apple of God's eye. If they are indeed
full of his fpirit, to behave unkindly or con-
temptuoufly to them, is doing no little defpite to
the fpirit of grace. Hereby likewife we feed and
increafe in ourfelves evil-furmifing and many
wrong tempers. To inftance only one. What
felf-fufficiency is this, to fet ourfelves up for
inquifitors general, for peremptory judges in
thefe deep things of God ? Are we qualified
for the office ? Can we pronounce in all cafes,
How far infirmity reaches ? What may, and
what may not be refolved into it ? What may
in

in all cricumftances, and what may not, confift
with perfect love ? Can we precifely determine,
How it will influence the look, the gefture,
the tone of voice.? If we can, doubtlefs we are
the men, and wifdom fhall die with us!

Q. But if they are difpleafed at our not believing them, is not this a full proof againft
them ?

A. According as that difpleafure is : if they are
angry; it is a proof againft them : if they are
grieved, it is not. They ought to be grieved,
if we difbelieve a real work of God, and thereby
deprive ourfelves of the advantage we might
have received from it. And we may eafily
miftake this grief for anger, as the outward ex-
preffions of both are much alike.

Q. But is it not well to find out thofe, who
fancy they have attained, when they have
not ?

A. It is well to do it by mild, loving examination. But it is not well to triumph even over
thefe. It is extremely wrong, if we find fuch an
inftance, to rejoice, as if we had found great
fpoils. Ought we not rather to grieve, to be
deeply concerned, to let our eyes run down with
tears ? Here is one who feemed to be a living
proof of God's power to *fave to the uttermoft.*
But alas ! It is not as we hoped ! He is *weighed
in the balance and found wanting !* And is this
matter of joy ? Ought we not to rejoice a thoufand

fand times more, if we can find nothing but pure love?

* " But he is deceived." What then ? It is a harmless miftake, while he feels nothing but love in his heart. It is a miftake which generally argues great grace, an high degree both of holinefs and happinefs. This fhould be a matter of real joy to all that are fimple of heart : not the miftake itfelf, but the height of grace which for a time occafions it. I rejoice that this foul is always happy in Chrift, always full of prayer and thankfgiving. I rejoice that he feels no unholy temper, but the pure love of God continually. And I will rejoice if fin is *fufpended*, 'till it is totally *deftroyed*.

Q. Is there no danger then in a man's being thus deceived?

A. Not at the time that he feels no fin. There was danger before, and there will be again, when he comes into frefh trials. But fo long as he feels nothing but love animating all his thoughts, and words and actions he is in no danger ! He is not only happy, but fafe, *under the fhadow of the Almighty.* And, for God's fake, let him continue in that love as long as he can ; mean time you may do well to warn him of the danger that will be, if his love grew cold and fin revive, even the danger of cafting away hope, and fuppofing, that becaufe he hath not attained yet, therefore he never fhall.

Q. But

Q. But what if none have attained it yet? What if all who think fo are deceived?

A. Convince me of this, and I will preach it no more. But underftand me right. I do not build any doctrine on this or that perfon. This or any other man may be deceived, and I am not moved. But if there are none made perfect yet, God has not fent me to preach perfection.

Put a parallel cafe. For many years I have preached, " There is a peace of God which paffeth all underftanding." Convince me, that this word has fallen to the ground, that in all thefe years none have attained this peace; that there is no living witnefs of it at this day, and I will preach it no more."

" O, but feveral perfons have died in that peace " Perhaps fo : but I want living witneffes. I cannot indeed be infallibly certain, that this or that perfon is a witnefs. But if I were certain there are none fuch, I muft have done with this doctrine.

" You mifunderftand me. I believe fome who died in this love, enjoyed it long before their death. But I was not certain, that their former teftimony was true, 'till fome hours before they died."

You had not an *infallible* certainty then. And a *reafonable* certainty you might have had before : fuch a certainty as might have quick-ened and comforted your own foul, and anfwered all other Chriftian purpofes. Such a certainty

as

as this any candid perſon may have, ſuppoſe there be any living witneſs, by talking one hour with that perſon in the love and fear of God.

Q. But what does it ſignify, whether any have attained it or no, ſeeing ſo many ſcriptures witneſs for it ?

A. If I were convinced, that none in England had attained what has been ſo clearly and ſtrongly preached by ſuch a number of preachers, in ſo many places and for ſo long a time, I ſhould be clearly convinced, that we had all miſtaken the meaning of thoſe ſcriptures. And therefore for the time to come, I too muſt teach that " ſin will remain 'till death."

. 20. * In the year 1762, there was a great increaſe of the work of God in London. Many, who had hitherto cared for none of theſe things were deeply convinced of their loſt eſtate. Many found redemption in the blood of Chriſt : not a few backſliders were healed. And a conſiderable number of perſons believed, that God had ſaved them from all ſin. Eaſily foreſeeing that Satan would be endeavouring to ſow tares among the wheat, I took much pains to apprize them of the danger, particularly with regard to *pride* and *enthuſiaſm.* And while I ſtayed in town, I had reaſon to hope they continued both humble and ſober-minded. But almoſt as ſoon as I was gone, enthuſiaſm broke in ; two or three began to take their own imaginations for impreſſions from God, and thence to ſuppoſe, suppofe, that they fhould never die. And thefe labouring to bring others into the fame opinion, occafioned much noife and confufion. Soon after, the fame perfons, with a few more, ran into other extravagances, fancying they *could not be tempted*, that they fhould *feel no more pain*, and that they had the gift of prophecy, and of *dif-cerning of fpirits*. At my return to London in autumn, fome of them ftood reproved: but others were got above inftruction. Meantime a flood of reproach came upon me almoft from every quarter: from themfelves, becaufe I was check-ing them on all occafions; and from others, "be-caufe, they faid, I did not check them." How-ever the hand of the Lord was not ftayed, but more and more finners were convinced: while fome were almoft daily converted to God, and others enabled to love him *with all their heart.*

21. About this time a friend at fome dif-tance from London, wrote to me as follows:

" Be not over alarmed, that Satan fows tares among the wheat of Chrift! It ever has been fo, efpecially on any remarkable out-pouring of his Spirit: and ever will be fo, 'till he is chained up for a thoufand years. 'Till then he will always ape, and endeavour to *counteract* the work of the Spirit of Chrift.

" One melancholy effect of this has been, that a world who is always afleep in the arms of the

evil

evil one, has ridiculed every work of the Holy Spirit.

"But what can real Chriſtians do ? Why, if they would act worthy of themſelves, they ſhould 1. Pray that every deluded ſoul may be delivered, 2. Endeavour to reclaim them in the ſpirit of meekneſs, and laſtly, Take the utmoſt care, both by prayer and watchfulneſs, that the deluſion of others may not leſſen their zeal in ſeeking after that *univerſal holineſs* of ſoul, body, and ſpirit, *without which no man ſhall ſee the Lord.*

" Indeed this *compleat new creature* is mere madneſs to a mad world. But it is notwithſtanding the will and wiſdom of God. May we all ſeek after it !

" But ſome who maintain this doctrine in its full extent, are too often guilty of limiting the Almighty. He diſpenſes his gifts juſt as he pleaſes : therefore it is neither wiſe nor modeſt to affirm that a perſon muſt be a believer for any length of time, before he is capable of receiving an *high degree of the ſpirit of holineſs.*

" God's *uſual method* is one thing, but his *ſovereign pleaſure* is another. He has wiſe reaſons both for haſtening and retarding his work : ſometimes he comes ſudden and unexpected : ſometimes not 'till we have long looked for him.

" Indeed it has been my opinion for many years, that one great cauſe why men make ſo little improvement in the divine life, is their own

coldneſs

coldness, negligence, and unbelief. And yet I here speak of *believers.*

" May the Spirit of Christ give us a right judgment in all things, and *fill us with all the fulness of God,* that so we may be *perfect and entire, wanting nothing.*"

About the same time five or six honest enthusiasts foretold the world was to end on the 28th of February. I immediately withstood them by every possible means, both in public and private. I preached expresly upon the subject, both at West-street and Spitalfields. I warned the society again and again, and spoke severally to as many as I could; and I saw the fruit of my labour: They made exceeding few converts: I believe scarce thirty in our whole society. Nevertheless they made abundance of noise, gave huge occasion of offence, to those who took care to improve to the uttermost every occasion against me, and greatly increased both the number and courage of those who opposed Christian Perfection.

22. Some questions now published by one of these, induced a plain man to write the following:

" Queries, humbly proposed to those who deny Perfection to be attainable in this life.

1. Has there not been a *larger measure* of the Holy Spirit given under the gospel, then under Jewish dispensation? If not, in what sense was *the Spirit not given* before Christ was *glorified?* *John* vii. 39.

2. Was

2. Was that *glory which followed the suffer-ings of Chrift,* 1 Pet. i. 11. an external glory or an internal, viz. the glory of holinefs ?

3. Has God any where in fcripture *commanded* us more than he has *promifed* to us ?

4. Are the promifes of God refpecting holi-nefs to be fulfilled *in this life,* or only in *the next ?*

5. Is a Chriftian under any other laws than thofe which God promifes to *write in our hearts, Jer.* xxxi. 31, &c. *Heb.* viii. 10.

6. In what fenfe is *the righteoufnefs of the law fulfilled in thofe, who walk not after the flefh but after the Spirit ? Rom.* viii. 4.

7. Is it impoffible for any one in this life, to *love God with all his heart, and mind, and foul and ftrength ?* And is the Chriftian under any law which is not fulfilled in this love ?

8. Does the foul's *going out of the body* effect its purification from indwelling fin ?

9. If fo, is it not fomething elfe, not *the blood of Chrift, which cleanfeth it from all fin ?*

10. If his blood cleanfeth us from all fin, while the foul and body are united, is it not *in this life ?*

11. If when that union ceafes ; is it not *in the next ?* And is not this too late ?

12. If in the article of death ; what fituation is the foul in, when it is neither *in the body,* nor *out of it ?*

13. Has

13. Has Chriſt any where taught us to pray for what he never deſigns to give?

14. Has he not taught us to pray, *Thy will be done on earth as it is done in heaven?* And is it not done perfectly in heaven?

15. If ſo, has he not taught us to pray for *perfection on earth?* Does he not then deſign to give it?

16. Did not St. Paul pray according to the will of God, when he prayed that the Theſſalonians might be *ſanctified wholly, and preſerved* (in this world, not the next, unleſs he was praying for the dead) *blameleſs in body, ſoul and ſpirit, unto the coming of Jeſus Chriſt?*

17. Do *you* ſincerely *deſire* to be freed from indwelling ſin *in this life?*

18. If you do, did not God give you that deſire?

19. If ſo, did he not give it you to mock you, ſince it is impoſſible it ſhould ever be fulfilled?

20. If you have not ſincerity enough even to deſire it, are you not diſputing about matters too high for you?

21. Do you ever pray God to *cleanſe the thoughts of your heart, that you may perfectly love him?*

22. If you neither *deſire* what you aſk, nor *believe* it attainable, pray you not as a fool prayeth?

God help thee to conſider theſe queſtions calmly and impartially!"

24. In the latter end of this year God called to himſelf

himself that burning and shining light, Jane
Cooper. As she was both a living and a dying
witness of Christian Perfection, it will not be at
all foreign to the subject, to add one of her own
letters, containing a plain and artless relation,
of the manner wherein it pleased God to work
that great change in her soul.

May 2, 1761.

" I believe while memory remains in me, gratitude will continue.—From the time you preached on Gal. v. 5. I saw clearly the state of my
soul.   That sermon described my heart, and
what it wanted to be, truly happy. You read M.
M.'s letter, and it described the religion which I
desired. From that time the prize appeared in
view, and I was enabled to follow hard after it.
I was kept watching unto prayer, sometimes in
much distress, at other times in patient expectation of the blessing. For some days before you
left London, my soul was stayed on a promise I
had applied to me in prayer, *The Lord whom ye
seek shall suddenly come to his temple.* I believed
he would, and that he would sit there as a re-
finer's fire. The Tuesday after you went, I
thought I could not sleep, unless he fulfilled his
word that night. I never knew as I did then
the force of these words, *Be still and know that I
am God.* I became nothing before him, and
enjoyed perfect calmness in my soul. I knew
not whether he had destroyed my sin: but

I desired

I defired to know, that I might praife him. Yet
I foon found the return of unbelief, and groaned,
being burdened. On Wednefday I went to
London, and fought the Lord without ceafing.
I promifed, if he would fave me from fin, I would
praife him. I could part with all things fo I
might win Chrift. But I found all thefe pleas
to be nothing worth, and that if he faved *me*, it
muft be freely, for his own name's fake. On
Thurfday I was fo much tempted, that I thought
of deftroying myfelf, or never converfing more
with the people of God. And yet I had no
doubt of his pardoning love: but " 'twas worfe
than death my God to love, and not my God
alone." On Friday my diftrefs was deepened.
I endeavoured to pray and could not. I went to
Mrs. D. who prayed for me, and told me, it was
the death of nature. I opened the bible on *The*
fearful and unbelieving fhall have their part in the
lake which burneth with fire and brimftone. I
could not bear it. I opened again on Mark xvi.
6, 7. *Be not afrighted: ye feek Jefus of Nazareth*
—Go your way; tell his difciples he goeth before
you into Galilee: there fhall ye fee him. I was
encouraged and enabled to pray, believing I
fhould fee Jefus at home. I returned that night
and found Mrs. G. She prayed for me: and the
predeftinarian had no plea, but " Lord, thou art
no refpecter of perfons." He proved he was not,
by blefling *me.* I was in a moment enabled to
lay

lay hold on Jefus Chrift, and found falvation by
fimple faith. He affured me, the Lord, the king
was in the midft of me, and that I fhould fee
evil no more. I now bleffed him who had vi-
fited and redeemed me, and was become my
*wifdom, righteoufnefs, fanctification and redemp-
tion.* I faw Jefus altogether lovely, and knew
he was mine in all his offices. And, glory be to
him! He now reigns in my heart without a
rival. I find no will but his. I feel no pride;
nor any affection but what is placed on him. I
know, it is by faith I ftand, and that watching
unto prayer muft be the guard of faith. I am
happy in God this moment, and I believe for the
next. I have often read the chapter you mention, (1 Cor. xiii.) and compared my heart and
life with it. In fo doing, I feel my fhort-com-
ings, and the need I have of the atoning blood.
Yet I dare not fay, I do not feel a meafure of the
love there defcribed, though I am not all I fhall
be. I defire to be loft in that *love which paffeth
knowledge.*—I fee *the juft fhall live by faith:* and
unto me, who am lefs than the leaft of all faints,
is this grace given. If I were an archangel, I
fhould veil my face before him, and let filence
fpeak his praife!"

25. The next year, the number of thofe who
believed they were faved from fin ftill increafing,
I judged it needful to publifh, chiefly for their

ufe,

use, " Farther Thoughts on Chriftian Perfection.".

Q. How is *Chrift the end of the law for righteoufnefs to every one that believeth ?* Rom. x. 4.

* *A.* In order to underftand this, you muft
underftand what law is here fpoken of. And
this I apprehend, is 1. The Mofaic law, the
whole Mofaic difpenfation ; which St. Paul continually fpeaks of as one, though containing
three parts, the political, moral, and ceremo-
nial : 2. The Adamic law, that given to Adam
in innocence, properly called, " the law of
works." This is in fubftance the fame with the
Angelic law, being common to angels and man.
It required, that man fhould ufe to the glory of
God, all the powers with which he was created.
Now he was created free from any defect, either
in his underftanding or his affections. His body
was then no clog to the mind : it did not hinder
his apprehending all things clearly, judging truly
concerning them, and reafoning juftly ; if he
reafoned at all. I fay, " If he reafoned :" for
poffibly he did not. Perhaps he had no need of
reafoning, till his corruptible body preffed down
the mind, and impaired its native faculties.
Perhaps till then, the mind faw every truth that
offered, as directly as the eye now fees the light.
Confequently this law, proportioned to his
original powers, required that he fhould always
think, always fpeak, and always act precifely
right,

right,-in every point whatever. He was well able fo to do. And God could not but require the fervice he was able to pay.

But Adam fell: and his incorruptible body became corruptible: and ever fince it is a clog to the foul, and hinders its operations. Hence at prefent no child of man can at all times apprehend clearly, or judge truly. And where either the judgment or apprehenfion is wrong, it is impoffible to reafon juftly. Therefore it is as natural for a man to miftake as to breathe; and he can no more live without the one than without the other. Confequently no man is able to perform the fervice which the Adamic law requires.

And no man is obliged to perform it: God does not require it of any man. *For Chrift is the end of the Adamic,* as well as the *Mofaic law.* By his death he hath put an end to both; he hath abolifhed both the one and the other, with regard to man; and the obligation to obferve either the one or the other is vanifhed away. Nor is any man living bound to obferve the Adamic, more than the Mofaic law. †

In the room of this, Chrift hath eftablifhed another, namely, The law of faith. Not every one that doeth, but every one that believeth, now receiveth righteoufnefs, in the full fenfe of the word, that is, he is juftified, fanctified and glorified.

D 5   Q. 2

---

† I mean, it is not the condition either of prefent or future falvation,

Q. 2. Are we then *dead to the law?*

A. We *are dead to the law by the body of Chrift* given for us, Rom. vii. 4. to the Adamic, as well as Mofaic law. We are wholly freed therefrom by his death: that law expiring with him.

Q. 3. How then are we *not without law to God, but under the law to Chrift?* 1 Cor. ix. 21.

A. We are without that law. But it does not follow that we are without any law. For God has eftablifhed another law in its place, even the law of faith. And we are all under this law to God and to Chrift. Both our Creator and our Redeemer require us to obferve it.

* *Q.* 4. Is love the fulfilling of this law?

A. Unqueftionably it is. The whole law, under which we now are, is fulfilled by love, Rom. xiii. 9, 10. Faith working or animated by love, is all that God now requires of man. He has fubftituted (not fincerity, but) love, in the room of angelic perfection.

Q. 5. How is *love the end of the commandment?* 1 Tim. i. 5.

A. It is the end of every commandment of God. It is the point aimed at by the whole, and every part of the Chriftian inftitution. The foundation is faith, purifying the heart, the end love, preferving a good confcience.

Q. 6. What love is this?

* *A.* The *loving the Lord our God with all our heart, mind, foul and ftrength:* and the *loving our neighbour,* every man as ourfelves, as our own fouls.

Q. 7. What are the fruits or properties of this love?

A. St. Paul informs us at large, love is long-suffering. It suffers all the weaknesses of the children of God, all the wickedness of the children of the world. And that not for a little time only; but as long as God pleases. In all it sees the hand of God, and willingly submits thereto. Meantime it *is kind.* In all, and after all it suffers, it is soft, mild, tender, benign. *Love envieth not:* it excludes every kind and degree of envy out of the heart. *Love acteth not rashly,* in a violent headstrong manner, nor passes any rash or severe judgment. It *doth not behave itself indecently,* is not rude, does not act out of character: *seeketh not her own* ease, pleasure, honour or profit: *is not provoked;* expels all anger from the heart: *thinketh no evil:* casteth out all jealousy, suspiciousness and readiness to believe evil: *rejoiceth not in iniquity;* yea, weeps at the sin or folly of its bitterest enemies; *but rejoiceth in the truth,* in the holiness and happiness of every child of man. *Love covereth all things,* speaks evil of no man; *believeth all things,* that tend to the advantage of another's character. *It hopeth all things,* whatever may extenuate the faults which cannot be denied, and it *endureth all things,* which God can permit, or men and devils inflict. This is *the law of Christ, the perfect law, the law of liberty.*

And this distinction between the *law of faith* (or love) and *the law of works,* is neither a *subtle,* nor an unnecessary distinction. It is plain, easy, and intelligible to any common understanding.

And

And it is abfolutely neceffary, to prevent a thoufand doubts and fears, even in thofe who do *walk
in love.*

* *Q.* 8. But do *we* not *in many things offend
all,* yea, the beft of us, even againft this law?

A. In one fenfe we do not, while all our tempers and thoughts, and words and works fpring
from love. But in another we do, and fhall do,
more or lefs, as long as we remain in the body.
For neither love nor the *unction of the Holy One*
makes us infallible. Therefore through unavoidable defect of underftanding, we cannot but
miftake in many things. And thefe miftakes
will frequently occafion fomething wrong, both
in our temper, and words, and actions. From
miftaking his character, we may love a perfon
lefs than he really deferves. And by the fame
miftake we are unavoidably led to fpeak or act
with regard to that perfon, in fuch a manner as
is contrary to this law, in fome or other of the
preceding inftances.

Q. 9. Do we not then need Chrift, even on
this account?

A. The holieft of men ftill need Chrift as their
prophet, as *the light of the world.* For he does
not give them light, but from moment to moment; the inftant he withdraws, all is darknefs.
They ftill need Chrift as their king. For God
does not give them a ftock of holinefs. But unlefs they received a fupply every moment, nothing but unholinefs would remain. They ftill
need Chrift as their prieft, to make atonement
for

for their holy things. Even perfect holiness is acceptable to God only through Jesus Christ.

Q. 10. May not then the very best of men adopt the dying martyr's confession, " I am in myself *nothing but sin, darkness, hell :* but thou art my light, my holiness, my heaven ?"

A. Not exactly. But the best of men may say, " Thou art my light, my holiness, my heaven. Through my union with thee, I am full of light, of holiness and happiness. But *if I were left to myself, I should be* nothing but sin, darkness, hell."

But to proceed. The best of men need Christ as their priest, their atonement, their advocate with the Father : not only, as the continuance of their every blessing depends on his death and intercession, but on account of their coming short of the law of love. For every man living does so. You who *feel all love*, compare yourselves with the preceding description. Weigh yourselves in this balance, and see if you are not wanting in many particulars.

Q. 11. But if all this be consistent with Christian Perfection, that perfection is not freedom from all sin : seeing *sin is the transgression of the law.* And the perfect transgress the very law they are under. Besides, they need the atonement of Christ. And he is the atonement for nothing but sin. Is then the term *sinless perfection* proper ?

A. It is not worth disputing about. But observe,

ferve, in what fenfe the perfons in queftion need the atonement of Chrift. They do not need him to reconcile them to God *afrefh :* for they *are* reconciled. They do not need him to *reftore* the favour of God, but to *continue* it. He does not *procure* pardon for them *anew,* but *ever liveth to make interceffion for them.* And *by one offering he hath perfected for ever them that are fanctified,* Heb. x. 14.

For want of duly confidering this, fome deny, that they need the atonement of Chrift. Indeed exceeding few : I do not remember to have found five of them in England. Of the two, I would fooner give up Perfection. But we need not give up either one or the other. The Perfection I hold, *Love rejoicing evermore, praying without ceafing, and in every thing giving thanks,* is well confiftent with it : if any hold a Perfection which is not, they muft look to it.

Q. 12. Does then Chriftian Perfection imply any more than *fincerity ?*

A. Not if you mean by that word, love fulfilling the heart, expelling pride, anger, defire, felf-will ; rejoicing evermore, praying without ceafing, and in every thing giving thanks. But I doubt few ufe *fincerity* in this fenfe. Therefore I think the old word is beft.

A perfon may be *fincere,* who has all his natural tempers, pride, anger, luft, felf-will. But he is not *perfect,* till his heart is cleanfed from thefe, and all its other corruptions.

To

To clear this point a little farther; I know many that love God with all their heart. He is their one defire, their one delight, and they are continually happy in him. They love their neighbour as themfelves. They feel as fincere, fervent, conftant a defire, for the happinefs of every man, good or bad, friend or enemy, as for their own. They rejoice evermore, pray without ceafing, and in every thing give thanks. Their fouls are continually ftreaming up to God, in holy joy, prayer, and praife. This is a point of faft. And this is plain, found, fcriptural experience.

But even thefe fouls dwell in a fhattered body, and are fo preft down thereby, that they cannot always exert themfelves as they would, by thinking, fpeaking, and acting *precifely right*. For want of better bodily organs, they muft at times, think, fpeak, or act wrong; not indeed through a defect of *love*, but through a defect of *knowledge*. And while this is the cafe, notwithftanding that defect, and its confequences, they fulfil the law of love.

Yet as even in this cafe there is not a full conformity to the perfect law, fo the moft perfect do on this very account need the blood of atonement, and may properly for themfelves, as well as for their brethren fay, *Forgive us our trefpaffes*.

Q. 13. But if Chrift has put an end to that
law,

law, what need of any atonement for their tranf-
greffing it ?

A. Obferve in what fenfe he has *put an end to*
it, and the difficulty vanifhes. Were it not for
the *abiding merit* of his death, and his *continual
interceffion* for us, that law would condemn us
ftill. Thefe therefore we ftill need, for every
tranfgreffion of it.

Q. 14. But can one that is faved from fin be
tempted?

A. Yes; for *Chrift was tempted.*

Q. 15. However, what you call temptation, I
call the corruption of my heart. And how will
you diftinguifh one from the other ?

A. In fome cafes it is impoffible to diftinguifh,
without the *direct witnefs* of the fpirit. But in
general one may diftinguifh thus :

One commends me. Here is a temptation to
pride : but inftantly my foul is humbled before
God. And I feel no pride : of which I am as
fure as that pride is not humility.

A man ftrikes me. Here is a temptation to
anger. But my heart overflows with love. And
I feel no anger at all : of which I am as fure, as
that love and anger are not the fame.

A woman folicits me. Here is a temptation to
luft. But in the inftant I fhrink back. And I
feel no defire or luft at all : of which I can be as
fure, as that my hand is cold or hot.

Thus it is, if I am tempted by a *prefent* object :
and it is juft the fame, if when it is abfent, the
devil

devil recalls a commendation, an injury, or woman to my mind. In the inflant the foul repels
the temptation, and remains filled with pure
love.

And the difference is ftill plainer, when I compare my prefent flate with my paft, wherein I
felt temptation and corruption too. ·

Q. 16. But how do you *know*, that you are
fanctified, faved from your inbred corruption?

A. I can know it no otherwife than I know
that I am juftified. *Hereby know we that we are
of God,* in either fenfe, *by the Spirit that he hath
given us.*

We know it by *the witnefs,* and by *the fruit* of
the Spirit. And firft, by *the witnefs.* As when
we were juftified, the *Spirit bore witnefs with our
fpirit,* that our fins were forgiven; fo when we
were fanctified, he bore witnefs, that they were
taken away. Indeed the witnefs of fanctification
is not always clear at firft ; (as neither is that of
juftification) neither is it afterward, ·always the
fame, but like that of juftification, fometimes
ftronger and fometimes fainter. Yea, and fometimes it is withdrawn. Yet in general, the latter
teftimony of the Spirit is both as clear and as
fteddy as the former.

Q. 17. But what need is there of it, feeing
fanctification is a *real change,* not a *relative* only,
like juftification ?

Q. But is the new-birth a *relative* change only ?
Is not this a *real* change ? Therefore if we need

no

no witnefs of our fanctification, becaufe it is a *real* change, for the fame reafon we fhould need none, that we are born of, or are the children of God.

Q. 18. * But does not fanctification fhine by its own light?

A. And does not the new birth too? Sometimes it does. And fo does fanctification: at others it does not. In the hour of temptation Satan clouds the work of God, and injects various doubts and reafonings, efpecially in thofe who have either very weak or very ftrong underftandings. At fuch times there is abfolute need of that witnefs: without which the work of fanctification, not only could not be difcerned, but could no longer fubfift. Were it not for this, the foul could not then abide in the love of God: much lefs could it rejoice evermore, and in every thing give thanks. In thefe circumftances therefore, a *direct teftimony* that we are fanctified is neceffary in the higheft degree.

" But I have no *witnefs* that I am faved from fin. And yet I have no doubt of it." Very well. As long as you have no doubt, it is enough; when you have, you will need that *witnefs*.

Q. 19. But what fcripture makes mention of any fuch thing, or gives any reafon to expect it?

A. That fcripture. 1 Cor. ii. 12, *We have received not the fpirit that is of the world, but the*
Spirit

*Spirit which is of God, that we may know the
thi·gs which are freely given us of God.*

Now surely fanctification is one of *the things
which are freely given us of God.* And no poffible
reafon can be affigned, why this fhould be excepted, when the apoftle fays, *We receive the
Spirit for this very end, that we may know the
things which are thus freely given us.*

Is not the fame thing implied in that well
known fcripture, Rom. viii. 15. *The Spirit itfelf witneffeth with our fpirit, that we are the
children of God?* Does he only wi nefs to thofe
who are children of God in the loweft fenfe?
Nay, but to thofe alfo who are fuch in the higheft fenfe. And does he not witnefs that they are
fuch in the higheft fenfe? What reafon have we
to doubt it?

What if a man were to affirm, (as indeed many
do) that this witnefs belongs *only to the higheft*
clafs of Chriftians? Would not you anfwer, the
apoftle makes no reftriftion. Therefore doubtlefs it belongs to all the children of God. And
will not the fame anfwer hold if any affirm, that
it belongs *only to the loweft* clafs?

Confider likewife 1 John v. 19. *We know that
we are of God.* How? *By the Spirit that he hath
given us.* Nay, *hereby we know that he abideth
in us.* And what ground have we either from
fcripture or reafon, to exclude the witnefs any
more than the fruit of the Spirit from being here
intended? By this then alfo *we know that we are*

of

of God, and *in what sense* we are so. Whether we are babes, young men, or fathers, we know, in the same manner.

Not that I affirm, that all young men, or even fathers, have this testimony every moment: there may be intermissions of the direct testimony that they are thus born of God. But those intermissions are fewer and shorter, as they grow up in Christ. And some have the testimony both of their justification and sanctification, without any intermission at all: which I presume more might have, did they walk humbly and closely with God.

Q. 20. May not some of these have a testimony from the Spirit, that they shall not finally fall from God?

A. They may. And this persuasion, that *neither life nor death shall separate them from* him, far from being hurtful, may in some circumstances be extremely useful. These therefore we should in no wise grieve, but earnestly incourage them, *to hold the beginning of their confidence stedfast to the end.*

Q. 21. But have any a testimony from the Spirit, that they shall *never sin?*

A. We know not what God may vouchsafe to some particular persons. But we do not find any general state described in scripture, from which a man cannot draw back to sin. If there were any state wherein this was impossible, it would be that of those who are *sanctified*, who are *fathers in Christ*,

who

who rejoice evermore, pray without ceasing, and *in every thing give thanks*. But it is not impossible for these to draw back. They who are *sanctified*, may yet fall and perish, *Heb*. x. 29. Even *fathers in Christ*, need that warning, *Love not the world*, 1 John ii. 15. They who *rejoice, pray*, and *give thanks without ceasing*, may nevertheless *quench the Spirit*, 1 Thes. v. 16. &c. Nay even they who are *sealed unto the day of redemption may yet grieve the Holy Spirit of God*, Eph. iv. 30.

Altho' therefore God may give such a witness to some patricular persons, yet it is not to be expected by Christians in general, there being no scripture whereon to ground such an expectation.

Q. 22. By what *fruit of the Spirit may we know that we are of God*, even in the highest sense ?

A. By *love, joy, peace* always abiding; by invariable *long-suffering*, patience, resignation ; by *gentleness*, triumphing over all provocation ; by *goodness*, mildness, sweetness, tenderness of spirit ; by *fidelity*, simplicity, godly sincerity ; by *meekness*, calmness, evenness of spirit ; by *temperance*, not only in food and sleep, but in all things natural and spiritual.

Q. 23. But what great matter is there in this ? Have we not all this when we are justified ?

A. What ! *Total resignation* to the will of God, without any mixture of self-will ? *Gentleness,*

tleness, without any touch of anger, even the
moment we are provoked ? Love to God, without the least love to the creature but in and for
God, excluding all pride ? Love to man, excluding *all* envy, *all* jealousy, and rash judging ?
meekness, keeping the whole soul inviolably calm ?
And *temperance* in all things ? Deny that any
ever came up to this if you please ; but do not
say all who are juftified, do.

Q. 24. But fome who are newly juftified do :
what then will you fay to thefe ?

A. If they really do, I will fay, they are fanctified, faved from fin in that moment : and that
they never need lofe what God has given, or
feel fin any more.

But certainly this is an exempt cafe. It is
otherwife with the generality of thofe that are
juftified. They feel in themfelves, more or lefs,
pride, anger, felf-will, and an heart bent to
backfliding. And till they have gradually mortified thefe, they are not fully renewed in love.

Q. 25. But is not this the cafe of all that are
juftified? Do they not *gradually* die to fin and
grow in grace, till at, or perhaps a little before
death, God perfects them in love?

A. I believe this is the cafe of moft, but not all.
God ufually gives a confiderable *time,* for men
to receive *light,* to grow in *grace,* to *do and* fuffer his will before they are either juftified or
fanctified. But he does not invariably adhere to
this. Sometimes he *cuts fhort his work.* He
does

does the work of many years in a few weeks: perhaps in a week, a day, an hour. - He juftifies or fanétifies both thofe who have *done*, or *fuffered* nothing, and who have not had *time* for a gradual growth either in *light* or *grace*. And may he *not do what he will with his own? Is thine eye evil, becaufe he is good?*

* It need not therefore be affirmed over and over, and proved by forty texts of fcripture, either that moft men are perfeéted in love *at laſt,* that there is a *gradual work* of God in the foul; or that, generally fpeaking, it is a long time, even many years, before fin is deftroyed. All this we know. But we know likewife, that God mãy, with man's good leave, *cut ſhort his work,* in whatever degree he pleafes, and do the ufual work of many years in a moment. He does fo, in many inftances. And yet there is a *gradual* work, both *before* and after that moment. So that one may affirm, the work is *gradual;* another, it is *inſtantaneous,* without any manner of contradiétion.

Q. 26. Does St. Paul mean any more by being *fealed with the Spirit,* than being *renewed in love?*

A. Perhaps in one place, 2 Cor. i. 22. he does not mean fo much. But in another, Eph. i. 13. he feems to include both the fruit and the witnefs; and that in a higher degree than we experience, even when we are firft *renewed in love, God fealeth us with the Spirit of promiſe,* by giving

ing

ing us *the full affurance of hope*; fuch a confidence of receiving all the promifes of God, as excludes the poffibility of doubting: with that *holy Spirit*, by univerfal holinefs, ftamping the whole image of God on our hearts.

* *Q*. 27. But how can thofe who are thus *fealed* grieve the Holy Spirit of God?

A. St. Paul tells you very particularly, 1. By fuch *converfation* as is not profitable, not to *the ufe of edifying*, not apt to *minifter grace to the hearers*; 2. By relapfing into *bitternefs* or want of *kindnefs*; 3. By *wrath*, lafting difpleafure, or want of *tender-heartednefs*; 4. By *anger*, however foon it is over, want of inftantly *forgiving one another*; 5. By *clamour* or bawling, loud, harfh, rough fpeaking; 6. By *evil-fpeaking*, whifpering, tale-bearing; needlefsly mentioning the fault of an abfent perfon, though in ever fo foft a manner.

Q. 28. What do you think of thofe in London, who feem to have been lately *renewed in love?*

* *A*. There is fomething very peculiar in the experience of the greater part of them. One would expect, that a believer fhould firft be filled with love, and thereby emptied of fin: whereas thefe were emptied of fin firft, and then filled with love. Perhaps it pleafed God to work in this manner, to make his work more plain and undeniable; and to diftinguifh it more clearly from that overflowing love, which is often felt even in a juftified ftate.

It

It feems likewife moft agreeable to the great promife, Ezek. xxxvi 25, 26, *From all your filthinefs I will cleanfe you ; a new heart alfo will I give you, and a new Spirit will I put within you.*

But I do not think of them all alike ; there is a wide difference between fome of them and others. I think moft of them with whom I have fpoken, have much faith, love, joy, and peace. Some of thefe I believe are renewed in love, and have the *direct witnefs* of it : And they manifeft the fruit above defcribed, in all their words and actions. Now let any man call this what he will. It is what I call *perfection.*

But fome who have much love, peace and joy, yet have not the direct witnefs. And others who think they have, are neverthelefs manifeftly wanting in the fruit. How many I will not fay : perhaps one in ten, perhaps more or fewer. But fome are undeniably wanting in *long-fuffering,* Chriftian refignation. They do not fee the hand of God in whatever occurs, and chearfully embrace it. They do not in every thing give thanks and rejoice evermore. They are not happy, at leaft, not *always* happy. For fometimes they *complain.* They fay, " This or that is *hard !"*

* Some are wanting in *gentlenefs.* They *refift evil,* inftead of turning the other cheek. They do not receive reproach with gentlenefs ; no, nor even reproof. Nay they are not able to bear contradiction without the appearance, at leaft, of refentment. If they are reproved, or contradicted, tho' mildly, they do not take it well. They behave with more diftance and referve than they did before. If they are reproved or contradicted harfhly, they anfwer it with harfhnefs; with a loud voice, or with an angry tone, or in a fharp and furly manner. They fpeak fharply or roughly, when they reprove others, and behave roughly to their inferiors.

* Some are wanting in *goodnefs*. They are not kind, mild, fweet, amiable, foft, and loving at all times, in their fpirit, in their words, in their look, and air, in the whole tenor of their behaviour; and that to all, high and low, rich and poor, without refpect of perfons: particularly to them that are out of the way, to oppofers, and to thofe of their own houfhold. They do not long, ftudy, endeavour by every means, to make all about them happy. They can fee them uneafy, and not be concerned: perhaps they make them fo. And then wipe their mouths and fay, " Why, they deferve it. It is their own fault."

Some are wanting in fidelity, a nice regard to truth, fimplicity, and godly fincerity. Their love is hardly *without diffimulation*; fomething like guile is found in their mouth. To avoid roughnefs, they lean to the other extreme. They are fmooth to an excefs, fo as fcarce to avoid a degree of fawning, or of feeming to mean what they do not.

* Some are wanting in meeknefs, quietnefs, of

fpirit,

fpirit, compofure, evennefs of temper. They are
up and down, fometimes high, fometimes low ;
their mind is not well balanced. Their affections are either not in due proportion: they have
too much of one, too little of another : or they
are not duly mixed and tempered together, fo
as to counterpoife each other. Hence there is
often a jar. Their foul is out of tune, and cannot make the true harmony.

Some are wanting in temperance. They do not
fteddily ufe that kind and degree of food, which
they know, or might know, would moft con-
duce to the health, ftrength and vigour of the
body. Or they are not temperate in fleep :
they do not rigoroufly adhere to what is beft both
for body and mind. Otherwife they would conftantly go to bed and rife early, and at a fixt hour.
Or they fup late, which is neither good for body
nor foul. Or they ufe neither fafting nor abftinence. Or they prefer (which are fo many forts
of intemperance) that preaching, reading or
converfation, which gives them tranfient joy
and comfort, before that which brings godly
forrow, or *inftruction in righteoufnefs*. Such joy
is not fanctified. It doth not tend to and terminate in the crucifixion of the heart. Such faith
doth not center in God but rather in itfelf.

So far all is plain. I believe you have faith,
and love, and joy, and peace. You who are
particularly concerned, know each for yourfelf

that

that you are wanting in the respects above-mentioned. You are wanting either in long-suffering, gentleness or goodness; either in fidelity, meekness or temperance. Let us not then on either hand, fight about words. In the thing we clearly agree.

You have not what I call perfection. If others will call it so, they may. However hold fast what you have, and earnestly pray for what you have not.

Q. 29. Can those who are perfect grow in grace?

A. Undoubtedly they can. And that not only while they are in the body, but to all eternity.

Q. 30. Can they fall from it?

A. I am well assured they can. Matter of fact puts this beyond dispute. Formerly we thought, one saved from sin could not fall. Now, we know the contrary. We are surrounded with instances of those who lately experienced all that I mean by perfection. They had both the fruit of the Spirit and the *witness*. But they have now lost both. Neither does any one stand, by virtue of any thing that is implied in the *nature* of the state. There is no such *height* or *strength* of holiness, as it is impossible to fall from. If there be any that *cannot fall*, this wholly depends on the promise of God.

Q. 31. Can those who fall from this state, recover it?

A. Why not? We have many instances of
this

this alfo. Nay, it is an exceeding common thing, for perfons to lofe it more than once, before they are eftablifhed therein.

It is therefore to guard them who are faved from fin, from every occafion of ftumbling, that I give the following advices. But firft I fhall fpeak plainly concerning the work itfelf.

I efteem this late work to be of God : probably, the greateft now upon earth. Yet like all others, this alfo is mixed with much human frailty. But thefe weaknefles are far lefs than might have been expected ; and ought to have been joyfully borne by all that loved and followed after righteoufnefs. That there have been a few weak, warm-headed men, is no reproach to the work itfelf, no juft ground for accufing a multitude of fober-minded men, who are patterns of ftrict holinefs. Yet (juft contrary to what ought to have been) the oppofition is great; the helps few. Hereby many are hindered from feeking faith and holinefs by the falfe zeal of others : and fome who at firft began to run well, are turned out of the way.

Q. 32. What is the firft advice that you would give them ?

A. Watch and pray continually againft pride. If God has caft it out, fee that it enter no more : it is full as dangerous as defire. And you may flide back into it unawares : efpecially if you think there is no danger of it. " Nay, but I afcribe all I have to God." So you may, and

E 3

be

be proud neverthelefs. For it is pride, not only
to afcribe any thing we have to ourfelves, but to
think we have what we really have not. Mr.
L—— for inftance, afcribed all the light he had
to God, and fo far he was humble. But then he
thought he had more light than any man living.
And this was palpable pride. So you afcribe
all the knowledge you have to God; and in this
refpect you are humble. But if you think you
have more than you really have; or if you think
you are fo taught of God, as no longer to need
man's teaching, pride lieth at the door. Yes, you
have need to be taught, not only by Mr. M.—d,
or me, but by the weakeft preacher in London:
yea, by all men. For God fendeth by whom he
will fend.

Do not therefore fay to any who would advife
or reprove you, " You are blind: you cannot
teach me." Do not fay, This is your *wifdom*,
your *carnal reafon:* but calmly weigh the thing
before God.

* Always remember, much grace does not imply much light. Thefe do not always go together. As there may be much light where there
is but little love, fo there may be much love
where there is little light. The heart has more
heat than the eye; yet it cannot fee. And God
has wifely tempered the members of the body together, that none may fay to another, " I have
no need of thee."

To imagine none can teach you, but thofe
who

who are themfelves faved from fin, is a very
great and dangerous miftake. Give not place
to it for a moment. It would lead you into a
thoufand other miftakes, and that irrecoverably.
No: *dominion* is not *founded in grace*, as the mad-
men of the laft age talked. Obey and regard
them that are over you in the Lord, and do not
think you know better than them. Know their
place, and *your own :* always remembering, Much
love does not imply much light.

The not obferving this has led fome into
many miftakes, and into the appearance, at leaft,
of pride. O beware of the appearance and the
thing. Let there *be in you that* lowly *mind which
was in Chrift Jefus.* And *be ye* likewife *cloathed
with humility.* Let it not only fill, but cover you
all over. Let modefty and felf-diffidence appear
in all your words and actions. Let all you fpeak
and do fhew that you are little, and bafe, and
mean, and vile in your own eyes.

As one inftance of this, be always ready to
own any fault you have been in. If you have at
any time thought, fpoke or acted wrong, be not
backward to acknowledge it. Never dream that
this will hurt the caufe of God: no, it will further
it. Be therefore open and frank when you are
taxt with any thing: do not feek either to evade
or difguife it. But let it appear juft as it is, and
you will thereby not hinder, but adorn the
gofpel.

E 4

Q. 33. What is the second advice which you would give them?

A. Beware of that daughter of pride, *enthufiafm!* O keep at the utmoft diftance from it: give no place to an heated imagination. Do not haftily afcribe things to God. Do not eafily fuppofe dreams, voices, impreffions, vifions or revelations to be from God. They may be from him. They may be from nature. They may be from the devil. Therefore *believe not every fpirit, but try the fpirits whether they be of God.* Try all things by the written word, and let all bow down before it. You are in danger of enthufiafm every hour, if you depart ever fo little from fcripture: yea, or from the plain literal meaning of any text, taken in connexion with the context. And fo you are, if you defpife or lightly efteem reafon, knowledge or human learning: every one of which is an excellent gift of God, and may ferve the noblest purpofes.

I advife you, never to ufe the words, *wifdom, reafon,* or *knowledge,* by way of reproach. On the contrary, pray that you yourfelf may abound in them more and more. If you mean *worldly* wifdom, *ufelefs* knowledge, *falfe* reafoning, fay fo: and throw away the chaff, but not the wheat.

One general inlet to enthufiafm is, expecting the end without the means; the expecting knowledge, for inftance, without fearching the fcripture, and confulting the children of God: the
expecting

expecting spiritual strength without constant prayer, and steady watchfulness: the expecting any blessing without hearing the word of God at every opportunity.

Some have been ignorant of this device of Satan. They have left off searching the scriptures. They said, " God writes all the scriptures on my heart. Therefore I have no need to read it." Others thought, they had not so much need of hearing, and so grew slack in attending the morning preaching. O take warning, you who are concerned herein. You have listened to the voice of a stranger. Fly back to Christ, and keep in the good old way, which was *once delivered to the saints :* the way that even an Heathen bore testimony of, " That the Christians rose early every day to sing hymns to Christ as God."

The very desire of *growing in grace* may sometimes be an inlet of enthusiasm. As it continually leads us to seek *new grace,* it may lead us unawares to seek something else new, besides *new degrees* of love to God and man. So it has led some to seek and fancy they had received gifts of a *new kind,* after a new heart, as 1. the loving God with all our mind. 2. with all our soul, 3. with all our strength, 4. oneness with God, 5. oneness with Christ, 6. having our life hid with Christ in God, 7. being dead with Christ, 8. rising with him, 9. the sitting with him in heavenly places, 10. the being taken up into his throne, 11. the being in the new Jerusalem, 12.

the

the feeing the tabernacle of God come down among men, 13. the being dead to all works, 14. the not being liable to death, pain, or grief, or temptation.

One ground of many of thefe miftakes is, the taking every frefh, ftrong application of any of thefe fcriptures to the heart, to be a gift of a *new kind:* not knowing that feveral of thefe fcriptures are not fulfilled yet; that moft of the others are fulfilled when we are juftified; the reft, the moment we are fanctified. It remains only, to experience them in *higher degrees.* This is all we have to expect.

* Another ground of thefe, and a thoufand miftakes is, the not confidering deeply, that love is the higheft gift of God, humble, gentle, patient love: that all vifions, revelations, manifeftations whatever, are little things compared to love: and that all the gifts above-mentioned are either the fame with, or infinitely inferior to it.

It were well you fhould be throughly fenfible of this; the heaven of heavens is love. There is nothing higher in religion: there is, in effect, nothing elfe: if you look for any thing but *more love,* you are looking wide of the mark, you are getting out of the royal way. And when you are afking others, Have *you* received this or that blefling? If you mean any thing but *more love,* you mean wrong; you are leading them out of the way, and putting them upon a falfe fcent.

ſcent. Settle it then in your heart, that from the moment God has ſaved you from all ſin, you are to aim at nothing more, but more of that love deſcribed in the thirteenth of the Corinthians. You can go no higher than this, till you are carried into Abraham's boſom.

I ſay yet again, beware of *enthuſiaſm*. Such is the imagining you have the gift of *propheſying*, or of *diſcerning of ſpirits*, which I do not believe one of you has; no, nor ever had yet. Beware of judging people to be either right or wrong, by your own *feelings*. This is no ſcriptural way of judging. O keep cloſe to *the law and to the teſtimony!*

Q. 34. What is the third?

A. Beware of *Antinomianiſm, making void the law*, or any part of it *through faith*. Enthuſiaſm naturally leads to this: indeed they can ſcarce be ſeparated. This may ſteal upon you in a thouſand forms, ſo that you cannot be too watchful againſt it. Take heed of every thing, whether in principle or practice, which has any tendency thereto. Even that great truth, that Chriſt *is the end of the law*, may betray us into it, if we do not conſider, that he has adopted every point of the moral law, and grafted it into the law of love. Beware of thinking, " becauſe I am filled with love, I need not have *ſo much* holineſs. Becauſe I pray always, therefore I need no *ſet time* for private prayer: becauſe I watch always, therefore I need no particular

ſelf

felf-examination." Let us *magnify the law*, the whole written word, *and make it honourable*. Let this be our voice, *I prize thy commandments above gold or precious stones. O what love have I unto thy law. All the day long is my study in it!* Beware of *Antinomian books* : particularly the works of Dr. Crifp and Mr. Saltmarfh. Thy contain many excellent things. And this makes them the more dangerous. O be warned in time! Do not play with fire : do not put your hand on the hole of a cockatrice den! I entreat you, beware of *bigotry*. Let not your love or beneficence be confined to *Methodifts* (fo called) only ; much lefs to that very finall part of them, who feem to be renewed in love : or to thofe who be'ieve your's and their report : O make not this your *Shibboleth*. Beware of *ftillnefs : ceafing*, in a wrong fenfe, *from your own works*. To mention one inftance out of many, " You have received, fays one, a great blefling. But you began to *talk* of it, and to *do* this and that. So you loft it. You fhould have been *ftill*."

Beware of *felf-indulgence :* yea, and making a virtue of it, laughing at *felf-denial*, and *taking up the crofs daily*, at fafting or abftinence. Beware of *cenforioufnefs* : thinking or calling them that any ways oppofe *you*, whether in judgment or practice, *blind, dead, fallen*, or " enemies to the work." Once more, beware of *Sclifidianifm* : crying nothing but " believe, believe :" and condemning thofe as *ignorant* or *legal*, who fpeak

in

in a more fcriptural way. At certain feafons indeed, it may be right to treat of nothing but repentance, or merely of faith, or altogether of
holinefs: but in general our call is, to declare
the whole counfel of God, and to prophefy according to the analogy of faith. The written
word treats of the whole, and every particular
branch of righteoufnefs, defcending to its minuteft branches, as to be fober, courteous, diligent,
patient to honour all men. So likewife the Holy
Spirit works the fame in our hearts, not merely
creating defires after holinefs in general, but
ftrongly inclining us to every particular grace,
leading us to every individual part of *whatfoever
is lovely*. And this with the greateft propriety:
for as *by works faith is made perfect*, fo the com-
pleating or deftroying the work of faith, and enjoying the favour, or fuffering the difpleafure of
God, greatly depends on every fingle act of obedience or difobedience.

Q. 35. What is the fourth?

A. Beware of *fins of omiffion*: lofe no opportunity of doing good in any kind. Be zealous of
good works: willingly omit no work, either of
piety or mercy. Do all the good you poffibly
can to the bodies and fouls of men. Particularly,
*thou fhalt in any wife reprove thy neighbour, and
not fuffer fin upon him.* Be active. Give no
place to indolence or floth: give no occafion to
fay, " Ye are idle, ye are idle." Many will fay
fo ftill; but let your whole fpirit and behaviour
refute

refute the flander. Be always employed : lose no fhred of time : gather up the fragments, that none be loft. And whatfoever thy hand findeth to do, do it with thy might. Be *flow to fpeak*, and weary in fpeaking. *In a multitude of words there wanteth not fin.* Do not talk much : neither long at a time. Few can converfe profitably above an hour. Keep at the utmoft diftance from pious chit-chat, from religious goffipping.

Q. 36. What is the fifth ?

A. Beware of *defiring* any thing but God. Now you defire nothing elfe. Every other defire is driven out : fee that none enter again. *Keep thyfelf pure* ; *let your eye remain fingle, and your whole body fhall be full of light.* Admit no defire of pleafing food, or any other pleafure of fenfe : no defire of pleafing the eye, or the imagination, by any thing grand, or new, or beautiful : no defire of money, of praife, or efteem ; of happinefs in *any creature.* You *may* bring thefe defires back ; but you *need* not ; you need feel them no more. O ftand faft in the liberty wherewith Chrift hath made you free !

Be patterns to all, of denying yourfelves, and taking up your crofs daily. Let them fee that you make no account of any pleafure, which does not bring you nearer to God ; nor regard any pain which does : that you fimply aim at pleafing him, whether by doing or fuffering ; that the conftant language of your heart, with regard to

pleafure,

pleafure or pain, honour or difhonour, riches
or poverty, is,

> All's alike to me, fo I
> In my Lord may live and die?

Q. 37. What is the fixth?

A. Beware of *fchifm*, of making a rent in the
church of Chrift. That inward difunion, the
members ceafing to have a reciprocal love *one
for another*, (1 Cor. xii. 25,) is the very root of
all contention, and every outward feparation.
Beware of every thing tending thereto. Beware
of a dividing fpirit : fhun whatever has the leaft
afpect that way. Therefore fay not, *I am of
Paul, or of Apollos*; the very thing which occafioned the fchifm at *Corinth*. Say not, this
is *my* preacher; the *beft* preacher in England.
Give me him, and take all the reft." All this
tends to breed or foment divifion, to difunite
thofe whom God hath joined. Do not defpife,
or run down any preacher. Do not exalt any
one above the reft, left you hurt both him and
the caufe of God. On the other hand do not
bear hard upon any by reafon of fome incohe-
rency or inaccuracy of expreffion: no, nor for
fome miftakes, were they really fuch.

Likewife if you would avoid fchifm, obferve
every *rule* of the *fociety*, and of the *bands*, for
confcience fake. Never omit meeting your clafs
er band; never abfent yourfelf from any public
meeting.

meeting. Thefe are the very finews of our fociety: and whatever weakens, or tends to weak-
en our regard for thefe, or our exactnefs in attending them, ſtrikes at the very root of our
community. As one faith, " That part of our
œconomy, the private weekly meetings for
prayer, examination, and particular exhortation, has been the greateſt means of deepening
and confirming every blefing, that was received
by the word preached, and of diffufing it to others,
who could not attend the public miniſtry; whereas, without this religious connexion and intercourfe, the moſt ardent attempts by mere preaching, have proved of no laſting ufe."

Suffer not one thought of feparating from your
brethren, whether their opinions agree with
your's or not. Do not dream, that any man
fins, in not believing *you*, in not taking *your
word :* or that this or that *opinion*, is effential to
the work, and both muſt ſtand or fall together.
Beware of *impatience of contradiction.* Do not
condemn or think hardly of thoſe, who cannot
fee juſt as you fee, or who judge it their duty to
contradict you, whether in a great thing or a
fmall. I fear fome of us have thought hardly of
others, merely becaufe they contradicted what
we affirmed. All this tends to divifion. And
by every thing of this kind, we are teaching
them an evil leffon againſt ourfelves.

O beware of touchinefs, of teſtinefs. not bearing to be fpoken to; ſtarting at the leaſt word;

and

and flying from thofe who do not implicitly receive mine or another's fayings !

* Expect contradiction and oppofition, together with croffes of various kinds. Confider
the words of St. Paul, *To you it is given in the
b half of* Chrift for his fake, as a fruit of his
death and interceffion for you, *not only to believe,
but also to fuffer for his fake,* Phil. i. 10. *It is
given!* God *gives* you this oppofition or reproach: it is a frefh token of his love. And will
you difown the giver ? Or fpurn his gift, and
count it a misfortune ? Will you not rather fay,
" Father, the hour is come, that thou fhouldeft
be glorified. Now thou giveft thy child, to fuffer fomething for thee. Do with me according
to thy will." Know that thefe things, far from being hindrances to the work of God, or to your
foul, unlefs by your own fault, are not only
unavoidable in the courfe of providence, but
profitable, yea neceffary for you. Therefore receive them from God (not from chance) with willingnefs, with thankfulnefs. Receive them from
men with humility, meeknefs, yieldingnefs, gentlenefs, fweetnefs. Why fhould not even your
outward *appearance* and *manner,* be foft ? Remember the character of Lady Cutts: " it was
faid of the Roman Emperor, Titus, never any
one *came difpleafed from him."* But it might be
faid of her, never any one *went difpleafed to* her.
So fecure were all, of the kind and favourable
reception,

reception, which they would meet with from her."

Beware of tempting others to separate from *you*. Give no offence which can possibly be a-voided : see that your practice be in all things suitable to your profession, adorning the doctrine of God our Saviour. Be particularly careful in speaking of yourself : you may not indeed deny the work of God : but speak of it when you are called thereto, in the most inoffensive manner possible. Avoid all magnificent, pompous words. Indeed you need give it no *general* name. Nei-ther " perfection, sanctification, the second blef-sing, nor the having attained." Rather speak of the *particulars*, which God has wrought for you. You may say, " At such a time I felt a change which I am not able to exprefs. And since that time I have not felt pride, or self-will, or anger, or unbelief : nor any thing but a full-nefs of love, to God and to all mankind." And answer any other plain question that is asked, with modefty and fimplicity.

And if any of you should at any time fall from what you now are, if you should again feel pride or unbelief, or any temper from which you are now delivered ; do not deny, do not hide, do not difguife it at all, at the peril of your foul. At all events go to one in whom you can confide, and speak juft what you feel. God will enable him to speak a word in feafon, which shall be health to your foul. And furely he will again

lift

lift up your head, and caufe the bones that have been broken to rejoice.

Q. 38. What is the laſt advice that you would give them?

A. Be *exemplary* in all things: particularly in *outward* things (as in *dreſs*) in *little* things, in the laying out of your *money*, (avoiding every need-leſs expence) in deep, ſteddy *ſeriouſneſs*, and in the *ſolidity* and *uſefu'neſs* of all your *converſa-tion*. So ſhall you be *a light ſhining in a dark place:* ſo ſhall you daily *grow in grace*, till *an entrance be miniſtered unto you abundantly, into the everlaſting kingdom of our Lord Jeſus Chriſt.*

26. * In the year 1764, upon a review of the whole ſubject, I wrote down the ſum of what I had obſerved, in the following ſhort propoſi-tions."

" 1. There is ſuch a thing as *perfection*; for it is again and again mentioned in ſcripture.

2. It is not ſo early as juſtification; for juſti-fied perſons are to *go on to perfection*. Heb, vi. 1.

3. It is not ſo late as death; for St. Paul ſpeaks of living men that were perfect, Phil. iii. 15.

4. It is not *abſolute*. Abſolute perfection be-longs not to man: nor to angels; but to God alone.

5. It does not make a man *infallible*: none is infallible, while he remains in the body.

6. Is

6. Is it *finlefs*? It is not worth while to contend for a term. It is *falvation from fin*.

7. It is *perfect love*, 1 John iv. 18. This is the effence of it ; its *properties*, or infeparable fruits, are *rejoicing evermore, praying without ceafing, and in every thing giving thanks*, 1 Thef. v. 16, &c.

8. It is *improveable*. It is fo far from lying in an indivifible point, from being incapable of increafe that one perfected in love, may grow in grace far fwifter than he did before.

9. It is amiffible, capable of being loft ; of which we have numerous inftances. But we were not thoroughly convinced of this till five or fix years ago.

10. It is conftanly both preceded and followed by a gradual work.

11. But is it in itfelf inftantaneous, or not ? In examining this, let us go on ftep by ftep.

An *inftantaneous change* has been wrought in fome believers : none can deny this.

Since that change they enjoy *perfect love*. They feel this and this alone. They rejoice evermore, pray without ceafing, and in every thing give thanks. Now this is all that I mean by perfection. Therefore thefe are witneffes of the perfection which I preach.

" But in fome this change was not inftantaneous." They did not perceive the inftant when it was wrought. It is often difficult to perceive the inftant when a man dies.

dies. Yet there is an inftant in which life ceafes. And if ever fin ceafes, there muft be a laft moment of its exiftence, and a firft moment of our deliverance from it.

"But if they have this love now, they will lofe it." They may; but they need not. And whether they do or no, they have it now: they now experience what we teach. They now are *all love*. They *now* rejoice, pray and praife without ceafing.

"However, fin is only *fufpended* in them; it is not *deftroyed.*" *Call* it which you pleafe. They are *all love* to day: and they take no thought for the morrow.

"But this doctrine has been much abufed." So has that of juftification by faith. But that is no reafon for giving up, either this or any other fcriptural doctrine! When you wafh your child, as one fpeaks, " throw away the water but do not throw away the child."

"But thofe who think they are faved from fin fay they have no need of the merits of Chrift." They fay juft the contrary. Their language, is,

> Every moment, Lord, I want
> The merit of thy death!

They never before had fo deep, fo unfpeakable a conviction of the need of Chrift, in all his offices as they have now.

Therefore all our preachers fhould make a point,

point, of *preaching perfection* to believers, con-
stantly, strongly and explicitly.

And all believers should *mind this one thing*,
and continually agonize for it.

27. * I have now done what I proposed. I have
given a plain and simple account, of the manner
wherein I first received the doctrine of perfection,
and the sense wherein I received, and wherein
I do receive and teach it to this day. I have declared the whole, and every part of what I
mean by that scriptural expression. I have drawn
the picture of it at full length, without either
disguise or covering And I would now ask any
impartial person, What is there so frightful
therein? Whence is all this outcry, which for
these twenty years and upwards, has been made
throughout the kingdom : as if all Christianity
were destroyed, and all religion torn up by the
roots? Why is it, that the very name of perfection has been cast out of the mouths of Christians ; yea, exploded and abhorred, as if it contained the most pernicious heresy? Why have
the preachers of it been hooted at, like mad
dogs, even by men that fear God? Nay, and by
some of their own children, some whom they,
under God, had begotten through the gospel?
What *reason* is there for this? Or what *pretence*?
Reason, sound reason there is none. It is impossible there should : but *pretences* there are, and
those in great abundance. Indeed there is a
ground to fear, that with some who treat us
thus,

thus, it is mere pretence: that it is no more than a copy of their countenance, from the beginning to the end. They wanted, they fought occasion againſt *me:* and here they found what they fought. " This is Mr. Weſley's doctrine! He preaches perfection!" He does: yet this is not *his* doctrine, any more than it is *yours;* or any one's elſe, that is a miniſter of Chriſt. For it is *his* doctrine, peculiarly, emphatically his; it is the doctrine of Jeſus Chriſt. Thoſe are *his* words, not mine, Ἔσεσθε ἐν τέλειοι ὡς ὁ Πατὴρ ὑμῶν ὁ ἐν τοῖς ὀρανοῖς τέλειός ἐςι. *Ye ſhall therefore be perfect, as your Father who is in heaven is perfect.* And who ſays, ye ſhall not? Or at leaſt, not till your foul is ſeparated from the body? It is the doctrine of St. Paul, the doctrine of St. James, of St. Peter, and St. John: and no otherwiſe Mr. Weſley's, than as it is the doctrine of every one who preaches the pure and the whole goſpel. I tell you, as plain as I can ſpeak, where and when I found this. I found it in the oracles of God, in the Old and New Teſtament: when I read them with no other view or deſire but to ſave my own foul. But whroſe ever this doctrine is, I pray you, what harm is there in it? Look at it again: furvey it on every ſide, and that with the cloſeſt attention. In one view it is pūrity of intention, dedicating all the life to God. It is the giving God all our heart; it is one deſire and deſign ruling all our tempers. It is the devoting, not a part, but all our foul, body, and ſubſtance

to

to God. In another view, it is all the mind which was in Chrift, enabling us to walk as Chrift walked. It is the circumcifion of the heart from all filthinefs, all inward as well as outward pollution. It is a renewal of the heart in the whole image of God, the full likenefs of him that created it. In yet another, it is the loving God with all our heart, and our neighbour as ourfelves. Now take it in which of thefe views you pleafe, (for there is no material difference) and this is the whole and fole perfection, as a train of writings prove to a demonftration, which I have believed and taught for thefe forty years, from the year 1725, to the year 1765.

28. Now let this *perfection* appear in its native form, and who can fpeak one word againft it? Will any dare to fpeak againft loving the Lord our God with all our heart, and our neighbour as ourfelves? Againft a renewal of heart, not only in part, but in the whole image of God? Who is he that will open his mouth againft being cleanfed from all pollution both of flefh and fpirit? Or againft having all the mind that was in Chrift, and walking in all things as Chrift walked? What man, who calls himfelf a Chriftian, has the hardinefs to object, to the devoting, not a part, but all our foul, body and fubftance to God? What ferious man would oppofe the giving God all our heart, and the having one defign ruling all our tempers? I fay again, let this perfection appear in its own fhape, and who will

fight

fight againſt it? It muſt be *diſguiſed*, before it
can be *oppoſed*. It muſt be covered with a bear-
ſkin firſt, or even the wild-beaſts of the people,
will ſcarce be induced to *worry* it. But whatever
theſe do, let not the children of God any longer
fight againſt the image of God. Let not the members of Chriſt ſay any thing againſt having the
whole mind that was in Chriſt. Let not thoſe who
are alive to God oppoſe the dedicating all our
life to him. Why ſhould *you*, who have his
love ſhed abroad in your heart, withſtand the
giving him all your heart? Does not all that is
within you cry out; " O who that loves can love
enough?" What pity that thoſe who deſire and
deſign to pleaſe him, ſhould have any other deſign or deſire? Much more that they ſhould
dread, as a fatal deluſion, yea, abhor, as an a-
bomination to God, the having this one deſire
and deſign, ruling every temper! Why ſhould
devout men be afraid of devoting all their ſoul,
body, and ſubſtance to God? Why ſhould thoſe
who love Chriſt, count it a damnable error, to
think we may have all the mind that was in him?
We allow, we contend, that we are *juſtified*
freely, through the righteouſneſs and the blood
of Chriſt. And why are you ſo hot againſt us,
becauſe we expect likewiſe, to be *ſanctified*
wholly through his Spirit? We look for no favour either from the open ſervants of ſin, or
from thoſe who have only the form of religion.
But how long will you, who worſhip God in

spirit, who are *circumcised with the circumcision not made with hands*, set your battle in array against those, who seek an entire *circumcision of heart*, who thirst to be cleansed *from all filthiness of flesh and spirit*, and to *perfect holiness in the fear of God?* Are we your enemies, because we look for a full deliverance from that *carnal mind, which is enmity against God?* Nay, we are your brethren, your fellow-labourers in the vineyard of our Lord, your companions in the kingdom and patience of Jesus. Although this we confess, (if we are fools therein, yet as fools bear with us:) we do expect to love God with all our heart, and our neighbour as ourselves. Yea, we do believe, that he will in this world to " cleanse the thoughts of our hearts, by the inspiration of his Holy Spirit, that we shall perfectly love him, and worthily magnify his holy name."

INSTRUCTIONS

INSTRUCTIONS

FOR

CHRISTIANS.

SECTION I.

LESSON I and II.

Of GOD.

HOW many Gods are there?
    One: who is God the Father, God the
Son, and God the Holy Ghoſt. Theſe three
are one.

2. What is God?
A Spirit.

3. What do you mean by a ſpirit?
One that cannot be ſeen or felt.

4. What ſort of a ſpirit is God?
One that always was, and always will be.

5. Where is God?
Every where.

F 2   6. What

6. What does God know?

Every thing.

7. What can God do?

Whatever he will.

8. Does God love you?

Yes: he loves every thing which he has made.

9. What has God made?

Every thing, and in particular, man.

LESSON III. and IV.

Of the Creation and Fall of man.

1. How did God make man?

His body out of the duft, his foul out of no-thing.

2. Why did God make man?

To know, love and be happy in God for ever.

3. Where did God put the firft man and woman?

In the garden of paradife.

4. What command did he give them there?

Not to eat of the tree in the midft of the gar-den.

5. Did they keep that command?

No, they did eat of it.

6. What hurt did they bring on themfelves thereby?

Sin and guilt, pain and death.

7. Did their fin hurt any befide themfelves?

Yes: all men that came from them.

8. How did it hurt *them?*

They

They are all born in fin and guilt, and fubject to pain and death.

9. How are men born in fin?

We are all born proud, felf-willed, lovers of the world, and not lovers of God.

LESSON V. VI. and VII.

Of the Redemption of Man.

1. By whom are we to be faved from fin?

By Jefus Chrift the eternal Son of God.

2. What did he do to fave us?

He was made man, and lived and died, and rofe again.

3. What may we gain by his living and dying for us?

Forgivenefs of fins, and holinefs and heaven.

4. When does God forgive our fins?

When we repent and believe in Chrift.

5. What do you mean by repenting?

Being thoroughly convinced of our finfulnefs, guilt, and helpleffnefs.

6. What is believing, or faith?

A conviction of thofe unfeen things which God has told us in the bible.

7. What is faith in Chrift?

A conviction that Chrift hath loved *me*, and gave himfelf for *me*.

8. By whom is this wrought in us?

By the Holy Ghoft.

F 3

9. What

9. What is holinefs?

The love of God, and of all mankind for God's fake.

10. Is he that believes and loves God, faved from fin?

Yes: from all finful tempers and words and works.

11. How is he faved from pride?

He is little and mean, and bafe and vile in his own eyes.

12. How is he faved from felf-will?

His heart continually fays, "Lord, not as I "will, but as thou wilt."

13. How is he faved from the love of the world?

He defires nothing but God.

14. How is he faved from finful words?

His words always fpring from the grace of God, and are fit to minifter grace to the hearers.

15. How is he faved from finful works?

By the Spirit of God which dwelleth in him, whether he eats or drinks, or whatever he does, it is all to the glory of God.

LESSON VIII. and IX.

Of the Means of Grace.

1. What is grace?

The power of the Holy Ghoft, enabling us to believe, and love and ferve God.

2. How are we to feek this?

In a conſtant and careful uſe of the means of grace.

3. Which are the chief means of grace?

The Lord's ſupper, prayer, ſearching the ſcriptures, and faſting.

4. How often did the firſt Chriſtians receive the Lord's ſupper?

Every day; it was their daily bread.

5. How often did they join in public prayers?

Twice a day, as many of them as could.

6. How often did they uſe private prayer?

Every morning and night, at leaſt.

7. How did they ſearch the ſcriptures?

They heard or read them every day, and meditated therein day and night.

8. How often did the old Chriſtians faſt?

Every *Wedneſday* and *Friday*, till three in the afternoon.

9. How long is every Chriſtian to uſe all theſe means of grace?

To his life's end.

LESSON X. and XI.

Of Hell.

1. Where do unbelievers go after death?
To hell.

2. What ſort of a place is hell?

It is a dark bottomleſs pit, full of fire and brimſtone.

3. How

3. How will they spend their time there?

In weeping and wailing and gnashing of teeth.

4. Will both their souls and bodies be tormented?

Yes: every part of them at once.

5. How will their bodies be tormented?

By lying and burning in flaming fire.

6. How will their souls be tormented?

By a sense of the wrath of God; by pride, self-will, malice and envy; by grief, desire, fear, rage, and despair.

7. Who will be their tormentors?

Their own consciences, the devils, and one another.

8. But will they have no rest from torment?

No, not for one moment, day or night.

9. How long will their torment last?

For ever and ever.

LESSON XII.

Of Heaven.

1. Where will believers go after death?

To heaven.

2. What sort of a place is heaven?

A place of light and glory.

3. How will good men live there?

In joy and happiness, greater than they can now desire or think.

4. Will they suffer nothing there?

No.

No. They will have no want, or pain, or fin.

5. What fort of bodies will they have then?

Spiritual bodies, fwifter than lightning, and brighter than the fun.

6. But wherein will their chief happinefs lie?

In the enjoyment of God.

7. How will they enjoy God?

They will know, and love, and fee God, face to face.

8. How will they fpend their time?

In finging praife to God.

9. How long will this happinefs laft?

As long as God lives, that is, for ever and ever. Lord! bring me thither! *Amen.*

SECTION II.

LESSON I.

Of God, and of the foul of man.

TAKE care you do not draw nigh to God with your lips, while your heart is far from him.

Never fay any thing to God, which you do not mean.

Do not dare to tell a lye to God, for he fees all that is in your heart.

Do

Do you know who God is?

· If you do not know God, how can you hope to pleafe God?

Think on this. Mind it well, for God is here. He minds you, if you do not mind him.

LESSON II.

God is an *eternal* Spirit, without beginning and without end.

He cannot be feen, or fully known by man.

He is *good*, and all good comes from him.

He has *power*, to do whatever he will.

He is *wife*, knowing all things, and doing all things well.

He is *happy*, and cannot want any thing.

He *loves* all things which he has made, and man above all.

It is his will, That all men fhould be faved, and come to the knowledge of his truth.

He is *juft*, to give to every man according to his works.

He is *true* in his promifes, and in his threatnings.

He is *merciful*, forgiving the fins of thofe who truly repent and believe.

LESSON III.

No man hath feen God at any time. The
Sen

Son of God who is in the bofom of the Father, he hath declared him unto us.

No one knoweth the Son of God, but the Father, and no one knoweth the Father but the Son, and he to whom the Son will reveal him.

All our reading, and the things we hear either at church, or any where elfe, cannot reveal God unto us.

* All the men in the world cannot give us the leaft fpark of the true knowledge of God, or of the things of God.

Only God himfelf can do this, by giving us his good Spirit.

He gives his grace and his light to thofe who pray earneftly for it.

* He declares himfelf to thofe who do his will, fo far as they know it already.

LESSON IV.

There is none good but One, that is God.

Every thing that is good, comes from God alone, whether it be in heaven or in earth.

If there be any thing good in any man, it all comes from God.

Therefore he alone ought to be praifed for it all.

All that we do without him, without his grace and his help, is evil.

Without God we can do nothing that is good.

He that has not God, has nothing that is

good ;

good; and is more unhappy than any words can tell.

LESSON V.

I know that God has power to keep what I commit to him, safe unto that day.

Our souls are now spoiled and destroyed by sin.

None can save us from our sins, but God who has all power.

Let us commit our souls wholly to him, to do with them what he will, and as he will.

Then he will keep us by his power, and defend us against every thing that would hurt us.

He is able to deliver us from all danger, and to keep our souls unto the great day.

And at that day he will restore in glory both our bodies and souls, and all that we had committed to his charge.

LESSON VI.

Do you know what your soul is ?

You have in you (though you cannot see it) a soul that will never die.

God made this, that he might come and dwell in it.

If God lives and dwells in your soul, then he makes it like himself.

* He makes the soul in which he dwells, good,

wife,

wife, juſt, true, full of love, and of power to do
well.

* He makes it happy. For it is his will, that
your ſoul ſhould rejoice in him for ever. He
made it for this very thing.

When a ſoul deſires God, and knows and en-
joys him, then it is truly happy.

But when a ſoul does not deſire God, nor
know and enjoy him, it is truly miſerable.

SECTION III.

LESSON I.

How to regulate our deſires.

THE gate by which God, with his holy
grace, comes into us, is the *deſire* of the
ſoul.

This is often called, the *heart*, or the *will*.

Unleſs our deſire be toward God, we cannot
pleaſe him.

All our knowledge without this, does but make
us the more like the devil.

* The deſire is to the ſoul, what the mouth
and the ſtomach are to the body.

It is by the mouth and the ſtomach that the
body receives its nouriſhment, whether good or
bad.

That

That our body may live, we muſt take care to put nothing but what is good into our mouth or ſtomach.

And that our ſoul may live, we muſt take care to deſire nothing but what is good.

LESSON II.

* Deſire was made for that which is good, that is, for God, who is the only good, and for his will, from which every good thing flows.

We ought to deſire nothing but God, and that which is according to his holy will.

And we ought to turn our deſire from every thing beſide.

For every thing, beſide God and his will, is evil.

Therefore no man ought to follow his own will.

As the will of God is the ſpring of all good, ſo our own will is the ſpring of all evil.

Take care, not to uſe yourſelf to do your own will.

No ſoul can ever be ſaved unleſs it renounces its own will, and its own deſires.

Father, let not my will be done, but thine!

We came into the world, not to do our own will, but the will of him that ſent us.

If we are already accuſtomed to do our own will, we muſt break that cuſtom without delay.

Our

O Lord, save us from our own will, or we perish.

LESSON III.

No one can do any thing good of himself, without the help of God.

All our own desires are only evil continually.

Therefore no man should desire to be esteemed, honoured, or praised by any man.

And no one ought to praise or esteem himself.

Rather we ought to despise ourselves: and we ought to desire to be thought by others, what we really are, that is, poor, weak, foolish, sinful creatures.

Then should we find help from God. For he resisteth the proud, but giveth grace to the humble.

* They who teach children to love praise, train them up for the devil.

Praise is a deadly poison to the soul; therefore never praise any one to his face.

Do not plant either in him or yourself that pride of heart, which is an abomination to the Lord.

LESSON IV.

You are of yourself nothing but sin, and deserve nothing but hell.

Therefore you ought to be content, though you should have little or nothing in the world.

And you ought not to desire any thing more
than

than you have; for you have now more than you deserve.

Chuse therefore the worst and meanest things: for even these are too good for such a sinner.

To raise any other desires in your heart, is to prepare you for hell-fire.

They that give you fine cloaths, are giving your soul to the devil.

They that humour you, do not love you.

If your father and mother give you every thing that you like, they are the worst enemies you have in the world:

By doing this, they make you slaves to the flesh, to vanity and corruption:

And so keep you as far from the Spirit of Christ, as the devil himself can wish.

LESSON V.

God is power, wisdom, goodness itself.

Therefore we should desire to praise, and honour him as he deserves, and to please him in every thing.

The end for which we were born is to praise and honour God.

And this we may do without ceasing, by continually lifting up our hearts to him.

This is the continual employment of the angels of God in heaven.

They sing day and night, to him that sitteth

upon

upon the throne, and to the Lamb for ever and ever.

Holy, holy, holy, Lord God of hosts! let all the earth be full of thy glory.

LESSON VI.

God is continually helping us, and pouring his benefits upon us.

All things come from him, our soul, our body, our life, our parents, our friends, and the good angels that guard us.

The earth on which we tread, the air we breathe, the sun which shines upon us, the food that keeps us alive, the cloaths that cover us, the fire that warms us, are all from him.

Therefore we should thank God for all these things, and for every one of them.

We ought to be thankful, even to a man, when he does us any good.

How much more ought we to be thankful to God, who made that man, and who does us good by him;

Thou art worthy, O Lord, our God, to receive glory, and honour, and power:

Because thou hast created all things, and for thy pleasure they are and were created.

And God not only has done us all this good, but he does us more and more good, continually.

For without his goodness, we, and all the world, should fall into nothing in a moment.

* We

* We are juſt like the brittle veſſel, which if it were not always upheld, would fall at once and break in pieces.

Therefore it ſhould be our deſire to be always thinking of God, becauſe he is always bleſſing us.

O God, our Father, teach us to give thee thanks, at all times, and for all things, through Jeſus Chriſt!

LESSON VII.

Thus God has been helping us this day. And we have no leſs need of his help for the time to come.

Above all, if we would be happy, we have need of his bleſſing upon our ſouls.

This he gives to them who truly deſire it and none elſe.

Therefore let us deſire of God to give us his grace, his good ſpirit, and the knowledge of himſelf.

* Let us aſk of him a meek and quiet ſpirit, a contented, humble, thankful heart.

If any man lack wiſdom let him aſk of God, who giveth to all men liberally, and it ſhall be given him.

Let us then take care, not to offend him, from whom we hope to receive ſo great bene-fits.

And let us always be ready to do his will; for
if

if any man honour God and do his will him he heareth.

LESSON VIII.

But we have often offended God already, and fo are unworthy of his grace and bleffings.

Therefore we ought with earneft defire to afk God to forgive our paft fins, for the fake of his Son who died for us, and to keep us from them for the time to come.

Thefe defires,

1. To praife God, for his power, wifdom, and goodnefs ;

2. To thank him for all his benefits :

3. To afk his grace, that fo we may pleafe him : and

4. To beg his mercy for the pardon of our fins ; are what we commonly call *prayer*.

We never pray but when we have really thefe defires in our heart.

If we fay ever fo many words without having thefe defires we are but like parrots before God.

Beware of this ; of drawing nigh unto God with your lips, while your heart (that is, your defire) is far from him.

LESSON IX.

What do you mean, when you pray to God, in the name of Jefus Chrift ?

The

The bare faying of thefe words fignifies nothing. It is only mocking God, if you do not
know what you fay.

We were all under the wrath and under the
curfe of God when Jefus Chrift the Son of God
died for us.

And for his fake, if we truly believe in him,
God is now reconciled to us.

Therefore all our truft fhould be in Jefus
Chrift, whenever we pray to God for any
thing.

For God would not hear us at all, but for the
fake of the blood of Chrift fhed for us.

Therefore we ought to pray always with an
eye to him, looking unto Jefus.

And our defires fhould all fpring from his grace
and be agreeable to his defires.

Then he offers our defires, as his own, to
God his Father, before whofe throne he ftands.

And God can refufe nothing to the defires and
the merits of his well-beloved Son.

When therefore you pray in the name of Jefus
Chrift, it is as if you fhould fay,

* " Lord I offer thee the defires which are
wrought in me by the grace of Jefus Chrift.

I pray, that thou wilt unite them to the defires
of thy Son, and regard them as his, who is pleading for me.

And grant me what I thus defire for his fake,
for thine own glory, and my falvation."

LES-

LESSON X.

Pray to God, in such words as come from your heart : It may be such as these :

* " My God, thou art good, thou art wise : thou art powerful : Be thou praised for ever !

‘ Give me grace to love and obey thee.

My God, I thank thee, for making and redeeming me.

My God, I thank thee, for giving me meat and cloaths, and for promising to give me thy love for ever.

My God, forgive me all my sins, and give me thy good Spirit.

Let me believe in thee with all my heart, and love thee with all my strength.

Let me be always looking unto Jesus Christ, who is pleading for me at thy right-hand.

Give me grace not to do mine own will, but thine.

Make me content with every thing. The least of all the good things thou givest me is far more than I deserve.

Give me, O my Lord, a lowly heart.

Let me not think myself better than any one.

Let me despise myself, and look upon myself as the very worst of all.

Let me hate all praise. Thou alone O my God, art worthy to be praised.

LESSON XI.

The beſt prayer in the world, is the prayer which our Lord Jeſus Chriſt himſelf has taught us.

Our Father which art in heaven, 1. Hallowed be thy name. 2. Thy kingdom come. 3. Thy will be done in earth, as it is in heaven. 4. Give us this day our daily bread, and, 5. Forgive us our treſpaſſes as we forgive them that treſpaſs againſt us. And 6. Lead us not into temptation, but deliver us from evil. For thine is the kingdom, and the power, and the glory, for ever and ever. Amen!

Do you underſtand what you have ſaid now?

How dare you ſay to God, you know not what?

Do you not know, that this is no prayer, unleſs you ſpeak it from your heart.

God is not pleaſed with your ſaying theſe words, unleſs there is in your heart at the ſame time a real deſire, that God ſhould be 1. Known and eſteemed. 2. Honoured and praiſed, 3. Obeyed by all men: 4. That he ſhould feed your ſouls with his grace and his love, 5. That he ſhould forgive you your paſt ſins, and 6. That he ſhould keep you for the time to come, from all ſin and from the ſnares of the devil.

SEC.

SECTION IV.

LESSON I.

How to regulate our Underſtanding.

OUR underſtanding was made for truth, that is, for God himſelf, for his word and his works.

Therefore we ſhould not deſire to know any thing but God, and what he has ſpoken and done for his own glory.

Accordingly, lying is the moſt abominable of all things. The devil is a liar, and the father of it.

We ſhould not deſire to know what men ſay or do. It is folly and vanity.

Curioſity is good for nothing.

It fills our mind with darkneſs: and makes us ſenſeleſs and unfit for the light of God.

What a loſs is this to fill thoſe veſſels with filth and dung, which were made to receive the pure light of God.

LESSON II.

The eye of the underſtanding, which ſhould ſee God, is quite ſhut in all men ſince the fall.

We are born quite blind to God, and the things of God.

And

And it is God alone that can open the eyes of our foul, to fee and know fpiritual things.

We could not fee or know the fun, the earth, or any other of the things of this world, if God had not given us bodily eyes.

And we can never know the things of God, if God do not reftore the fpiritual eyes of our foul.

This he does for thofe and thofe only, who flee from evil, and learn to do good.

Give me underftanding, O Lord, and I will keep thy law; yea, I will keep it with my whole heart.

Open thou mine eyes, that I may fee the wondrous things of thy law.

'Till God opens our eyes to fee the things above, we muft believe what God has told us, though we fee it not.

But we muft not believe what the world tells us about the things of God; for all men who have not his Spirit, are blind and liars.

We muft truft in God, as to thofe things which as yet we cannot comprehend:

And wait and defire, that he would open the eyes of our underftanding, and give us his light, that we may fee all things clearly.

LESSON III.

* A blind man, though he could reafon ever fo well, yet could not by this means, either know or fee the things of the world.

Aud

And with all his reafon he could have only very dark, grofs, nay, and falfe conceptions of them.

* In like manner, though all the men in the world fhould reafon with all their might concerning them: yet could they not by this means know either God or the things of God.

Nay, with all their reafon they could only have dark, foolifh, falfe conceptions of them.

Before God can be known, he muft give other eyes to the foul and other light than man can give.

We may paint the fun or fruits in a picture; but this painted fun cannot warm or give us light.

And thofe painted fruits cannot nourifh us, nor give us any ftrength.

Juft fo we may draw pictures, as it were in our mind, of God, and of the things of God.

But thefe pictures can give us no true light. Neither can they nourifh our fouls, or give us any ftrength to ferve God.

They are only dead fhadows, cold and empty, barren and unfruitful.

We can build nothing upon them but the wind, which ferves only to puff men up, and to drive each againft the other in endlefs difputes, till they burft of themfelves or dafh in pieces one againft another.

LESSON IV.

Our underſtanding, or reaſon without the grace and ſupernatural light of God, is like a blind man who draws wild, random pictures of things he never ſaw nor can ſee.

The natural man diſcerneth not the things of the ſpirit of God.

They are fooliſhneſs unto him, neither can he know them, becauſe they are ſpiritually diſcerned.

No one knoweth the things of God, but the Spirit of God ! and he to whom God revealeth them by his Spirit.

Offer therefore your underſtanding to God, with a ſincere deſire to do his will only.

And pray him earneſtly, to give you his light, and to open the eyes of your ſoul.

LESSON V.

* Endeavour to ſee God in all things, and to give a reaſon for every thing, from the perfections of God.

For example. Why was the world made ? To ſhew the goodneſs, and wiſdom, and power of God.

Why do men die ? Through the juſtice of God.

Men having abuſed the life he gave, it was juſt to take it away.

Why

Why is it our duty to obey our parents ? Becaufe it is the will of God.

Why ought we not to return evil for evil ? Becaufe God would have us do like him; who is continually doing good unto us, even when we ourfelves do evil.

Why may we not defpife or judge our neighbour ? Becaufe God is the judge of all.

Thus we fhould accuftom ourfelves to have God always before our eyes, and to walk continually in his prefence.

Thus every thing may fhew us the power, wifdom or goodnefs, the truth, juftice or will of God ;

And fo every thing may fhew us the weaknefs, ignorance, folly, and wickednefs of men.

LESSON VI.

What do you believe of God ?

I believe in God the Father Almighty, maker of heaven and earth.

And in Jefus Chrift, his only Son, our Lord.

Who was conceived by the Holy Ghoft, born of the Virgin *Mary*;

Suffered under *Pontius Pilate*, was crucified, dead and buried ; he defcended into hell ;

The third day he rofe again from the dead.

He afcended into heaven, and fitteth at the right hand of God the Father Almighty :

From

From whence he shall come to judge the quick and the dead :

I believe in the Holy Ghost,

The holy Catholic church,

The communion of saints,

The forgiveness of sins,

The resurrection of the body, and the life everlasting.

You may learn from those words. 1. To believe in God the Father, who is powerful, and wise, and good; who made you and all things visible and invisible, temporal and eternal.

You may learn, 2. To believe in God the Son, who lived and died to redeem you and all mankind ;

And 3. To believe in God the Holy Ghost, who restores fallen man to the image of God in which he was made.

LESSON VII.

All which comes to this. Almighty God, the maker of all things, made man to this intent, that desiring God alone, God might fill him with his knowledge, with his love, and joy, and glory, for ever.

But man turned his desire from God, and his will, and so became both guilty, wicked and miserable.

The Son of God was made man, lived and died, and rose again, to buy forgiveness for us,

and

and to fhew us how we ought to renounce onr
own will and defires, and to give ourfelves up
to the holy will of God.

This the Holy Ghoft works in us, inlighten-
ing our underftanding, and filling our fouls with
a divine peace and joy.

Hereby we are joined again with all that is
holy either in earth or heaven.

We rejoice together with them in the common falvation, in the benefits and graces of
Jefus Chrift.

And after the body is dead and rifen again,
we fhall live together in eternal glory.

LESSON VIII.

We cannot now comprehend how thefe three
are one, God the Father, the Son, and the Holy
Ghoft.

But tho' we do not comprehend it, yet we believe it, becaufe God hath faid it.

The true knowledge of all the things of God
is wrought in our fouls by his holy Spirit.

This is a faving knowledge, when it works by
love, and brings us to imitate God.

So we are taught by St. Paul, be ye followers
of God. as dear children, and walk in love as
Chrift alfo hath loveth us, and given himfelf
for us.

For every one that loveth (faith St. John) is
born of God, and knoweth God.

But

But he that loveth not, knoweth not God; for God is love.

So likewife if a man fay, he knows Jefus Chrift and keeps not his commandments, he is a liar, and the truth is not in him.

We then favingly know God the Father, the maker of all things, when we love him with obedient reverence :

When we confidently give ourfelves up into his hands, and rely on his providence :

And when we imitate his goodnefs in all things and towards all men.

We then favingly know God the Redeemer, when we live as thofe whom he has bought with his blood.

And when all our tempers and words and actions fhew, that he has redeemed us from the prefent evil world.

We favingly know God the fanctifier when we are holy, as he is holy.

When he hath purified both our hearts and lives by faith, fo that we continually fee and love God.

SECTION V.
LESSON I.
How to regulate our Joy.

MEN are poor, ignorant, foolifh finners that will fhortly rot in the earth.

And

And all that is in the world is perifhable and vain, and will foon be deftroyed by fire.

Therefore we ought by no means to place our joy and delight, on any of thefe things.

Neither ought we to rejoice or delight in pleafing men, who will quickly turn to duft ;

Nor in being handfome or well dreft, or well provided with all things; for all this will perifh for ever.

God alone is great, good, and the giver of all good things.

Therefore we ought to rejoice and delight in him alone, and in the fulfilling of his good and holy will.

And we fhould now accuftom ourfelves to this: to rejoice and delight in God and his holy will.

LESSON II.

For example, we fhould rejoice that we have for our true father, an eternal and almighty God.

We fhould rejoice that this God has made us, to fill us with divine and eternal joy.

That is, if you believe in Jefus and do his holy will:

If we will love and obey him, and not love either the honours, riches, or pleafures, that pafs away like a dream.

And this we may do by the power of his grace,

by

by the Holy Ghoft, which he is ready to give unto us.

We fhould rejoice that God is happy and glorious in himfelf, that he is greater than we can think:

That he knows every thing, and can do every thing:

That he is juft and good: that he is true in all his promifes; and wife to teach and govern us well:

We fhould rejoice, that God alone deferves to be defired, known, loved, praifed, and glorified for ever.

We fhould rejoice that the Son of God took our nature upon him, in order to take us with him to heaven for ever.

And that even now he will come and dwell in our heart, if we defire it, and believe in him, and do his will.

LESSON III.

When any thing is done according to the will of God, we ought to rejoice in it.

But when any thing is done according to our own will, we ought not to rejoice but be forry for it.

Therefore we ought greatly to be troubled and deeply forrow, for the fins committed againft God, whether by ourfelves or others:

For

For in sinning we follow our own will, and despise the will of God.

Likewise, when any one praises us, if we are wise, we should be ashamed and sorry; and should say,

O Lord, thou art good, and thou alone. Thou alone art worthy to be praised.

O Lord it is a shameful theft for a poor creature to take to itself the esteem and praise which belongs to thee only.

On the contrary; when we are despised or ill-used, or when we have not things as we would have, we should rejoice.

We should take all as from the hand of God, and be well content, saying unto him,

O Lord, I deserve nothing but pain and contempt: I rejoice that thy justice gives me what I deserve.

I desire to thank thee for it with all my heart, and to rejoice that thy holy will is done upon me.

It is thy will that we should be like Christ: and he was despised and hated of men.

He lived in contempt, and want, and pain. O let me rejoice to tread in his steps.

Let me be content, let me rejoice to suffer with him, that I may reign with him.

LESSON IV.

One that is sick, if he is wise, will rejoice to take a good medicine, be it ever so bitter.

Espe.

Especially if he knows it is given him by a wife physician, and that it will restore his bodily health.

In like manner, if we are wife, we shall rejoice to take what God sends us, be it ever so bitter.

For we are sure it is given us by the wife physician of our souls, in order to restore them to health and life everlasting. On the contrary,

It would be folly and madness in a sick man, to rejoice in taking the things that please his taste, though they would kill him.

And the same folly and madness it is in us, to rejoice in taking the things that please our corrupt will.

.Because the end of these things is death, even the destroying both body and soul in hell.

LESSON V.

When you are glad of any thing that is given you, be sure to remember, that all this comes from God.

Therefore thank him for it, and think in yourself, God has a thousand and a thousand times more than this, to give them that love and obey him.

And be ready to leave all these little things, whenever it is his will.

If any say to you, ' See what a pretty thing
                                                    here

here is,' ' Look, here is a pretty thing for you,' they are fools, and know not what they do.

This is the way to make you fond of such foolish things, but if you love these, you cannot love God.

If any one ever said to you, ' Did it hurt you? Give me a blow for it,' they were then teaching you to serve the devil.

For this was teaching you to revenge your-self; and to revenge ourselves in serving the devil.

If any one used to say to you, when you did any thing, ' It was not my child, was it? Say, it was I.'

Then they were leading you the way to hell; for all liars go to hell.

And whoever they are that teach their chil-dren lying, pride, or revenge, they offer their sons and their daughters unto devils.

LESSON VI.

Above all, beware of the love of money; for it is the root of all evil.

Money is now the God of this world. The aim of men is to get and keep this. And herein they place their welfare and joy.

This is an idolatry no less damnable than that of the Heathen world.

There would be little or no use for money, if Love governed the world.

G 6   And

And even now money is good for nothing, but as it is a means of procuring among men of the world, the things needful to sustain life.

Neither ought we to desire it any farther, than as it is needful for this end.

God to whom it belongs (as do all things) will require us to give a strict account of it.

His will is, that when we have used what is needful of it for ourselves, we should give all the rest to the poor, and for his glory.

Do not use yourselves therefore to lay it up, but give what you can spare to the poor.

Or else buy a little meat or cloaths for them, or some good books for their instruction.

And rejoice when you use your money thus; because this is for the glory of God.

LESSON VII.

Joy was made for God. Therefore we are taught in his word, to rejoice in the Lord always.

We should look upon God and his grace, as a great treasure; and thence we may learn how to rejoice in him

When we possess a vast treasure, so that we cannot possibly lose it, then our joy is perfect.

Such will be the joy of the saints in heaven, because then they cannot possibly lose this treasure any more.

But when we possess a vast treasure in such a

manner,

manner, that we may lofe it every moment, it is plain that our joy therein fhould be tempered with a very ferious fear.

And fo it is with us. We may lofe the grace of God, yea, every moment, by divers ways.

We may lofe it by our own wilful fins, by our negligence, or by our prefumption.

To thefe we are tempted continually, by an infinite number of malicious and fubtle enemies.

Thefe furround us at all times, and in all places, and they never reft day or night.

Day and night the devil goeth about as a roaring lion, feeking whom he may devour.

Therefore bleffed is the man that feareth always.

And accordingly the fame apoftle, who teaches us to rejoice in the Lord always,

Teaches us at the fame time, to work out our falvation with fear and trembling.

And fo St. Peter, fpeaking to thofe who rejoice in Chrift with joy unfpeakable and full of glory;

Advifes them to remember him, who would judge them according to their works, and pafs the time of their fojourning in fear.

LESSON VIII.

If we have loft this great treafure by our own fault, we have nothing in its place but poverty and mifery.

But

But God has promised to give it to us again, if we are thoroughly sensible of our loss:

If we repent, bring forth fruits meet for repentance, and truly believe in Jesus Christ.

So there is room for us, still to rejoice in hope; yet with a lively sense of our past sins, and present misery.

For to such alone is the promise made : thus saith the Lord, to this man will I look, even to him that is poor, and of a contrite spirit, and that trembleth at my word.

And our Lord says, Blessed are they that mourn, for they shall be comforted.

A broken and a contrite heart, O God, thou wilt not despise.

LESSON IX.

Even religious joy, if it be not thus mixed with fear, will soon be a mere nest of self-love.

It will cover the greatness of our corruption, and so hinder us from seeking to be cured of it.

It will make us carnally presume that we have the treasure of grace, while indeed we are far from it.

So the church of Laodicea said, I am rich and increased in goods, and have need of nothing.

But Christ answered, Thou knowest not that thou art wretched, and miserable, and poor, and blind, and naked.

And

And it is to such that he says, Wo unto you that are rich; for ye have received your confolation.

Wo unto you that are full; for ye fhall hunger.

Wo unto you that laugh now; for ye fhall mourn and weep.

Thefe are they to whom St. James fays, Be afflicted, and mourn and weep:

Let your laughter be turned to mourning, and your joy to heavinefs.

Bleffed is the man that feareth the Lord; for the fear of the Lord is the beginning of wifdom.

Therefore learn to ferve the Lord in fear, and to rejoice in him with reverence.

SECTION VI.

LESSON I.

How to regulate our Practice.

OUR body and our life belong to God. Therefore we ought to difpofe of them according to his will, not according to our own.

Our own will naturally inclines to our own profit, our own honour, and our own pleafure.

And

And thus it begets in us the deadly vices of covetoufnefs, pride, and fenfuality.

They hinder the workings of God in us, and the falvation of our fouls.

Therefore, we ought to accuflom ourfelves, with God's help, to deny ourfelves in all tbings:

We fhould accuftom ourfelves to do all we do in a fpirit of charity, and for the good of others:

In a fpirit of humility, without any defign or defire of being efteemed.

And in a fpirit of penitence, without any regard to our own pleafure, either of body or mind.

In all things we fhould aim at being made conformable to our crucified Saviour.

This is the true fpirit of the Chriftian life and practice. This is true Chriftianity.

But it is wholly oppofite to the fpirit of the world, and of corrupt nature.

By which, alas! one fuffers one's felf to be fo foftly drawn into hell, and drop fmiling into everlafting perdition.

LESSON II.

It is the will of God, that we fhould do nothing but to pleafe him.

It is his pleafure to be glorified by our falvation.

His glory fhould be our fupreme, abfolute, and univerfal end.

The

The glory of God is advanced in this life, when we gives ourselves up to Jesus Christ.

Then his power works through us, many holy actions ; for which he alone is to be honoured and praised.

Without me, saith our Lord, ye can do nothing. But he that abideth in me bringeth forth much fruit.

Herein is my Father glorified, that ye bear much fruit.

This is to be understood of all sorts of actions and things : for every thing we do is to be done to the glory of God.

And nothing can be done well but in the name, that is, in the strength, and through the blessing of Jesus Christ.

Whether ye eat or drink, or whatever ye do, do all to the glory of God.

Whatsoever ye do in word or deed, do all in the name of the Lord Jesus.

LESSON III.

So for example, we eat and drink to the glory of God, and in the name of Jesus Christ, when we are enabled by him to do it on a right principle, and in a right manner, so as to say to him from the heart,

Suffer me not O Lord to eat and drink like a brute beast, only by a brutal appetite :

Much

Much lefs do thou fuffer me to follow herein the motions of my corrupt nature.

But grant me, thro' the Spirit of thy Son, to eat and drink fo much as is needful to fupport my life.

And let me fpend that life wholly in blefling thee, and in loving and obying thee.

So likewife you fpeak to the glory of God, and in the name of Jefus Chrift, when by his ftrength, you fay nothing but what is guided by him, and directed according to his will :

When you fpeak nothing but what is needful and proper to give men good thoughts and turn them from fuch as are wicked and vain.

And thus, in all things, let this be your fingle aim, That God may be glorified through Jefus Chrift.

LESSON IV.

What are the ten commandments of God?

1. Thou fhalt have no other God but me.

2. Thou fhalt not make to thyfelf any graven image nor the likenefs of any thing that is in heaven above, or in the earth beneath, or in the waters under the earth, thou fhalt not bow down to them, nor worfhip them : for I the Lord thy God, am a jealous God, and vifit the fins of the fathers upon the children unto the third and fourth generation of them that hate me, and fhew mercy unto thoufands in them that love me, and keep my commandments.

3. Thou

3. Thou ſhalt not take the name of the Lord thy God in vain: for the Lord will not hold him guiltleſs that taketh his name in vain.

4. Remember that thou keep holy the ſabbath day. Six days ſhalt thou labour and do all that thou haſt to do, but the ſeventh day is the ſabbath of the Lord thy God: in it thou ſhalt do no manner of work, thou and thy ſon and thy daughter, thy man ſervant and thy maid ſervant, thy cattle and the ſtranger which is within thy gates. For in ſix days the Lord made heaven and earth, the ſea and all that in them is, and reſted the ſeventh day: therefore the Lord bleſſed the ſeventh day, and hallowed it.

5. Honour thy father, and thy mother, that thy days may be long in the land which the Lord thy God giveth thee.

6. Thou ſhalt do no murder.

7. Thou ſhalt not commit adultery.

8. Thou ſhalt not ſteal.

9. Thou ſhalt not bear falſe witneſs againſt thy neighbour.

10. Thou ſhalt not covet thy neighbour's houſe, thou ſhalt not covet thy neighbour's wife, nor his ſervant, nor his maid, nor his ox, nor his aſs, nor any thing that is his,

LESSON V.

Conſider, the law of God is a ſpiritual law. Therefore all theſe commandments are to be ſpiritually underſtood.

The

The first commandment means. Thou shalt not think, believe, or own any thing to be God but me.

Thou shalt not fear any thing but me.

Thou shalt not seek after witches or wizards, or practife any fuch abomination.

Thou shalt not put thy truft in any creature.

Thou shalt not love any thing but me, or for my fake.

God likewife herein commands thee to believe in him, and to acknowledge him in all thy ways.

He commands thee to thank him for all thou haft, and to make him thy only fear and dread:

To be in the fear of the Lord all the day long, and to truft in him with all thy heart:

To defire him alone; to rejoice in him always, and to love him with all thy heart, and with all thy foul.

The fecond commandment teaches us, not to fancy that God is like the thoughts or imaginations of our dark reafon:

It teaches us alfo, not to worfhip or bow to any image or picture, but to glorify God both with our bodies and with our fpirits.

LESSON VI.

If we will keep the third commandment,

We muft never fwear falfely : and if we have fworn to do any thing, we muft furely do it.

We

We muſt never uſe the name of God at all, but with reverence and godly fear.

We muſt not value ourſelves upon his name, his covenant, or the knowledge of him in vain:

That is, without profiting thereby, without bringing forth ſuitable fruits.

We muſt not cover over our own will, or paſſions, or deſigns, with the holy name of God, of his truth, or his glory.

By the fourth commandment you are taught, to do no worldly buſineſs on the Lord's day.

But to ſpend it wholly in prayer, praiſe, hearing or reading the word of God, and other works of piety and charity.

The fifth commandment teaches you theſe things,

Shew all lowlineſs and reverence to your father and mother, and do whatever either of them bids you.

If need be, relieve them, and never let them want any thing you can help them to.

Eſteem the miniſters who are over you in the Lord, very highly in love for their work ſake.

Obey them, and ſubmit yourſelves to them; for they watch over your ſouls.

Honour the king. Obey magiſtrates. Pray for kings, and all that are in authority.

If you have a maſter or miſtreſs, be obedient to them in ſingleneſs of heart, as unto Chriſt.

LES-

LESSON VII.

The fixth commandment forbids not only the killing or hurting any one, but all anger, hatred, malice, or revenge.

It forbids all provoking words, all ftrife and contention, all gluttony and drunkennefs.

The feventh commandment forbids not only all outward uncleannefs, but even the looking on a woman to luft after her.

It forbids alfo the ufing any thing merely to pleafe ourfelves. For this is a kind of fpiritual fornication.

The eighth commandment forbids not only the taking from another what is his, either openly or fecretly;

But likewife the ftealing from God (to whom they all belong) either our affections, or our time, or our goods, or our labour, by employing any of them any otherwife than for him.

The ninth commandment requires us, to put away all lying, and to fpeak the truth from our heart.

It requires us to fpeak evil of no man, but to put away all back-biting and tale-bearing.

It requires us alfo, to judge no man, that we be not judged ; but to leave every one to God, the judge of all.

The tenth commandment requires us to be content with what we have, and to defire nothing more.

LES-

Thefe are thofe laws of God, fo wonderful and holy, of which David fpeaks fo often with love and admiration.

Thefe all the fcriptures recommend as the fpring of life, the light of the heart, the treafure of fouls: yea, our Lord calls them life everlaft-ing, John xii. 50.

Thefe the Holy Spirit has promifed to write in the hearts of thofe that truly believe in Jefus.

They may all be fummed up in three.

1. To love God; 2. To love Jefus Chrift him-felf, his crofs and his tribulation, his reproach, the fellowfhip of his fufferings, and the being made conformable to his death.

3. To love our neighbour.

Our heart therefore fhould always be full of reverence for thefe. The love of them fhould be fixed in the very marrow of our bones.

We fhould labour after this, by earneft prayer, by reading, and by meditating on thofe deep words:

The law of the Lord is an undefiled law, (the law of love) converting the foul: the teftimony of the Lord is fure, and giveth wifdom to the fimple.

The fear of the Lord is clean and endureth for ever, the judgments of the Lord are true and righteous altogether.

More to be defired are they than gold; yea,

than

than much fine gold; fweeter alfo than honey and
the honey-comb.

LESSON IX.

In a word: with regard to God, always live
and act, as being in the prefence of God.

Remember he is continually looking upon you.

And he will bring into judgment, all that you
have done, faid, or thought, whether it be good
or evil.

For all which, you will be either rewarded or
punifhed everlaftingly.

Never fail to pray to God morning and evening, as well as before and after you eat or drink.

Often lift up your heart to God at other times,
particularly before any work or bufinefs.

Defire his blefling and help, and afterwards
give him thanks, and offer it up to God and his
glory.

Hear the truths of God with attention and reverence, whether at home or at church.

But do not think you have ferved God, barely
becaufe you have heard them, or have got them
by heart.

Pray to God to give you a true underftanding
of them, and to enliven them by the working of
his Spirit.

Pray him to give you an humble, fubmiffive,
fimple, and obedient heart.

As to your father and mother, and fuperiors,

Pray

Pray to God for them, love and reverence them, obey them without murmuring, even in thofe things which do not pleafe you, unlefs they are plainly fins.

Do nothing without their knowledge, or without their leave.

LESSON X.

With regard to your neighbours, and your companions,

Pray to God for them alfo, wifh them as well as you do yourfelf ; and do to them, as you would have them do to you.

Think every one better than yourfelf: live in peace with them, help them : if they have done you wrong, forgive them, and pray heartily to God for them.

With regard to yourfelf,

Pray to God that you may always think meanly of yourfelf.

Eat nothing between meals.

At your meals eat moderately, of whatever is given you, whether you like it or not.

Defire nothing fine. Do not defire abundance of any thing. Be content with a little.

Employ your time as you are directed. Never be doing nothing. Idlenefs tempts the devil to tempt you.

Do not difpute, do not contradict any one, do not talk unlefs there be a neceffity.

Do not seek to excuse yourself when you have done wrong, but be always ready to confess your fault, both to God and man.

For God will not forgive your sin so long as you strive to excuse it.

LESSON XI.

If you do any thing well, thank God for it, and say,

I praise thee, O Lord, for giving me grace to do this. Without thee, I can do nothing but evil.

And take care not to value yourself upon it. If you do, it destroys your soul.

When you do wrong, without knowing it, perhaps it may be excused : especially, if you are glad to be taught better.

But whatever fault you commit willfully, knowing it to be a fault, it cannot be excused.

So you must always be punished for lying, for calling names, for disobedience, or for striking any one : For you know, this is a sin against God, and you must be punished for it, out of love to you and for your good.

You deserve punishment, both in the sight of God and man.

If this fault was not punished now, it would grow upon you and carry you to hell.

To prevent this, it is good to let you suffer

a

a punifhment now a hundred thoufand million of times lefs than that.

If you do this again, you muft be punifhed again; but pray to God that you may do it no more.

That foolifh love which would fpare you now, would be indeed the moft cruel hatred.

LESSON XII.

Some may think the rules before laid down, to be either impoffible or ridiculous.

They would not appear impoffible to us, but becaufe we have not been accuftomed to them.

If we had we fhould find, by the grace of God, that nothing can be eafier.

Neither can any think them ridiculous, unlefs it be thofe to whom the crofs of Chrift is foolifh-nefs.

They are indeed ridiculous to the world, be-caufe the world is an enemy to God.

But the wifdom of the would is foolifhnefs with God, as the wifdom of God is foolifhnefs to the world.

Be not conformable then to this prefent world. And love not the world nor the things of the world. If any man love the world, the love of the father is not in him.

How unhappy therefore are they who bring

up

up their children according to the rules of the world ?

They who train them up, as it is called, to make their fortunes in the world !

That is indeed, to perish with the world, to be turned into hell, with all that forget God.

They will be reproached and curfed to all eternity by thofe whom they thus trained up for the devil. Together with whom they will have their lot in everlafting burnings.

But happy are thofe who defpifing the rules of the diabolical and antichriftian world,

Train up the precious fouls of their children, wholly by the rules of Jefus Chrift.

CHRISTIAN REFLECTIONS.

Tranflated from the *French*.

* 1. THE firft motions of turning to God, are ufually like a fpark of fire dropped on ice, with the wind blowing on all fides ; which muft therefore be quickly extinguifhed, unlefs God is pleafed to keep it alive.

2. If you defire to give yourfelf up to God, be not difcouraged at hindrances, temptations, oppofitions : but confider, the grace of God in the foul grows by degrees, like a grain of muftard-feed in the earth.

3. It

3. It is not said, *Bleſſed is the man that hath not ſinned*: but he *to whom the Lord imputeth it not.*

4. Read a little at a time, and offer it to God on your knees. Thus David prayed ſeven times a day.

* 5. The grace we receive ſoon vaniſhes away, if it be not nouriſhed and increaſed by holy exerciſes, which are the very firſt fruits, or rather the firſt bloſſoms of converſion.

6. Retirement from the world, joined with prayer and proper employ, are means of mortifying our ſenſes, without which prayer profits little.

* 7. The beſt helps to mortification are the ill uſage, the affronts, and the loſſes which befal us. We ſhould receive them with all humility, as preferable to all others, were it only on this account, That our will has no part therein, as it has in thoſe which we chooſe for ourſelves.

8. Wo to them that ſeek comments to obſcure the bible, and to widen the narrow way of ſalvation ! For none can change the word of our Lord, *I have given you an example, that ye may do as I have done:* Neither that word, *What I ſay unto you, I ſay unto all.*

9. When we would give ourſelves to God, we ſhould not be eager at the beginning, to hear long diſcourſes on the ſublime truths of Chriſtianity; ſince it is not then the time for deep knowledge, but for good-works and ſufferings. Thoſe who are juſt turning to God, may even

receive

receive prejudice from such an employment of their yet feeble minds. It suffices for them now, to know what they ought to do, and instead of multiplying knowledge, to multiply good-works.

10. We should bear not only with patience but with joy, loss of goods, pleasures, and the evils of earth, seeing Christ has taught us by his example, that there is no other way of attaining the glory of heaven.

* 11. The souls of men are things so great and precious, that having need, according to the divine wisdom, of an invisible guardian, and a visible guide, they can neither have an angel to guard, nor a man to guide them, but those whom God himself gives, by a peculiar appointment.

* 12. The language of love and grace is upon earth, the beginning of the language of heaven.

* 13. Those who feel that they are always upon the verge of death, and who have eternity in their heart, will not find any thing very alluring or agreeable in the world. And he to whom God is all, looks on every thing upon earth as nothing.

* 14. True virtue consists in a thorough conformity to the whole will of God: who wills and does all (excepting sin) which comes to pass in the world. And in order to be truly holy, we have only to embrace all events, good and bad, as his will.

15. Except the fight of glory, and the participation of grace (the light of God) all is darkness in this world and in the other. We need not therefore so much lament over those, who want their bodily fight, as over them who being quickfighted

in

in this life, will in the other be blind for ever.

16. God is not honoured as God, in a manner worthy of him, but by the voluntary oblation which we make him of our life. His Son made an oblation of his own to God; which obliges us if we are real Chriſtians, to give him our life, and that of thoſe who are ſo dear to us, that they are as our ſecond ſoul.

* 17. In the greateſt afflictions which can befal the juſt, either from heaven or earth, they remain immoveable in virtue, and perfectly ſubmiſſive to God, by an inward loving regard to him, uniting all the powers of their ſoul.

* 18. Such is the condeſcenſion of God, that he requires us to love him even more than we fear him. 'Many fear without loving him: but no one loves without fearing him, and being ready to die rather than offend him. Among perſons of every age, and every profeſſion, there are but few of this diſpoſition: but what of piety appears in them, reſembles the bloſſoms which we ſee in ſpring, that adorn the trees for a-while, but ſoon diſappear, and leave no fruit behind them.

* 19. Whether we think, or ſpeak to God, whether we act or ſuffer for him, all is prayer, when we have no other object than his love and the deſire of pleaſing him.

* 20. That ſilence of ſpirit which cuts off all thoſe thoughts and words, that might ſpring from the affliction we feel, on the loſs of them who are moſt near and dear to us, is the beſt ſubmiſſion

H 4

we can pay, to that empire over the living and the dead, which God has referved to himfelf. And the beft devotion we can practife on thefe occafions, is, as far as poffible to efface from our minds, thofe images which difquiet and afflict us, that God alone may fill our heart, and remain for ever the object and the mafter of our paffions and of our thoughts.

* 21. We ought to confider, at the death of thofe whom we love the moft, and even of them from whom we receive life, that all the names of tendernefs and refpect, which proceed from flefh and blood, are loft at the moment of their feparation from us, to return to God as their principal: to the end that the ftream running no more, we may have recourfe to the fountain ; that ceafing to fee them, we may feek to him, of whom they were only the image; and that fo we may now have no other Father than him which is in heaven, of whom we are inceffantly to afk the bread of life, and eternal inheritance.

22. The moft magnificent houfes and palaces are only trophies of human vanity, which in a little time will perifh in flames with the world. Let us provide an habitation, in the eternal palace of paradife, by now purifying ourfelves in the flames of divine love.

23. In the world, the fathers muft die, before their children can enter upon their inheritance. But in the church, the children muft die, to

enter

enter into the inheritance of their heavenly
Father.

24. If the death of them we love, does not
make us enter into ourselves, correct that which
displeases God, and ask of him light to discover
the delusions of the world and the devil: we
have reason to fear that nothing will, but that we
shall live and die without wisdom.

25. Grace from within and affliction from
without, destroy the sins of those souls, who cast
themselves into the arms of God, and sincerely
desire to be given up to him.

26. The language of love, even when it speaks
the most strongly, ought to be decent and courteous, there being no courtesy like that which
we learn from the holy scripture.

27. We need not affect elaborate reasonings in
matters of grace, because the principle of this is
faith, which does not reason at all, but goes simply where God points out the way.

28. The way to find nothing grievous in this
world, is to have eternity always in our thoughts.
For then all of grand and magnificent which we
see here, appears a mere shadow, a nothing.
How natural a reflection is this, when great men
die in the prime of life ! What can shew in a
stronger light the vanity of all, which men admire so much and leave so soon !

* 29. We ought to honour those holy ones
which God honours, and to expect more assis-
tance from them than from others, at the time

when

when he manifefts their holinefs; becaufe they are then as it were new fountains, which God caufes to appear in his church, and who will foon (as other faints have done) retire into God their fource, after they fhall have watered a few more of his children.

30. God hates nothing fo much as the forgetting the favours which he does to them whom he deigns to name his friends.

31. The whole life of a Chriftian confifts in following God; who manifefts his will more and more, according to our faithfulnefs to him.

32. When one is willing fimply to follow the truth, there is no trouble in deciding the greateft difficulties.

33. God himfelf inftructs thofe who follow him with fimplicity, and fhines in their hearts when they regard none but him. To arrive at this hapyy ftate, we muft defire only that which God gives us from his own hand, and beg him with fervent prayer, to keep us always in the defire of him alone, and of his grace.

* 34. It is fcarce conceivable, how ftrait the way is, wherein God leads them that ferve him, and how dependent upon him we muft be, unlefs we will be wanting in our faithfulnefs to him.

35. It is God's part to prevent us, and ours to adore and ferve him in perfect fubjection to his will.

36. Few perfons go to God with that fulnefs of heart, which makes them walk with vigour in the narrow way to heaven.

37. As a fingle foul furpaffes in excellence all bodies, how beautiful fo ever they are; fo a fingle fpiritual fin often furpaffes in guilt a multitude of bodily fins. And fpiritual fins are the more dangerous, in that bodily fins ufually come to a period by age, by change of fortune, by the removal of the occafions, by the difgufts that accompany, or the evils that follow them: but it is quite otherwife with fpiritual: nothing being fo fruitful as the fins of the fpirit.

38. There is nothing fo bitter that love does not fweeten. And if one fees that the covetous, the ambitious, the voluptuous, turn their greateft labours into their greateft pleafures, is it ftrange that the love of God, and the forrow for having offended him, are capable of fweetening whatever he has ordained for the healing of our fouls?

39. God gives his children a kind of fpiritual air to breathe, namely, the influence of his fpirit. And this never fails them that love him, how weak fo ever they are.

40. The grand truths of repentance, and the prefent kingdom of heaven, are unveiled under the new law. The gofpel always joins them together; and it is impoffible to put them afunder.

* 41. As a very little duft will diforder a clock, and the leaft fand will obfcure our fight, fo the

least grain of sin, which is upon the heart, will hinder its right motion toward God.

* 42. It is scarce credible, of how great consequence before God the smallest things are, and what great inconveniences sometimes follow those, which appear to be light faults.

* 43. We ought to be in the church, as the saints are in heaven; and in the house as the holiest men are in the church; doing our work in the house as they pray in the church, worshipping God from the ground of the heart.

* 44. There is no love of God without patience, and no patience without lowliness and sweetness of spirit. It is by this alone, that we are able to pass the days of winter, as those of summer; that is, the afflictions we meet with from time to time, as well as the joys and consolations.

45. God loves nothing so much as gratitude and thankgiving. And, as this is the first act of our piety, it ought to be the most constant, and to begin and conclude all our prayers.

46. To continue in grace, we must pray without ceasing, since we cannot continue, unless we grow therein. Hence it is, that many of those who receive it, lose it immediately: because their commerce with the world, does not permit them to pray often; or if they do, it is with a thousand distractions, which dishonour the majesty of God, whom we should hardly approach, but with the lowest prostration both of body and soul.

foul. He difpenfes indeed with that of the body, becaufe our weaknefs does not permit us to be always in that pofture: but our inmoft foul fhould be always bowed down before him in the loweft humiliation.

* 47. The evils of the body cure themfelves in time, but not thofe of the fpirit; becaufe they partake of its nature, which is immortal, and for this cure they can rely on none but God; who is the only phyfician of fouls, as it is he alone who creates them.

48. The bearing men, and fuffering evil in peace and filence, is the fum of the whole Chriftian life. Without this a man is a captive though at liberty, and with this he is free though a captive.

49. A true Chriftian is not a common thing. And he who is fuch, is unfpeakably happy.

50. To be habitually prepared for the Lord's table, we muft walk in the narrow way, at a diftance from the world, nourifh our fouls with the truths of God laid down in the gofpels, and in the epiftles, which are a kind of commentaries upon them: meditate on them in the fecret of our heart, and grow in love as well as in knowledge.

51. Truths refemble money, all the value whereof depends upon the proper ufe of it.

52. Humility and patience are the fureft proofs of the increafe of love.

53. In-

53. Inſtead of reading much, to ſatisfy our curioſity, we ought to content ourſelves with reading a little, in order to make a full uſe thereof, and turn it, as it were, into our ſubſtance. Otherwiſe by filling our heads with knowledge, we drive the grace of God from our hearts.

54. Both at the beginning and end, and even in the midſt of our reading, we ſhould lift up our hearts to God, whether with words or without, that he would pleaſe to convert what we read into ſpiritual food, ſuch as by means of his truth may nouriſh and ſtrengthen us more and more in his love.

55. The truths of religion are like eſſences, of which we give the ſick a little at a time, becauſe being full of ſpirits, all parts of the body are affected by the little that is taken. This occaſioned our bleſſed Lord to ſay, *My words are ſpirit and life.* And accordingly one of his divine truths, ſuffice a man to nouriſh his ſoul for a whole day.

56. One may ſay of the knowledge of ſublime truths, what the apoſtle ſays of the goods of this world, that they may not hurt a Chriſtian, he ought to poſſeſs them not: that is, without any attachment to them, without any reliance upon them.

57. Nothing is ſo capable of deſtroying the grace of God, even in retirement, as idleneſs.

* 58. Agree with the poor quickly while thou

art in the way with them. Make them friends by the mammon of unrighteoufnefs. For they will be as princes in paradife, where they will receive the rich into the everlafting habitation.

59. The whole Chriftian religion is only love, pure and fervent as the fire at pentecoft.

60. Inftead of bufying our mind with dwelling on the grievous part of what is paft and to come, we fhould remember, that the gofpel does not permit us to dwell on any thing, but the prefence and love of God, who fills our foul, provided we do not difquiet ourfelves with vain thoughts. But we cannot, either in earth or heaven, inhabit any other than a peaceful heart.

61. Sweetnefs joined with ftrength are the two marks of the Spirit of God.

62. As God is well pleafed, that they who love him fhould form defigns for his glory, we ought to labour therein with all our power; and yet not to be any way difcompofed, when he breaks in pieces our beft defigns, fo our heart is ftill fixed to be his entirely, and to live to his glory.

63. The whole of Chriftian religion is love. This alone deftroys the defire of the goods, and the fear of the evils of this world. We fhould labour to increafe it, without defiring and without fearing any thing.

64. The love of God has its forrows and tears, as well as its joys and confolations.

65. As love, which is the foul of our foul and
life

life of our life, is at firſt only a ſingle ſpark, we ſhould take care that nothing remain in our ſoul, that hinders its growth and enlargement.

* 66. God is the firſt object of our love : its next office is, to bear the defects of others. For as he is inviſible to us, it is his will, that we ſee and love him in our neighbour. And we ſhould begin the practice of this love, amidſt our own houſhold.

67. The littleneſs of things does not hinder their being greatly pleaſing to God, when we do them with all our heart : as on the contrary, great things done lazily, are little in his ſight : Becauſe in all our works, he regards the ſpirit abundantly more than the matter.

68. Let none imagine he is virtuous becauſe he talks of virtue with pleaſure. Virtue without practice is a mere illuſion.

69. Thoſe who ſeek God find him, in practiſing the exerciſes which he has preſcribed in the goſpel. The ſum of which is, love, obey, be humble, ſuffer his will.

70. God is ſo great, that we know not how to pray to him, but by his own Spirit, and the movement which he gives us.

71. Great virtue conſiſts in trying to vary and multiply the marks of our gratitude for all the mercies of God.

* 72. One obſerves, that whereas there is but one devil who perſecutes the innocent, there are ſeven that perſecute the penitent.

73. Chriſt

73. Chrift charges himfelf with our temporal affairs, provided we charge ourfelves with thofe that regard his glory.

74. The fmalleft things of religion are great, becaufe the Spirit of God is in them.

75. The main of Chriftianity confifts, in not following our own fpirit, and being given up to God by renouncing ourfelves. Accordingly, there is nothing more profitable for a Chriftian than ficknefs, which joins obedience with faith.

76. Our one defire fhould be, to have no other defire in this world but to be faithful to God.

* 77. Humility alone unites patience with love, without which, it is impoffible to draw profit from fuffering, or indeed to avoid being difcontented at being afflicted: efpecially when we think that we have given no occafion for the evil which men make us fuffer. If we then fall into impatience, it is for want of humility, whatever love we may appear to have.

78. Perfect humility is a kind of felf-annihilation; and this is the center of all virtues.

79. When we let the time of affliction pafs, without profiting by it, we commit three faults: that is, to defpife God; to forget ourfelves; and to overlook the great leffon which religion teaches, viz. What we are in this world, and what we fhall be in the other.

80. The firft thing we ought to do when great

affliction

affliction befals us is, to examine the state of our souls: and if we find ourselves culpable in any thing, whatever it costs, to make our peace with God.

81. There is none who comforts Christians but the Spirit of God; the word itself, separate from him is useless. He is therefore peculiarly stiled the Comforter; because he is come down on the earth, on purpose to heal our sorrows and cares, by shedding his love abroad in our hearts.

* 82. The readiest way to escape from our sufferings is, To be willing they should endure as long as God pleases.

83. They who have known most of the ineffable greatness of God have had the deepest reverence for it. The sense of this ought to make us work out our salvation with fear and trembling, and distrust ourselves in our best undertakings, particularly in those which regard the service of the church; because they require the highest purity of heart, in all that are employed therein.

* 84. As painters chuse and prepare the ground, which they design for their choicest works, so God prepares the ground of those souls, by whom he intends to do great things; Thus he prepared St. Paul, even from his mother's womb.

85. We ought earnestly to pray to God, before we undertake any thing, though we feel such love in our heart, that there are no poor whom we would not relieve, no sick whom we

would

would not heal, and none afflicted whom we would not succour, even at the expence of our life. For experience shews, that in order to do good, it is not enough to have a loving heart : And that God sometimes gives these desires and yet does not bring them to effect.

86. Our own houshold gives us too great occasion to know, the greatness and depths of our inward wounds, by the falls into which we are so often betrayed, by their, perhaps involuntary defects. How ought we to watch over ourselves, in order to resist these temptations, which (how little soever the occasions be) are great, because they are continual ?

87. The bare sight of men in the world, impresses I know not what of evil on the hearts of good men : there is a kind of contagious air hid in the spirit of the ungodly, which communicates itself to the soul more insensibly, than the infection of the plague communicates itself to the body. In order therefore to solid Christian holiness, we must keep at a distance from these men.

88. The world is an enemy to truly good works, particularly the great change which God works in the soul.

89. Flattery is a poison which is the more dangerous, the more sweet and insensible it is. Those therefore who are just setting out in religion, should carefully shut their ears to praise, even to that which the best of men sometimes give.

give, without thinking of the mifchief it may do.

90. Virtue is like a cryftal, on which the leaft word of praife imprints a blot, which muft be effaced.

91. We fhould be continually labouring to cut off all the ufelefs things that furround us. And God ufually retrenches the fuperfluities of our foul, in the fame proportion as we do thofe of our bodies.

92. As the devil will not be fhut up in the abyfs till the judgment of the great day, he makes, meantime, an abyfs of the fouls of wicked men, into which he plunges himfelf with whole legions.

93. As man has nothing excellent but love, he gives God nothing, unlefs he gives him this. Even as all the reft of God's gifts would be ufelefs to man, did he not give him his love alfo.

94. The devil is fo hideous, that he could not deceive us, nor make himfelf beloved by us, did he not cover himfelf with the beauty, and the fweet and agreeable appearances of the creatures.

95. The beft means of refifting the dev il is, to deftroy whatever of the world remains in us, in order to raife for God, upon its ruins, a building all of love. Then fhall we begin in this fleeting life to love God, as we fhall love him in eternity.

96. The love of God and the love of the world
cannot

cannot fubfift together in one heart. It muft needs be, that one of them will conquer and deftroy the other.

97. St. Auguftine fays, There is danger, left after fin is killed, it comes to life again, if it be not buried.

98. If we would be fuperior to the goods and evils of this world, the things that are feen, ought to be to us as if they were not feen: and, on the other hand, the things that are not feen, as if they were always before our eyes.

* 99. Nothing fhews the real ftate of our foul, like perfecution and affliction. And if we fuffer them with that humility and firmnefs, which only the grace of God can work in us, we attain a larger meafure of conformity to Chrift, by a due improvement of one of thefe occafions, than we could have done by imitating his mercy, in abundance of good works.

100. The fcripture fpeaks of the earth as a wildernefs, an hofpital, a prifon, an image of hell. Therefore wo unto them that are attached to it; who do not labour to die to all below, and to afpire after nothing but heaven, where alone is true life, and all that deferves the name of good or pleafure.

101. How real foever the things of earth appear, they are no other than veils that deceive us. The ills thereof hide eternal goods from us, and the goods hide from us eternal evils.

102. The true marks of love are, an hunger
and

and thirst after the word and the life of Chrift.

103. God often deals more rigoroufly, with thofe whom he loves than with others. And his will is, that the afflictions which he fends them, fhould ferve to difengage them, from whatever attached them to the world, that they may be more free to cleave to him.

* 104. We fcarce conceive, how eafy it is to rob God of his due, in our friendfhip with the moft virtuous perfons, until they are torn from us by death. But if this lofs produce lafting for-row, it is a clear proof, that we had two trea-fures, between which we had divided our heart.

105. The devil is enraged only at thofe who fight again him, and his rage increafes, when he fees the increafe of grace in them. But he cannot conquer us, if we continue to fight, and to have fteady dependance on God, who fights for and in his children, and can never be conquered.

106. We are to labour as if we had no depend-ance on the grace of God: and to truft as in-tirely in his grace, as if we did not labour at all. The one preferves us from negligence, the other from prefumption.

107. There are fome peculiar occafions that rarely occur, which we ought to manage with the utmoft care ; becaufe one of thefe is of far more value before God, than many ordinary ones.

108. Even the weaknefs which remains in us is, by the teftimony of God, one of the moft

powerful

powerful means, of making us more ftrong than ever, more immoveable in his fervice.

109. If we were not weak and impotent, our good works would be to us our own property; juft as the corn he produces out of the earth belongs to the hufbandman. Whereas now they belong wholly to God, becaufe they proceed from him and his grace, which triumphs over our weaknefs, when raifing our works and making them all divine, honours himfelf in us through them.

110. When men have fown the feed in the ground, they ceafe awhile from their labour. But when Jefus Chrift has fown his grace in our hearts, we fhould befeech him to labour with us ftill, and to perfect that which he has begun: otherwife there will be no fruit. For the devil omits nothing which may hinder the good feed from growing up, and bringing forth fruit to perfection.

* 111. If we do not teftify to God, by a continual care for our falvation, that we efteem his grace above all things, the leaft confent to an evil thing, makes it retire by little and little, into the bofom of Chrift, from whence it came. Yet he is fo gracious, that after we are truly humbled, he gives us new grace.

* 112. God, in order to cure fome fouls of thofe fins which are the greateft of all in his fight, fuffers them to fall into others, which are greater in the fight of men.

112. Chrif-

113. Chriſtian friendſhip is the refinement of that love which we bear to a fellow-chriſtian, to whom God unites us by an affection which cannot be well known but by thoſe who truly love God.

114. The Holy Spirit, having made of all Chriſtians one ſoul, they ought to have the ſame joys and ſorrows. But if it pleaſes him (of which alſo we have examples in ſcripture) to make of two or more Chriſtians one heart and one ſoul, there ought to be an increaſe of joy in their holy affections, as much greater as their friendſhip is more perfect than that of other Chriſtians.

115. One of the principal rules of religion is, to loſe no occaſion of ſerving God. And ſince he is inviſible to our eyes, we ought to ſerve him in our neighbour, which he receives as done to himſelf in perſon, ſtanding viſibly before us.

116. The way to advance more and more in love, is to practiſe it to the uttermoſt.

117. The chief worſhip we owe to God, is to love him with all our heart without ſharing it between him and the creatures. They ought to ſerve us only for ſteps, to lift us up toward him.

118. Love has this in common with ſacrifice, that it ought to be offered to God alone.

* 119. To preſerve the life of the ſoul, prayer ought to be joined with the other ordinances, as it is the channel which reaches to heaven, and
brings

brings down into the foul that breath of God, without which it cannot live.

* 120. Charity cannot be practifed right, unlefs firft, We exercife it from the moment God gives the occafion; and fecondly retire the inftant after, and offer it to God by humble thankfgiving. And this for three reafons; the firft, To render to him what we have received from him; the fecond, To avoid the dangerous temptation which fprings from the very goodnefs of thefe works; and the third, To unite ourfelves to God, in whom the foul expands itfelf in prayer, with all the graces we have received, and the good works which we have done, to draw from him new ftrength againft the bad effects which thefe very works may produce in us, if we do not make ufe of the antidotes which God has ordained againft thefe poifons. The true means, to be filled anew with the riches of grace, is thus to ftrip ourfelves of it: and without this it is extremely difficult not to grow faint in the practice of good works.

* 121. We ought to know, that we have no part in the good which we do; and that accordingly, as God hides himfelf in doing it by us, we ought alfo, as far as is poffible, to hide it from ourfelves, and in a manner to annihilate ourfelves before him, faying, "Lord, we are nothing before thee; but thou art all to us. We continue to be as nothing, after thou haft by thy double mercy, drawn us out of nothing and out of fin:

the proof whereof we inceffantly bear in ourfelves, in our continual weaknefs and helpleffnefs. We fee ourfelves in the midft of an ocean : for thou art the true and boundlefs ocean of nature and of grace, which neither ebbs nor flows, but is permanent and immoveable. Thou fpreadeft abroad as it pleafeth thee, the celeftial waters in all ages, and draweft them back and fendeft them again into the fouls thou loveft, by fluxes and refluxes, ineffable and divine. Thy Spirit is the only wind that blows, and that reigns over the infinite ocean. And as we fee the waters on earth, which ceafe to run, though but for a little while, are immediately corrupted, we have reafon to fear, left the fame thing befal our fouls, if inftead of caufing thefe heavenly waters to return to thee their fource, we retain, and ftop them in their motion, though it were but for a moment. For whereas the rivers of earth corrupt themfelves when they ftop, but without corrupting the channel through which they flow, the rivers of thy grace, though ftopt, are never themfelves corrupted, but the fouls, the channel through which they pafs. We find therefore, O God, it is more difficult to reftore to thee, by an humble thankfulnefs, the graces we have received from thee, than to attract them into our fouls by prayer ; and that accordingly thefe refluxes toward the fountain, are greater favours than the effluxes therefrom. Wherefore the only grace which we implore from thee, and which comprehends all others,

others, is, That thy grace may never defcend to us, but to re-afcend toward thee: and that it may never re-afcend, but to defcend, into us again: fo that we may be eternally watered by thee, and thou be eternally glorified."

* 122. Good works do not receive their laft perfeftion, till they as it were lofe themfelves in God. This is a kind of death to them, refembl-ing that of our bodies, which will not attain their higheft life, their immortality, till they lofe themfelves in the glory of our fouls, or rather of God, wherewith thy will be filled. And it is only what they had of earthly and mortal, which good works lofe by fpiritual death.

* 123. Fire is the fymbol of love: and the love of God is the principle and end of our good works. But as truth furpaffes figure, the fire of divine love has this advantage over material fire, that it can re-afcend to its fource, and rife thither with all the good works which it pro-duces. And by this means it prevents their be-ing corrupted by pride, vanity, or any evil mix-ture. But this cannot be done otherwife than by making thefe good works, in a fpiritual manner die in God, by deep gratitude, which plunges the foul in him as in an abyfs, with all that it is, and all the grace and works for which it is in-debted to him: a gratitude, whereby the foul feems to empty itfelf of them, that they may re-turn to their fource, as rivers feem willing to

empty

empty themfelves, when they pour themfelves with all their waters into the fea.

124. The natural admiration of man flows from ignorance: but that of a Chriftian from knowledge.

* 125. When we have received any favour from God, we ought to retire, (if not into our clofet, into our heart) and fay, " I come, Lord, to reftore to thee what thou haft given, and I freely relinquifh it, to enter again into my own nothingnefs. For what is the moft perfeft crea-ture in heaven or earth in thy prefence, but a void capable of being filled with thee and by thee, as the air which is void and dark is capable of be-ing filled with the light of the fun ? Grant there-fore, O God, that I may never appropriate thy grace to myfelf, any more than the air appropri-ates to itfelf the light of the fun; who withdraws it every day to reftore it the next, there being nothing in the air that either appropriates its light or refifts it. O give me the fame facility of re-ceiving and reftoring thy grace and good works : I fay thine ; for I acknowledge the root from which they fpring, is in thee, and not in me."

* 126. As all that we can properly call our own, is the evil which is natural to us, they who are truly touched by the Spirit of God, have no right to complain of any reproach, whether they are guilty of the thing or not. It fuffices, that they

have

have in them the principle of all the faults which are, or can be laid to their charge.

127. There is no true charity which is not accompanied with humility, courage and patience.

* 128. We fhould chiefly execife our love toward thofe who moft check either our way of thinking, or our temper, or our knowledge, or the defire we have, that others fhould be as virtuous as we would wifh to be ourfelves.

* 129. As God once fubfifted without any creature in his own infinite fulnefs, fo love will one day fubfift in itfelf, without any outward works: which are now only the ftreams, whereof love is the fource, the fhoots of which this is the root, the rays whereof love is the fun, the fpark of which this is the fire, always acting, always confuming, and yet preferving the foul wherein it dwells.

* 130. The defire of exercifing charity, obliges us to purify ourfelves by all forts of holy exercifes, that we may be filled with the gifts of God, and capable of imparting them to others, without lofing any thing of our own fulnefs. By thus exercifing our charity, we increafe it. This alone, when it fills the heart, has the advantage of giving always and by giving enriching itfelf.

131. One of the greateft evidences of the love of God, to the fouls he hath touched with his love,

is to fend them afflictions, with grace to bear them.

132. There is no affliction which befals the righteous, of which God is not the author. And whereas the ills of other men have no mixture of good, God mingles with the fufferings of the righteous, thofe feeds, which although bitter at firft, yet afterward bring forth peaceable fruit.

133. Ever in great ficknefles or afflictions we ought to teftify to God, that in receiving them as from his hand, we feel pleafure in the midft of the pain, from being afflicted by him who loves us, and whom we love.

134. If we are perfuaded, that God does not afflict us, but to make us ftill more capable of loving him, by purifying our hearts through that fire which he came to bring into the world, we fhould take pleafure in fuffering our afflictions, and confuming, by that divine fire, this fire of the earth, which makes us love too well our bodies, our health, our own will and the things of the world.

135. There would be danger in ever mentioning to any perfon, any good work which he had done : if he was not humble, and his heart abafed before God, by a deep fenfe of his favours.

136. God ufually mingles pains with the fignal

nal graces which he gives, or will give to them he loves. And his thus casting them down is the ordinary token, that he is about to raise them up.

137. Happy are they who are sick, or lose their life, for having done a good work.

138. The souls of the just re-enter into God by death, as the venal blood re-enters the heart.

139. Most of those who die well in the judgment of men, die ill in the judgment of God.

140. The weightiness of our words and actions is an effect of simplicity joined with prudence.

141. Nothing gives us so great confidence in speaking, as speaking from the fulness of our heart. And when it is filled with love, this confidence is so great that we can hardly refrain from speaking.

142. He who loves none but God, thinks of him always, and that which is not God, cannot please him.

143. " If I grieve, O Lord, it is because loving thee as I do, I do not see thee."

144. God is so great that he communicates his greatness to the least things which are done for his service.

135. To live as a Christian, one must act

only

only by the fpirit of God : otherwife we live as Heathens.

146. God hardly gives his fpirit even to thofe whom he has already eftablifhed in grace, if they do not afk it of him on all occafions not only once, but many times.

147. The firft fruit of faith is prayer, the lifting up the foul to God to implore his af-fiftance even in the fmalleft things, which it would undertake for his fervice.

148. Faith teaches us two things at the fame time: one, that we ought to do nothing but for God : the other, that he muft engage us in thofe good works which we would carry on and finifh well.

149. As far as we advance in obedience, fo far we advance in faith. And fo far as we advance in faith, we advance in love, which is the heart, the life, the foul of faith.

150. We fhould do nothing without afking confent of God ; and we fhould take care not to prevent his anfwer, by thofe almoft infenfible defires which lie hid in the foldings of our heart.

* 151. All is clear to us, in proportion as we walk in the bright path of faith, obedience, prayer, love, and Chriftian fidelity.

152. God teaches the fouls he loves, and that love him, in a far more excellent manner than men can do. For whereas they fpeak
only

only to the ear, he fpeaks to the heart. They can only propofe what ought to be done: he gives power to execute, light and heat at once.

153. When a Chriftian is fick his bed is his church.

154. We fhould be prepared by purity of heart to fpeak of God, left we fhould wound his truths. We are to give a ftrict account of our leaft idle words : and fhall we not give a ftrict account of his !

155. Great men have herein more of the image of God than others, that they have more means of doing good. And one may fay, that they are born for that end, To do good in the world.

156. God never hears our prayers without increafing our love to him and our neighbour.

* 157. All that a Chriftian does, even his eating and fleeping, is prayer, when it is done with fimplicity, according to the order of God, without either adding to, or diminifhing from it, by his own choice.

158. Love is the only virtue which has no bounds.

* 159. The three greateft punifhments which God can inflict on finners in this world, are, 1. To let loofe their own defires upon them ; 2. To let them fucceed in all they wifh for, and 3. To fuffer them to continue many years in the quiet enjoyment thereof.

160.

160. The Heathen philofophers well knew that man is the world in miniature. But they did not know, that every fingle man is a world of corruption. And that all the impurity which is in the creation, flows from the impurity contained in our fouls.

161. If the greateft philofophers can hardly account for the conflicts that rife in the air, how can they account for thofe that rife in our fouls, the depth of which furpaffes that of the fea? This ignorance is one of the greateft exercifes of our patience; and of the moft ufeful, if we fuffer, but not confent to it.

* 162. God confiders our outward good works, only according to the good difpofitions of our hearts. And as this is fometimes like the trees in winter, full of warmth within, though producing nothing without, he loves this barrennefs, caufed only by outward hindrances, more than men do flowers and fruits.

164. True friendfhip obliges us to have no lefs regard to the defires of our friends than to their needs.

165. Happy the foul in which love never fleeps, and to which it ferves for a perpetual fpur.

166. It is obferved, that the actions which proceed from love, are done without difficulty. How much more if they proceed from the love of God, fince it is himfelf who does them in us?

167.

167. God, in creating vifible things, only gave us a picture of things invifible.

168. There are three ways to edify our neighbour: the firft, to treat well, at leaft in words, all evil men, particularly thofe who feek to do us evil: the fecond, To judge no man, though appearances are againft him; and even when the fault is proved, as far as we can, either to excufe or cover it by a modeft filence: and the third, Unlefs there be a plain neceffity, not to fpeak of ourfelves, good or bad.

* 169. Love fhews courtefy to young and old, good and bad, wife and unwife: indeed to all the world. But it ufes no flattery either to others or ourfelves.

* 170. Love fafts when it can, and as much as it can. It leads to all the ordinances of God, and employs itfelf in all the outward works whereof it is capable. It flies as it were, like Elijah, over the plain, to find God upon his holy mountain.

* 171. We ought to fuffer with patience whatever befals us, to bear the defects of others, and our own, to own them to God in fecret prayer, or with groans which cannot be uttered: but never to fpeak a fharp or peevifh word, nor to murmur or repine.

172. If to avoid occafions of fin, and to ftrengthen our weaknefs, we would now and then retire from the world, it is incredible, what help

I 6

we fhould receive from God, and what increafe in the fruits of his Spirit.

* 173. The fea is an excellent figure of the fulnefs of God, and that of the bleffed fpirits. For as the rivers all return into the fea, fo the bodies, the fouls and the good works of the righteous, return into God, to live there in his eternal repofe.

* 174. What the fcripture terms *the finger of God*, is no other than the Holy Spirit, who engraves in our hearts what pleafeth him.

175. Nothing is more oppofite to falvation than the love of riches; for in the fame proportion as thefe increafe, all experience fhews, the love of pleafure, and the defire of honour increafes alfo.

176. One that is truly *poor in fpirit* loves poverty, as much as other men love riches.

177. At firft the Chriftians were wholly diftinct from the world. But as they are now mingled with it, and of the fame fpirit, thofe who ferioufly defire falvation, ought fo far as they can, to feparate themfelves from all that have the fpirit of the world.

* 178. It is full as glorious to die for charity as for truth; nor will it have a lefs recompence from God.

* 179. Death entered by the ear into the foul of our firft mother: by the eye chiefly it enters the fouls of her children. But whereas Eve, after having hearkened to the ferpent, took the

forbidden

forbidden fruit, her children generally, after having seen it, hearken to the counsels of the devil. And indeed, if the few words of that unhappy spirit ruined Eve, even in a state of innocence, what can we expect, if in our state of sin and impotence, we pass our life in perpetual converse with the world, and in the continual fight of creatures under which the devil conceals himself far better than under the form of a serpent?

* 180. To conceive still better the danger we are in, while we remain in the corruption of the world, confider on the one hand, Eve, with her strength and innocence, in the paradise of God : on the other, men weak and sinful, the creatures all infectious, all instruments of sin, and that are as a veil with which the devil covers himself, to tempt us the more effectually ; and lastly, the world, which is the place of banishment with regard to our bodies, a prison with regard to our souls, and an hell with regard to those evil spirits, who remain there, continually mingled with men, till the judgment of the great day.

181. The world which we are to hate, is not this heaven and this earth which we behold, but the infection which sin has spread through them and all the creatures which they contain. So that whereas at their creation they were the objects that excited man's praise, admiration and devotion

tion toward God, they are now the objects of his concupiscence and irregular desires.

* 182. The great, will, after their death, look upon the pomp and pleasures wherein they had lived, just as those who awake from a deep sleep do on the riches, honours, and pleasures which they saw in their dream.

183. There is no other way to find God, than to despise all things else, to love him alone in the unity of his being, the trinity of persons, and the incarnation of his Son.

184. Although all that is created lives in and by God, as the birds live in and by the air, nevertheless this universal system of beings has not yet acquired its last perfection. It bears, deeply engraven in all its parts, the marks of Adam's disobedience; which render it altogether unworthy of our desires and affections.

185. God has not given man an heart so vast and so capable of loving, but in order to fill it with his love, and with himself alone. Accordingly we ought to use the creatures as so many steps to raise us up to the Author of our being, that we may render him not only for ourselves, but for them also, a perpetual homage, by acknowledging all the wonders and benefits for which they are indebted to him.

* 186. As on many occasions some of the senses correct the others, and reason corrects them all; so faith which is in Christians a superior reason, ought to correct the judgment which purely

purely human reason forms of the goods and evils of this world.

187. If the whole earth is no more than a point compared with the heaven that surrounds it, what is it when compared to the superior sphere which surrounds all the lower heavens? What is the littleness then of any or all of the things which the earth contains?

* 188. All that is good here below flows from above. And if but one drop could fall into our heart of the happiness of heaven, pure as it is in its source, earth would become a paradise. Nor would there be then need to put off the body; because the least part of those heavenly goods, received in its fulness, would render us blessed and immortal, even in this world.

* 189. Although all the grace of God depends on his mere bounty, yet is he pleased generally to attach them to the prayers, and good instructions, the good examples and the holiness of those among whom we are brought up. And if we knew the secret of the grace of Christ, and the strong though invisible attractions whereby he draws some souls through their intercourse with others, we should beware to whom we intrusted the education of our children.

190. When the world displays all its grandeur and goods before us, we should say to it, as our Lord to Satan, when he shewed him all the kingdoms of the earth and the glory of them:

Get

Get thee behind me, world, for it is written, Thou shalt worship the Lord thy God, and him only shalt thou serve.

191. There is nothing in the world that is not in a continual flux, and with so rapid a motion, that one cannot possess it, but part by part, and from moment to moment.

* 192. To prepare the mind for prayer it ought to be at liberty, in tranquility, in humility, in confidence, in simplicity, and in an entire dependence on God: not troubled, not divided, not wavering, neither preventing the will of God by any secret passion.

* 193. Prayer continues in the desire of the heart, though the understanding be employed on outward things.

194. We should not be impatient to receive of God, but to give him our heart, the only thing he requires.

195. Those words of St. Paul, *No man can call Jesus Lord but by the Holy Ghost*, shew us the necessity of eying God in our good works, in our prayers, and even in our minutest thoughts, knowing that none are pleasing to him but those which he forms in us and with us. From hence we learn, that we cannot speak to him or serve him, unless he uses our tongue, hands, and heart, to do by himself, and by his Spirit, whatever he would have us do.

196. All devotion depends on that new heart, which God gives us when it pleases him. In

order

order to receive it, the soul should be disengaged, from all that shuts up the door of our heart against the Spirit. We are continually as asleep, unless he awakens us.

197. By retirement and abstractedness from the world, we should remove all hindrances to those secret conversations, those visits, unknown to men of the world, and those divine impressions, which make us groan and sigh, love and desire, pray and importune God to give us the continual influence of his Spirit, without which the soul remains dry, and barren, as trees are in winter, though there may be life in their root.

198. Whenever God ceases to inspire us with his holy Spirit, we lie open to the corruption of our own spirit, and the malice of the wicked one. And this he frequently does if we discontinue our watching, or are not instant in prayer.

* 199. God's command, To pray without ceasing, is founded on the necessity we have of his grace, to preserve the life of God in our soul, which can no more subsist one moment without it, than the body can subsist without continual supplies of air.

200. If even those who have known the grace of God, do not continually watch unto prayer, the evil root of sin will have more influence on them than the good seed of grace.

201. God in his excellent wisdom raises in us good thoughts, and then inspires us with prayer,

to aſk of him thoſe graces, which he is reſolved to give, when we aſk with a full ſubmiſſion to his will. Therefore in order to know, if we ſhall obtain what we aſk, we have only to conſider, Do we ſeek our own pleaſure, or merely the grace of God in our prayers? If this only, we ſhall have the petitions we aſk of him.

* 202. As the moſt dangerous winds may enter at little openings, ſo the devil never enters more dangerouſly into the ſouls of good men, than by little amuſements, and little unobſerved incidents, which ſeeming to be nothing, yet inſenſibly open the heart to great temptations.

203. To make our reading uſeful, it ſhould be incloſed between two prayers, at the beginning and the end of it.

* 204. The chief deſire of Chriſtian parents ſhould be, for the ſalvation of their children. Without this, all they do for them ſerves only to draw the curſe of God upon themſelves; ſince they are as guardian angels that ought to conduct to heaven, thoſe to whom they have given life. 'Tis a great miſtake to ſuppoſe, they can pleaſe God by any other good works while they neglect this.

205. True piety conſiſts in doing, not what we chuſe, but what God chuſes for us.

206. The holieſt men are troubled, when God ever ſo little turns away his face from them. And from thence ariſes the neceſſity of continually watching and prayer.

* 207. The perfection we are inceffantly to prefs after, is no other than perfect love : and love cannot increafe in the foul, but by a difengagement from fenfible and pleafing objects. Otherwife our love is falfe, our courtefy deceitful, and our condefcenfion to others only a fnare to ourfelves; becaufe inftead of flowing from the love of God, they flow from felf-love, and the love of the world.

* 208. The readieft way which God takes to draw a man to himfelf is, to afflict him in that which he loves the moft, and with good reafon; and to caufe this affliction to arife from fome good action done from a fingle eye : becaufe nothing can more clearly fhow him the emptinefs of what is moft lovely and defirable in the world.

209. Separation from the world is the firft ftep towards heaven, and the beginning of our commerce with God, who advances towards us when he fees we eftrange ourfelves from others to go to him.

* 210. God does nothing but in anfwer to prayer: and even thofe who have been converted to God, without praying for it themfelves, (which is exceeding rare) were not, without the prayers of others.

211. As our wants are continual, fo fhould our prayers be, chiefly in the beginning of our good refolutions : as there is no time wherein we have greater need of peculiar help from God.

* 212. To prayer fhould be added continual employment; for grace flies a vacuum as well as nature, and the devil fills whatever God does not fill.

213. One ought to read the holy fcriptures with fo deep a refpect, and fo abfolute a fubmif-fion, as fhew that we are thoroughly perfuaded it is the Holy Ghoft that fpeaks. And we ought to receive with all humility what he is pleafed to difcover to us, to profit thereby, leaving the reft in the treafure of his infinite knowledge. Such reading is no lefs ufeful than prayer, and brings a bleffing with it, which is the principle of our good works, and of the conduct of our whole life.

* 214. One of the greateft faults which pa-rents can commit, and which is the fource of numberlefs diforders in families and in common-wealths, is, that inftead of bringing up their children as thofe that are now the children of God, by the fecond birth which they received in baptifm, they think only of giving them fuch an education as is fuitable to their firft birth. They take great care of them as they are children of Adam, but none at all as they are children of God. Thus they are murderers of their own children, ftifling the life of God which was begun in their fouls.

215. If we would be obeyed by our domeftics we muft not only command, but endeavour to gain their heart. For God himfelf to make
himfelf

himfelf obeyed, does not barely give commandments, but alfo infpires his love into the fouls of thofe who are to fulfil them.

* 216. Uniformity of life and fymetry of action, is effential to Chriftian holinefs. It is like a circle, which is confidered as the firft of figures, becaufe of the equality of all its parts.

* 217. It is highly dangerous to grow in the knowledge of the things of God, and not in the love of God.

* 218. God does not love men that are inconftant, nor good works that are intermitted. Nothing is pleafing to him but what has a refemblance of his own immutability.

219. God, who is a Spirit, will dwell no where on earth but in our fpirits, which are his palaces. But he does not confider them as fuch, unlefs they are wholly devoted to him.

220. The truly devout fhow, that paffions as naturally flow from true as from falfe love : fo deeply fenfible are they of the goods and evils of thofe whom they love for God's fake. But this can only be comprehended by thofe who underftand the language of love; which to all others, how wife or learned foever, is ftrange and barbarous.

221. Truft in God, who every moment affifts thofe, who give themfelves up to him. If we will be always thinking of what is paft and what is to come, we fhall be under continual apprehenfions.

222. To

222. To desire to grow in grace which is the greatest thing in the whole world, and yet not to strive and labour after it, is desiring to establish an order contrary to that of God, which is immoveable as himself.

223. Can we be troubled when we know that God does all, and that not an hair falls from our head without his permission?

* 224. The bottom of our soul may be in repose, even while we are in many outward troubles; just as the bottom of the sea is calm, while the surface is strongly agitated.

225. Christianity is summed up in being throughly willing that God should treat us in the manner that pleases him. As by becoming Christians we are become his lambs, we ought to be ready to suffer even to the death, without complaining.

226. We ought never to make a law of the advices we give, but leave those to whom they are given to their own choice.

* 227. God frequently conceals the part which his children have in the conversion of other souls. Yet one may boldly say, that a person who long groans before him for the conversion of another, whenever the soul is converted to God, is one of the chief causes of it; especially if it is a mother who prays and groans for her child.

* 228. A constant attention to the work with which God intrusts us, is the greatest mark of solid piety.

229. When

229. When God afflicts us, we ought, if possible, to add something to our usual exercises of piety, to harden ourselves against that little relaxation which our present circumstances· may require.

230. If after having renounced all, we do not incessantly watch over our actions, and beseech God to accompany our vigilance with his, we shall be again entangled and overcome.

231. The more pure the heart is, the more capable it is of prayer.

232. When we know the pride of our heart, we should offer it to God, as a sickness which he alone can cure.

233. This is humility, to serve God in the state wherein we are, waiting till he shall make us better.

* 234. We are to bear with those whom we cannot amend, and to be content with offering them to God. There is no greater exercise of charity than this, nor of true resignation. And since God has borne our infirmities in his own person, we may well bear those of each other for his sake.

235. Seeing Christ has given his life for our salvation, it is just that they who love souls for his sake, sometimes hazard their own life for him, to repay some part of his unexampled love.

236. Where there is love, there humility, long-suffering, patience, and all other virtues

meet

meet together : inafmuch as thefe are only the branches whereof love is the root.

237. Chriftians generally defire to have only fweet medicines for the diftempers of their fouls, not confidering that we ufe fharp and bitter ones to cure the difeafes of our bodies.

* 238. Nothing is more to be lamented, than that the wounds of the foul are invifible like herfelf: and that we are fo far from being fenfible of them as foon as we have received them, that for a long time we find pleafure in our misfortune, and fancy we are well, though we are fick unto death.

239. We cannot keep the Spirit of God after we have received it, but by increafing it by conftant exercifes of piety. Nor can we increafe it, but by keeping ourfelves at a diftance from the world.

240. To abandon all, to ftrip one's felf of all, in order to feek and follow Jefus Chrift, naked in Bethlehem when he was born, naked in the hall when he was fcourged, and naked when he died on the crofs. is fo great a mercy, that neither the thing nor the knowledge of it is given to any, but through faith in the Son of God.

* 241. As devils and the fouls of men are both of the fame, of a fpiritual nature, and accordingly the former well underftand what paffes in the latter, they find it eafy to tranfmit from one foul to another the corruption and infection

fection they meet with there, by means of the
evil converfation and friendly intercourfe there
is between them.

242. There is no faithfulnefs like that which
ought to be between a true guide of fouls and
the perfons directed by him. They ought continually to regard each other in God, and clofely to examine themfelves whether all their
thoughts are pure, and their words conducted
with Chriftian difcretion. Other affairs are only
the affairs of men, but thefe are peculiarly the
things of God.

* 243. The fears which the firft appearance of
the great truths of God raife in the minds of
young converts, refemble thofe which are occafioned at firft by the apparition of good angels:
but they foon pafs away, and leave the foul in
peace and joy in the Holy Ghoft.

244. Of all converfions, the moft apoftolical
is that which is wrought by the very words of
the gofpel. By thefe God has converted both
the Jews and Heathens, and has formed and does
ftill form his church.

245. The foul wherein God has fhed abroad
his grace, no longer knows any language but that
of grace.

246. The words of the gofpel are the words of
life. All others are only dead words, whatever
vigour they may feem to receive from the eloquence of him that fpeaks them.

247. Grace renders fweet to the foul not only

the harfheft truths, hard fayings which we could
not bear before, but alfo the moft difficult actions and the moft grievous fufferings.

248. Jefus Chrift alone opens the ears of the
heart ; and then we run in his ways after the
odour of his ointments.

* 249. Jefus Chrift renews his own life every
hour in the bodies and fouls of real Chriftians.
They are living images of him, and reprefent
him in a more excellent manner than the writings of the gofpel itfelf. For the dead charac-
ters of the gofpel (though living in another fenfe,)
contains only the paft life of Chrift : whereas
true Chriftians contain alfo his prefent life, and
that in living charaders : which caufed the
apoftle to declare, *I live not, but Chrift liveth in
me.*

250. Every new victory which the foul gains
is the effect of a new prayer.

251. It is very poffible for a man to love any
of the creatures, without their contributing to
it ; but it is not poffible for him to love God,
unlefs God himfelf waters him from moment
to moment.

252. The clouds which frequently rife in the
fouls of thofe who are truly converted to God,
do not hinder the continuance of that joy which
his prefence produces in them : but thefe clouds
are all fcattered by a frefh fupply of faith, and of
the Spirit of Jefus Chrift.

* 253. It is not good for a babe in Chrift,
either

either to converse much with the world, or to be wholly alone.

* 254. Employment frequently holds the place of mortification, and produces the same effects.

255. Those who write by the Spirit of God do not follow their memory so much as their heart.

* 256. Our continuance in good works is the best means to retain a continual sense of the love of God.

257. We cannot continue in good works, unless we renounce all desire of the goods, honours, and pleasures of the world.

258. Let the things of earth roll under our feet, as those of heaven roll over our heads.

259. God hates sloth as much as presumption.

260. It is frequently necessary to serve God, and abandon ourselves to him, though we see but darkly what is his will concerning us, without waiting for particular revelations. For we cannot expect in the order of grace, as in that of reason, to have evidence and demonstration at every step.

261. Truth cannot so well be found by disputing, as by holy meditation.

262. Every one has his peculiar gift from God, according to which he ought to conduct himself. At the same time he should labour with sobriety, to acquire the knowledge of divine things, so he

does

does it with a single eye, that he may profit thereby, and be more deeply grounded in love.

263. They that cannot fast one way, may fast
another. And those who are truly devoted to
God, have a great liberty, to do or not to do
those outward things which are in themselves indifferent.

* 264. The sympathies formed by grace, far
surpass those formed by nature.

265. The love of God leads us first to the true
love of ourselves, and thence to the love of our
neighbour.

266. It is good to renew ourselves from time
to time, by closely examining the state of our
soul, as if we had never been renewed before.
For nothing tends more to the full assurance of
faith, than to keep ourselves by this means in
humility and the exercise of all good works.

* 267. God considers us only according to
what we are in our hearts, in the secret movements of our soul, in our hidden intentions and our
passions imperceptible to others. The goodness
of all our works depends on the purity and simplicity of our heart, which is at it were the spirit,
the invisible soul of this visible body.

268. We should disengage ourselves from all
those pleasures, which if otherwise innocent, yet
fill the capacity of the heart, which should be
filled by grace only.

* 269. If we do not devote all we do to God,
there is nothing in our best works but what is human

man or pagan : becaufe we regard only ourfelves·
therein, and while we do what is good in appearance, we in effect put ourfelves by a fecret felf-
complacence in the place of God.

270. In the greateſt temptations, a fingle look
to Jefus Chriſt, or the bare prounouncing his·
name, fuffices to overcome the wicked one,
fo it be done with confidence and calmnefs of
fpirit.

271. There is nothing either in earth or hell·
that can poſſibly hurt a foul, which regards Jefus
Chriſt, with a lively faith, either in his death,
or in his refurrection.

* 272. Thankfgiving is as it were the foul of
prayer, with which it fhould begin, continue, and
end.

273. The hindrances of our thankfulnefs,
when we conquer them, increafe inſtead of diminifhing it.

* 274. God frequently gives a foul that ardent-
ly loves him, a difpenfation from thofe laborious
works, which it would do, to teſtify its gratitude
by laying obſtacles in the way which makes
them impoſſible.

275. In fouls filled with love, the defire to
pleafe God is a continual prayer.

* 276. Nothing is more true, than that *the
yoke of Chriſt is eafy, and his burden light.* For
one need only love, to fulfil the whole law, even
when it cannot be outwardly accomplifhed. And
yet it is true, that this difpenfation from outward

K 3   works,

works, which proceeds from providential hindrances, is often a greater trial to fouls full of love
than the moſt painful of thofe works would have
been.

277. God does not always fuffer himſelf to be
overcome by his children (as he was by Jacob)
in the fecret combats of faith and love, wherein
they wreſtle with him. He often remains victor-
ious over the foul, which defires to labour, to
fuffer, to die for him ; that he may attach her
more and more to his love by hindering the effects of that love which ſhe bears him. But however the combat is, ſhe is ſo much the happier
through the increaſe of her love by thofe very
oppofitions, as torrents are raiſed by the obſtacles
which they meet with. And the faith which
guides her love, gives her to underſtand that ſhe
fucceeds in the moſt excellent manner, by contributing to the fuccefs of God's defigns, by the
difappointment of her own.

278. God only requires of his adult children
that their hearts be throughly purified, and that
they offer him continually the wiſhes and vows,
that naturally fpring from perfect love. For thofe
defires being the firſt genuine fruits of love, are
the moſt perfect prayers which can fpring from
it.

279. The neceffity of continual watching
unto prayer rifes hence, that the devil is continually watching to furprize us, and to deſtroy us
by

by thofe very victories which we gain over him.

* 280. As the furious hate which the devil bears us is termed, the roaring of that lion, fo our vehement love may be termed, crying after God.

281. Thofe who know the greatnefs and holinefs of the church, count nothing therein little.

282. On every occafion of uneafinefs, we fhould retire to prayer, that we may give place to the grace and light of God, and then form our refolutions, without being in any pain what fuccefs they may have.

283. Thofe who clofely follow God, eafily judge of the manner wherein they ought to act in fpiritual things. They need walk but a little in the ftrait way, to fee before them the light which difperfes the clouds.

284. Nothing of that which is in the order of God, ought to be accounted troublefome.

* 285. A foul returned to God, ought to be attentive to every thing which is faid to him on the head of falvation, with a fecret defire to profit thereby.

286. The whole life of grace confifts in dependence upon God.

287. There is no furer mark of a true converfion, than to be greatly tempted of the devil. The beft means of overcoming him is, to have no dependence upon ourfelves, but to throw

ourfelves

ourfelves wholly upon God, with an abfolute dependence on his will.

288. The *juſt ſhall live by faith*. By his continual regard to God he draws thofe graces and influences from heaven, without which the moſt righteous man upon earth could not fubfiſt one moment.

289. Ignorance of the truths which exalt God, and abafe man, (convinced that in whatever ſtate he is, he has continual need of new grace, which God gives to thofe only that humble themfelves more and more) has caufed the ruin of many, who were much admired in the firſt ſtages of their converfion.

290. Jefus Chriſt, becoming man out of love to us, fatisfied the juſtice of his Father, by an humility, an obedience, and a patience as incomprehenfible in the human nature, as God in his divine nature, was, is, and always will be, to all but himſelf.

291. We ought to defire the Lord's fupper with the fame earneſtneſs as we defire to preferve the health we enjoy, or to recover that we have loft.

292. He to whom the Lord's fupper ferves chiefly for food, fhould prepare himfelf by another food, the word of God. He to whom it ferves chiefly for a medicine, fhould prepare himfelf for it by repentance.

293. God impofes one kind of penance on every penitent, by giving him various afflictions:

and

and anothor kind, in the unavoidable inconveniences which. attend every calling whatever. And none is duly prepared for the Lord's fupper, but he that acquits himfelf well in affliction and in his calling.

294. None is duly prepared for it, who does not daily examine the ground of his confcience, with an earneft defire to judge himfelf that he may not he judged of the Lord.

295. They whom God has preferved from grofs fins, ought to have tender compaffion and great patience toward thofe whom God has fuffered to fall into them, and whom he has left in them for a feafon. It is thus they are to fhew their humulity and gratitude to God, and their charity to their neighbour.

296. Of the fins which God has pardoned, let nothing remain but a deeper humility in our heart, and a ftricter regulation in our words, in our actions, and in our fufferings.

297. A natural goodnefs and eafinefs of temper, often hinder our growing in grace; making us do almoft all good works rather from inclination, than by the Spirit of God.

298. Examples are to be followed with caution; but the gofpel rules without referve. St. Paul advifes to follow him, only fo far as he followed Chrift.

299. It is of no ufe to love the brightnefs of truth, unlefs we fhew the warmth of it in our practice.

K 5

300.

300. The warmth of love refembles that of the heart, which extends itfelf to the fmalleft parts of the body.

* 301. If the love of God does not increafe in us, in the fame degree as we increafe in knowledge, the ftronger principle will overcome the weaker, and knowledge will ftifle love. This has occafioned men of the greateft learning, almoft to envy their happinefs, who know little, but love much.

* 302. The body increafes without decreafing, till it comes to a certain age. But there is no limited time wherein the foul may not either increafe or decreafe.

303. Silence of fpirit confifts in cutting off all vain and ufelefs thoughts.

304. One may be intemperate in fpeaking as well as in eating. And as after we have fafted long, we are apt to eat too much, fo are we to fpeak too much after we have been long filent.

305. It is not reafonable to defire they fhould love us, who do not love God.

306. We would every day gain fomething upon ourfelves, and be a little more difengaged from the objects that furround us.

307. When we fhould counfel our friends, filence is no lefs blameable than indifference.

308. The holy fcripture is the mirror wherein we fee God, and wherein we may fee the fmalleft fpots upon our fouls.

309. Death is the greateft affair of human life.

life. We muſt prepare for it while we are in
reſt and health.

310. In whatever way of life we are, we depend on the mercy of God. And it is far better
humbly to truſt in him, though with ſomething
of uncertainty, than to truſt in ourſelves with
the utmoſt aſſurance. Adam, left to himſelf,
fell. Whereas thouſands of his offspring, though
ſinful, and feeble, ſtand through the grace of
Jeſus Chriſt.

* 311. If one cannot faithfully ſerve an earthly
prince without expoſing himſelf to many dangers
in his court, and to death in his armies, it is far
more reaſonable that thoſe who ſerve God in the
church, which is the court of his Son, ſhould
expoſe themſelves to all the dangers, and ſuffer
all the evils that occur in his ſervice : eſpecially
as he who has eſtabliſhed this kingdom, was
himſelf hated of men, and has foretold, that the
war, which they who preached the goſpel after
him, need make upon the world, would cauſe
them likewiſe to be hated of all men, for his
name's fake.

* 312. A true guide of ſouls, ought to be as
the heart, the tongue, and the hand of God, to
labour by his aſſiſtance for the ſalvation of them
that are under his care. For it is not he that
prays, that ſpeaks, that wiſhes, ſtrives, ſuffers;
but it is the Spirit of God which does all this,
when the miniſter is united to him, and calls
upon him continually.

313. There is this difference in the minifters of the church and of the world, that the latter affume pomp and grandeur, whereas the former are always covered with charity and humility.

* 314. There ought nothing to come out of the mouth or the heart of a preacher of the gof-pel, but what is not only reafonable but chriftian, and animated by the holy Spirit.

* 315. Between the phyficians of the foul and thofe of the body, there is a great difference in this. The latter are more and more hardened, by the fight of more patients and difeafes ; whereas the hearts of the former, by the fight of fpiritual difeafes, grow more and more tender.

316. A man muft have courage more than hu-man, to make war on all the world both within and without him.

* 317. The only way to undertake the preach-ing of the gofpel, is, To enter upon it by the infpiration of God, without having any regard to the world, or of what is either agreeable or difagreeable in it, and to forget even our own houfe and relations juft as Abraham did, in order to love God alone, as if he alone were our world, our relations, our all.

* 318. It is the glory of all true minifters of Chrift, to refemble the angels of God. They nearly refemble them, by having renounced the body, in order to regard the foul only : by their life all fpiritual, uniform throughout, all from

God,

God, all for God, and all proceeding from
the Spirit of God, as is that of the angels in heaven.

319. The government of fouls, particularly
in that which regards the fpiritual life, is not a
government of dominion and empire, but of love
and tendernefs. It confifts in following the
movements of God in the perfons committed to
us, after having difcerned by his light, that thefe
movements come from him.

320. God is the mafter of fouls: he moves
and guides them as he pleafes, according to the
depth of his judgments. We who are only his
fervants and helpers of thefe fouls, depend far
more on what he works in them, than they do
upon us.

* 321. He who is honoured with the minif-
try, ought to be and to appear as far feparate
from common Chriftians, as common Chriftians
ought to be and to appear feparate from Heathens.

* 322. A preacher fhould earneftly beg of
God, that his being accuftomed to facred offices
may no ways abate the folemn awe which he at
firft experienced in them. There is the utmoft
need that he fhould have as much of this to the
end (if not more) as at the beginning.

323. It is often improper to declare our fentiments haftily and abruptly. It may put it out of
our power to defend the truth; at leaft with any
profit.

324. Ministers, above all other men, should have those words continually before their eyes, *The kingdom of heaven suffereth violence, and the violent take it by force.*

* 325. The dispensation which God indispensibly requires of all that would minister his word, excludes every other design but that which springs from his grace and the motion of his Spirit.

* 326. Christ has always reserved in his church some ministers who bear in their souls the character of his divinity, so as to do nothing which is not suitable to his greatness, and far distant from the corruption which not only overflows the world, but even the church, the generality of his ministers.

327. None ought to believe himself worthy of the ministry.

328. A minister ought to avoid contention.

329. Nothing increases grace so much as the ministry, when it is exercised by the Spirit of God.

* 330. Faith has a peculiar force in an house where several souls consecrated to God are joined together.

331. The life of a minister ought to be uniform, to render it exemplary. * And if his example does not edify the world, neither will his writing benefit the church.

332. When we speak to others of the things

of

of God, we ought always to speak to ourselves, so as to take to ourselves at least an equal part of the instructions which we give them.

333. Those who have surmounted the desire of the flesh, have still to surmount that of the tongue and of the understanding: particularly at this time, wherein knowledge is so frequently found separate from virtue.

* 334. When any one writes for God, he should seek for no other eloquence than that which God gives in the simplicity of his Spirit. He would corrupt this, were he to mix it with human eloquence; and he should never forget, before, in, and after his work, to cry to God, that he may have his heart continually lifted up to him, who ought to be the source of all the thoughts and all the conversation of every minister.

* 335. While a man is alienated from God, he makes little account of that natural inclination which such an one as to some good works, or his aversion to some sins. But from the moment that he is converted to God, he sanctifies this inclination and this aversion, and serves himself of it in order to increase it: and nevertheless, the ease with which we do those good works, and avoid those evil ones, does not at all diminish the reward or value of them. Thus what was only virtuous Heathenism before, becomes true Christian virtue, by the infusion of love, which is in us as it were a second soul, all divine, and which

which transforms into itſelf that which before animated the body.

* 336. How clear-ſighted ſoever a man is in other reſpects, he hardly ſees all that love requires to be done, whether in reſpect of God or his neighbour, but while he feels that love in his heart.

INSTRUCTIONS

FOR

MEMBERS

OF

RELIGIOUS SOCIETIES.

Tranſlated from the FRENCH.

---

1. MEMBERS of religious ſocieties, who ought to be ſo holy, who have ſo many helps for becoming ſo, frequently fall ſhort of it, through the exceſſive confidence they are taught to place in external rules. They do not know that true holineſs flows neither from the will, nor from the efforts of man. They are not ſenſible that their corruption is above all remedies except only the grace of Chriſt : that all outward helps reach not the deep and inviſible wound of
the

the heart, and that they are defperately fick, who fancy they can be cured by their own cares or labours. Thefe do not hold by the root of all true good, which is Jefus Chrift. They are fevered from the principle of health and life: and it is for this reafon that they are fo weak, fometimes fo fenfual, and always fo proud, becaufe they do not receive that influence which gives ftrength, purity, and humility, in the fpirit of grace and love. This is therefore highly needful for them to confider, that neither *the ftaff of the prophet* nor *his fervant* is able to raife the dead: but only the prophet himfelf ftretched upon the body; that is, Chrift become man for us.

2. It is of deep importance, that they fhould underftand the connexion there is between their vows and the gofpel.† ＊ Suppofe they did not vow obedience to their Superior, they muft dread their own will as the fource of all vices. For in any ftate we are not at our own difpofal, we are not to live to ourfelves, or permitted to reft in ourfelves, or to be our own rule and end. We need not make a vow of poverty; but in every ftate the love of riches is forbidden; covetoufnefs is idolatry; and truft in our goods is incompatible with a due truft in God. We muft limit ourfelves to the neceffities of nature; difpenfe the reft with the moft exact fidelity, and use

† This letter was originally defigned for thofe of a Religious Houfe in France.

ufe even what we allow ourfelves as though we ufed it not. We need not bind ourfelves to a fingle life : but the laws of chaftity are fo ftrict in every ftate ; faults of this kind are fo dangerous ; the occafion of them are fo frequent in the world ; and it is fo juft to be afraid of that fin which may be committed even by a look, that it is eafier to abftain from all, than to ftop precifely at the point where innocence ends. See what is the ground of refolving upon a fingle life. And we fhould infinitely deceive ourfelves, if we regarded chaftity as a thing indifferent before we made the refolution. The dangers we are in, an holy fear, the care of an ineftimable treafure lodged in a brittle veffel, and the defire of pleafing Chrift by giving him an undivided heart, were, or ought to have been, our only motives for making fuch a refolution. It is becaufe we do not conceive this, that we are fo little guarded againft the tender connexions, and fo feebly refift that defire of pleafing ; fo often attach ourfelves to perfons whom we ought not to fee, but in order to become more pure ; that we nourifh in our hearts a thoufand ufelefs and frivolous defires ; fuffer our comfort to depend on the moft trifling things ; and fall into the incomprehenfible folly of having renounced what is lawful, the love of a fpoufe, and of children, to put filly, little, forbidden attachments in the place of thefe innocent and even holy ties.

3. Obferve the difference between the rules
which

which are merely of human authority and the laws of God. The former may on several occasions be difpenfed with; whereas the laws of God are indifpenfable : nor can their obligation be weakened either by cuftom, or by example, or authority. Neither can we excufe ourfelves on account of ignorance, becaufe that ignorance itfelf is a fin. Accordingly we may not on any pretence lofe time in trifling difcourfe, love worthlefs things, fuffer ourfelves to be betrayed into murmuring and impatience, or follow our pride, or felf-will in any thing. Thefe would be fins, though we were not fo peculiarly devoted to God: and our profeffion of religion only adds a new degree of guilt to them.

* 4. It is then of great moment to diftinguifh between thofe rules which feem purely arbitrary, and thofe which all muft impofe upon themfelves, if they purpofe to fave their fouls. Such are ftated hours of private prayer, reading, and meditation; conftant and ferious employment; plain and modeft apparel, and a carriage ftill more plain and modeft; a fteady uniformity of behaviour; following the counfel of fome guide who is taught of God ; an habitual dread of foftnefs and pleafure, and a love of penitence. Nothing of this is arbitrary. Piety partly confifts in thefe things, partly depends upon them. If you was in no religious fociety, you would be equally obliged to thefe; but you would be deprived

prived of the valuable helps of rule, of inſtruc-
tion, and of example, which you now enjoy.

* 5. And even thoſe rules which appear quite
arbitrary and indifferent, are uſually neceſſary
in order to the keeping of others, as the huſk
preſerves the corn, and as the letter preſerves
the ſpirit. It ſeems indeed to men of the world,
that theſe are little things : but pride and worldly wiſdom are ill judges of what is little or great
in the eyes of God. There are abundance of
things neceſſary in order to diſcipline, precious
helps for humility and fervency of ſpirit, which
the world deſpiſes, but which the children of
God know the value of.

* 6. Above all things, we muſt labour to convince ourſelves throughly, that we can never fill
up the charaſter of a life conſecrated to the ſervice of God, without an univerſal renunciation
of all things ; that it avails nothing to ſhut all the
other gates, if we leave one open for the devil ;
that we only make him rage the more, unleſs
we reſiſt him more valiantly in every point :
that the leaſt vice indulged brings back all the
reſt : that the ſelf-love which leads us to except
any thing, leads us afterwards to reſume all ; that
whatever takes up a part of our heart, neceſſarily wounds and weakens it : that the parting it,
when we owe and have promiſed the whole, is
no leſs than ſacrilege ; that the death of Ananias
ought to make all thoſe tremble, who keep back
a part : that the command to Lot and his wife,

Not

Not to look back, is renewed by Chrift in the gofpel; that it is eafy, by our defires, to turn back to the world; and that one cannot even thus return to it, without rendering ourfelves unworthy to enter into the promifed land; that we cannot conceive the fury of the devil againft thofe who undertake to live an angelic life in a mortal body; we cannot conceive therefore how neceflary it is to redouble our vigilance againft his unwearied efforts, and to be as unwearied and as diligent as him; otherwife he muft prevail.

*7. Let us be throughly perfuaded, that Chriftianity implies a general oppofition to all the falfe notions of the world, to its maxims and fentiments; that it knows no other pattern than Jefus Chrift and him crucified; that his difgraces and griefs are all its riches, and all its confolations: that confequently nothing is more oppofite thereto than pride and the love of pleafures, and that the only way for Chriftians to become great, is to be fincerely willing to be the leaft of all; that is, the moft unknown, the moft defpifed, the moft dependent, the leaft accommodated, and yet the moft patient and the moft fatisfied; not through an idea of our own virtue, which would be the height of pride, but from a confcioufnefs of our own unworthinefs, and from a deep love of the truth, which makes us fenfible of it.

8. Let us take care to preferve all the fervor and all the exactnefs which we find in the community, to look upon ourfelves as charged with

this

this depofitum, and obliged to tranfmit it to others; never to give it the leaft fhock, either by our example or advice; to be infinitely afraid of the great guilt implied in weakening piety or regularity in any point; to tremble at the thought of the fatal confequences that the leaft relaxations draw after them, which are ufually without remedy, and which terribly fwell the account of thofe which open the door for them. It is often but a fmall thing, in appearance: but all is precious and important; and a perfon devoted to God is to look upon nothing as little or indifferent.

9. Be convinced of the neceffity of leading a ferious life, and of loving none but ferious employments: regard every thing which is but a frivolous fpending of time, as an amufement unworthy of you: fly every employment which conduces only to luxury or vanity: refufe not that which is troublefome and humbling: place your honour, not in being ferved, but in ferving others: labour ufefully, as far as ever your ftrength will permit; have nothing of little, of weak, of childifh, in your inclinations: have on the contrary, fomething grand and manly in your fentiments, raifed above the weaknefs of your fex‖, which naturally leads to amufements and trifles.

* 10. Accuftom yourfelf to do nothing without defign, without reflection, without a lively

fentiment

‖ This was originally written for women.

sentiment of piety : not to suffer any of your
actions to be lost ; not to lose the fruit of any of
your prayers : Never to appear before God in
public service, without summoning all your
faith ; to esteem nothing great but for the holy
dispositions with which it is performed : Never
to separate your actions or your sufferings from
those of Jesus Christ, from which they derive all
their value : to count for nothing all, either virtue or wisdom, which is not grounded on Jesus
Christ, which has more of show than of truth,
which swells self-love, not the love of God : to
distrust all virtues which do not render you more
humble, more detached from yourselves, more
ready to yield to all the world : To dread
in that which is good, the vain satisfaction which
is almost inseparable, and which is the poison of
it : To be truly humbled by your faults ; to preserve with great care, the desire of future bliss,
the sense of the mercies of God, the remembrance of your sins and miseries, and the spirit of
compunction, which is the very soul of religion.

* 11. Guard early against the temptations and
dangers which might one day weaken you. Few
continue as they have begun ; fewer advance in
virtue. There are even in the most holy re-
treats, what are almost certain means of enfeebl-
ing the soul : and it is a great misfortune, either
not to know them, or when one does know
them, not to guard against them. It is impossible to set down here, every thing which may

slacken

flacken the foul. A thoufand imperceptible
ways, a thoufand infenfible declenfions, a thoufand flight lóffes, a thoufand fecret fnares, may
occafion this. Natural inconftancy and fickle-
nefs, lukewarmnefs in prayer, union with perfons that are not fervent in fpirit, attachment to
any thing wrong, which God punifhes, the flight-
ing of little duties, of little faults, of the checks
of an enlightened confcience; the forgetting the
reafons and motives which induced us to chufe
the ftate wherein we are; a fecret difguft at our
fuperior: too quick a fenfe of fome flight or re-
fufal; too great liberty in examining the defects
of our brethren; liftening to murmurers; any
fecret unfaithfulnefs not acknowledged; any
thing done with a doubting confcience; any
temptation on which we have not had the humility to afk advice; any fear of raillery in doing our duty; any flight diffipation; but above
all any fecret pride: for it is this fin which almoft always leads to the reft. And one cannot
too much recommend to them who would be all
devoted to God, an humility proportioned to
the graces they have need of, in order to advance in virtue and perfevere to the end.

12. Labour to extinguifh in yourfelf, to the
very root, the defire to pleafe, which finks even
to the marrow, and which is the moft invinci-
ble obftacle to the pure love of God. This driven
out on one fide, returns on another. It lives
equally on vice and on virtue: it does not for-

get the body, but to avail itself more of the qualities of the mind : it is humble and yet fierce : it is full of self-will, and affects to will nothing : it often deceives itself, and is the source of a thousand errors and seductions.—Happy he who is aware of such an enemy, who combats it sincerely, yet who has no hopes of conquering it otherwise than by the almighty grace of Jefus Christ. All the imperfections of religious societies, all their irregularities, flow from this poisoned fountain. Where discipline is wanting, it produces grofs evils. It produces evils no lefs dangerous, though spiritual, wherever true piety is not sufficiently known, and where the depth of human misery is covered, not healed, by superficial remedies.

. * 13. As persons usually know only the outside of chastity, and are little informed of its inward ground and its extent, it is of importance to consider, that this virtue resides chiefly in the heart; that it extinguishes all desire to have a place in the heart of another ; that it is an enemy to pleasure, to all that gratifies the senses, to all superfluity, to all that satisfies curiosity or softnefs, to all that weakens the soul and makes it bend earthward, to all that wounds the most severe modesty, to all that disturbs the peace and tranquillity necessary for prayer, to all that is capable of creating or recalling dangerous images ; in fine, to all that strengthens the chains which attach the soul to the body, and the inclination which

which it is so hard to lay aside, of seeking our repose in sensible things.

* 14. In order to be agreeable in a family, we ought not to suffer in ourselves any defect which we can correct. We should be neat in our cloaths, in our chamber, in all that we do either for ourselves or others. Our gait, our way of speaking, our whole behaviour, should be reformed with care. There may be much of simplicity therein, and yet much of dignity. We should not give ourselves leave to laugh, to speak, to admire any thing, in a flat and disgusting manner. We should carefully avoid every thing that is coarse, clownish, or indecent, and every way of expressing joy or friendship which is not quite well-bred and modest. Shun betimes little habits which give pain to others, and which age and negligence may increase. Accustom yourself to reflect upon every thing which might incommode another; to avoid with care, and not to slide into it either through hurry or forgetfulness. On the other side, we ought to bear with sweetness whatever incommodes us in another; to exact nothing; to excuse every thing, and to be patient ourselves and studious for the good of the family, purely from a motive of Christian love; regarding as mere worldly politeness whatever is done with a lower view, or from purely human motives.

* 15. The chief dispositions of mind, which are necessary in every member of a Christian fa-

mily,

mily, are goodnefs, fweetnefs, patience, the
defire of obliging, the fear of grieving or hurting
any one, a care to preferve love in himfelf and
others; a pain to fee any breach therein: hu-
manity toward the weak either in mind or in body; a joy in taking the burdens of others upon
ourfelves; a love of the religious exercifes
which are performed in common; an avoiding
all needlefs fingularity: an unfpeakable averfion
to complaints and murmurs; a fincere, refpect-
ful and tender union, firft with our fuperior,
and afterwards with all our brethren. We cannot but beftow different degrees of love and efteem upon thefe, according to their different
gifts and graces. But we fhould be very wary,
as to the public marks whereby we fhew our inward preference of fome to others.

Directions to preferve fervency of fpirit.

* 1. IF we would preferve our fervour unabat-
ed, we muft particularly attend to thofe
things which have at all times led to wearinefs
and weaknefs of fpirit, and to thofe which tend to
infpire zeal and fervor, and to rekindle languid defires. We fhould regard the former as certain mif-
chiefs, whatever pretences may be made to excufe
them, and the latter as invaluable helps, however

ever little or trifling they may appear to falfe
wifdom.

* 2. Frequently reflect on the infenfible de-
cays by which our piety is weakened. Dread
the confequences of the leaft relaxations, which
at the beginning appear fo far removed from the
point to which they lead. Be affured, that all
faults which are neglected are punifhed, the little ones by great, the inward by outward, lukewarmnefs by infenfibility. Be always faithful
to your confcience, to the firft cry of charity, to
that clear decifion which you hear in your heart
upon every duty. Do not confound with your
reafon this fupreme rule of reafon. Reverence
it as the voice of God. Do not deliberate on
the obedience you owe to it. Give no entrance
to the enemy, by reafoning upon any command
or prohibition of the Holy Spirit. By refifting
the beginning of temptations, you eafily conquer them, whereas after the firft moment, you
are almoft difarmed and vanquifhed.

3. Love prayer, and do all that in you lies,
that it may be continual. We receive nothing
from God but by this; it is the hand that knocks
and that receives. The gifts of God do not come
to us without this: when this languifhes all is
languid: and it is always by lukewarmnefs in
prayer, that we fall into that general lukewarmnefs which is without remedy.

4. Prize the holy and happy liberty of your

ftate:

ftate : † the freedom from every other duty, but that of loving and ferving Chrift; the exemption from the pain of the firft woman, though you have had a part in her fin. Be thankful to God, that he has brought you to an afylum, of which your weaknefs had fo great need: where the eyes of a whole community enlighten and obferve you; where you are animated by example : and where the infirmities of others exercife your patience and feed your charity. Beware you be not like the Ifraelites of old, who *thought fcorn of the pleafant land*; and do not give way to the leaft defire of turning back into Egypt.

5. Check every thought which tends to this, under what pretext foever it comes. It is a dangerous temptation, to dwell on fome rules which we diflike, and would have taken away; on certain defects which are common in focieties, which lead infenfibly to repent of being joined therein; on the weaknefs, the ignorance, the want of underftanding or of education in fuch and fuch, who therefore cannot be of ufe to us; on a difcipline which fometimes appears ufelefs, embarraffing, contrary to the liberty of the Spirit of God: on fomething either uneven or imprudent in the conduct of our fuperiors: in a word, on any thing which abates the love of our ftate, and tends to extinguifh our thankfulnefs for it. All thefe thoughts fhould be reprefl, the moment

† That of a fingle life. This tract too was originally directed to fingle women, living in one community.

moment they appear. If we give them an hearing we are fallen : and if the heart is not exactly clofed againſt them, they furprize and poiſon it.

* 6. Make it a point of duty, to do nothing out of humour, that is, without any reaſon but inclination. Be faithful in the uſe of every means, independently on relifh or difrelifh. When you are heavy, look for the return of grace and unction : when you have moſt ferrour, prepare for temptation. Look on thefe inward viciſſitudes as you do on thofe of bodily health. Do not neglect them ; and yet beware of being difcouraged thereby. Only redouble your diligence and your care in proportion to the length and violence of your trials. And from the moment that light appears again, be fo humble and fo thankful that you may keep it.

* 7. The efteem, confidence, and friendſhip of others ferve only to weaken you, if they leſſen that compunction and contempt of yourſelf which is the ſource of true ſtrength. Unlefs love or neceſſity require it, be not forward to talk of thofe things which you know the beſt. Eſteem fimplicity and purity of heart more than the fineſt underſtanding. Do not cheriſh the defire of either having or ſhewing this. Never ſhew in your converfation an air of capacity and fufficiency. Cure the prejudices of perfons lefs enlightened than you, by a modeſt, calm, loving behaviour, and draw no other advantage from

being

being more knowing, than that of being more humble.

* 8. Be fweet, even, courteous, from a motive of faith and love, not from a defire to pleafe. The more capable virtues of this kind are of attracting efteem and friendfhip, the more vigilance and jealoüfy over ourfelves is needful, that they may be pure and holy. For it is eafy to feduce the heart of others, even though we are clear ourfelves. And it is a great affliction to one who loves God, to be the occafion of another's loving him lefs, or in a lefs noble and lefs perfect manner.

* 9. Regard then thofe advantages which draw love and efteem, only as fnares and fources of temptation, without that extraordinary grace which is feldom given, becaufe men are feldom humble enough to obtain it. Be abafed before God for whatever diftinguifhes you in the fight of men; as it expofes you to pride, the moft fhameful of all vices in a poor, finful wretch. Efteem only that which God efteems; praife only that which he praifes. Make little account of all the fhining virtues which are found even in reprobates. Regard piety and humility as the only ones which diftinguifh the children of God from the children of wrath.

* 10. Preferve with the utmoft care the fpirit of piety, recollection, watchfulnefs, and compunction. Do nothing in hafte and with diffipation. Speak nothing but what is neceffary.

Never

Never speak without watching over your words and the motive which leads you to speak. Talk not even on useful subjects but with a single eye; otherwise you may lose the treasure which is in your heart by shewing it from a wrong motive.

* 11. Let none of your actions, not even the smallest be lost. Do them all from views which spring from faith. Accordingly, know why you do them. Do not walk by chance, without seeing your mark or without aiming at it. Despise nothing, because every action may become of great price. Make all noble, all grand, all divine. Nothing is little when one loves much, and nothing is great when one loves but little.

* 12. When you are doing a thing, never depend on doing it better another time; but at this time give it all possible attention. When you are doing one thing, do not think on another, that is to follow it. Always limit yourself to the present moment, and distrust projects which cause you to flight the present work, by promising wonders in time to come.

13. Esteem no virtues, if they do not spring from the Spirit of Christ; if they are not an effect of his grace; if they do not terminate in him. Reason and wisdom separate from faith are mere folly; and pride under the disguise of virtue is vice still. While we abide in the heart of Christ we are alive; if we are out of this divine fountain of all good, out of this vine, we

can

'can bear no fruit, or none which deferves any thing but death.

* 14. Do not wait till the evening before you examine all your actions and all your motives. Keep one part of your foul continually attentive on what the other does. Let not your whole foul be taken up with any thing, except prayer, which is then moft pure when one leaft reflects upon it. Never lofe ferenity of mind and peace of heart; becaufe when your foul is ruffled you no longer know what you do, whither you go, nor where your danger lies. Stop the very moment you begin to be no longer your own mafter. That moment fly to prayer, and continue therein till peace returns to your foul.

15. Do not love your faults, but love the profitable humiliation which follows them. Let none of them pafs lightly over; but do not ftrive to correct them out of pride. Be more afraid of the glare of virtue, and the admiration it draws, than of your greateft infirmities: for the greateft of fins is pride of heart and a vain fatisfaction in your own righteoufnefs, of which thofe outward imperfections may be the remedy. When you fall into any of them, you ought immediately to think of God, and not of men; quietly to ftay yourfelf on him, and not to fink ftill lower by being difheartened, or by evil fhame.

* 16. Never be under fo much apprehenfion as when you do any good, when you fpeak with wifdom

wifdom and reafon; becaufe you are then on the brink of that moſt ſlippery and dangerous precipice, vanity. After having felt more fervor and enlargement of heart in any ordinance, or having ſuffered any thing with more patience and ſweetneſs than uſual, labour to be more humble; for the devil is watching to ſteal away the fruit as ſoon as it appears: and it is juſt in God to ſuffer it ſo to be, if you are robbing him of his glory. Always receive commendations and marks of eſteem which a ſecret reluctance, for fear left God ſhould blaſt theſe vain applauſes with an hidden curſe. On the contrary, eſteem yourſelf happy in being neglected, deſpiſed, yea, reproached, how ſeverely ſoever; becauſe God generally ſhews himſelf moſt preſent and moſt gracious at thoſe precious moments.

LONDON, *Feb.* 26, 1768.

THOUGHTS

THOUGHTS

ON

A SINGLE LIFE.

1. THE *forbidding to marry*, as it is well known the church of Rome does, and has done for feveral ages (in which *marriage* is abfolutely *forbidden*, not only to all religious orders, but to the whole body of the clergy) is numbered, by the great apoftle, among the *doctrines of devils*. And among the fame we need not fcruple to number, the *defpifing*, or *condemning marriage*: as do many of thofe in the Romifh church, who are ufually termed *myftic* writers. One of thefe does not fcruple to affirm: " Marriage is only *licenfed fornication*." But the Holy Ghoft fays, *Marriage is honourable in all, and the bed undefiled*. Nor can it be doubted but perfons may be as holy in a married, as in a fingle ftate.

II. In

II. In the latter clause of the sentence, the apostle seems to guard against a mistake, into which some sincere Christians have fallen; particularly, when they have just found such a liberty of spirit, as they had not before experienced. They imagine a *defilement* where there is none, *and fear where no fear is.* And it is possibly this very fear of sin, may betray them into sin. For it may induce married persons to *defraud each other*, forgetting the express determination of the apostle, *The wife hath not power of her own body, but the husband; and the husband hath not power of his own body, but the wife,* 1 Cor. vii. 4.

III. And yet we must not forget what the apostle subjoins in the following verses. *I say to the unmarried and widows: it is good for them, if they abide even as I,* ver. 8. *Art thou bound unto a wife? Seek not to be loosed: art thou loosed from a wife? Seek not a wife. But if thou marry, thou hast not sinned.—Nevertheless such shall have trouble in the flesh,* ver. 27, 28. *I would have you without carefulness. He that is unmarried careth for the things of the Lord, how he may please the Lord! But he that is married careth for the things of the world, how he may please his wife.—The unmarried woman careth for the things of the Lord, that she may be holy both in body and spirit: but she that is married careth for the things of the world, how she may please her husband. And this I speak*

for

*for your own profit, that you may attend upon the
Lord without distraction,* ver. 32, 35.

IV. But though *it is good for a man not to touch
a woman,* (ver. 1.) yet this is not an univerfal
rule. *I would,* indeed, fays the apoftle, *that all
men were as myself,* ver. 7. But that cannot be. For
*every man hath his proper gift of God, one after
this manner, another after that. If* then *they
cannot contain, let them marry; for it is better to
marry than to burn,* ver. 9. *To avoid fornication, let
every man have his own wife, and let every woman
have her own husband.* Exactly agreeable to this
are the words of our Lord. When the apoftle
faid, *If the cafe be fo, it is good not to marry,* he
*faid unto them, All men cannot receive this faying,
but they to whom it is given. For there are fome
eunuchs, who where fo born from their mother's
womb; there are fome, who were made eunuchs by
men; and there are eunuchs who have made themfelves eunuchs, for the kingdom of heaven's fake.
He that is able to receive it, let him receive it.* Matt.
xix. 11, 12.

V. But who is *able to receive this faying?* To
abftain from marriage, and yet not *burn?* It behoves every one here to judge for himfelf; none
is called to judge for another. In general, I
believe, every man is *able to receive it,* when he is
firft juftified. I believe every one then receives
this gift: but with moft it does not continue
long. Thus much is clear: it is a plain matter
of fact, which no man can deny. It is not fo
clear,

clear, whether God withdraws it of his own good pleafure, or for any fault of ours. I incline to think, it is not withdrawn, without fome fault on our part. But be that as it may, I have now only to do, with thofe who are ftill *able to receive this faying.*

VI. To this happy few I fay, 1. Know the advantages you enjoy, many of which are pointed out by the apoftle himfelf. You may be *without carefulnefs.* You are under no neceffity of *caring for the things of the world.* You have only to *care for the things of the Lord, how you may pleafe the Lord.* One care alone lies upon you, how you *may be holy both in body and fpirit.*

You may *attend upon the Lord without diftraction. While others, like Martha, are cumbered with much ferving, and drawn* hither and thither by *many things,* you may remain centred in God, fitting, like *Mary,* at the mafter's feet and liftening to every word of his mouth.

You enjoy a bleffed liberty from the *trouble in the flefh,* which muft more or lefs attend a married ftate, from a thoufand namelefs domeftic trials which are found fooner or later in every family. You are exempt from numberlefs occafions of *forrow* and *anxiety,* with which heads of families are intangled : efpecially thofe who have fickly, or weak, or unhappy, or difobedient children. If your fervants are wicked, you may put them away, and your relation to them ceafes.

ceafes. But what could you do with a wicked
fon or daughter? How could you diffolve that
relation?

Above all, you are at liberty from the greateft
of all intanglements, the loving *one* creature
above all others. It is *poffible*, to do this without
fin, without any impeachment of our love to
God. But how inconceivably *difficult?* To
give God our *whole heart*, while a creature has
fo large a fhare of it? How much more eafily
may we do this, when the heart is tenderly indeed, but equally attached to more than one?
Or at leaft, without any great inequality? What
angelic wifdom does it require, to give *enough* of
our affection, and not *too much*, to fo near a relation?

And how much eafier is it (juft to touch on
one point more) wholly to conquer our *natural
defires*, than to gratify them exactly *fo far*, as
Chriftian temperance allows? Juft fo far as
every pleafure of fenfe prepares us for taking
pleafure in God.

VII. You have *leifure*, to improve yourfelf,
in every kind, to wait upon God in public and
private, and to do good to your neighbour in
various ways, as Chriftian prudence fhall fuggeft.
Whereas thofe who are married are neceffarily
taken up with the things of the world. You may
give *all* your *time* to God without interruption, and need afk leave of none but yourfelf fo
to do. You may employ every hour in what

you

you judge to be the moſt excellent way. But
if you was married, you may aſk leave of your
companion: otherwiſe what complaints or dif-
guſt would follow? And how hard is it even to
know (how much more, to act ſuitably to that
knowledge) how far you ought to give way, for
peace ſake, and where to ſtop? What wiſdom
is requiſite, in order to know, how far you can
recede from what is moſt excellent, particularly
with regard to converſation that is *not to the uſe
of edifying*, in order to pleaſe your good-natured
or ill-natured partner, without diſpleaſing God?

VIII. You may give *all* your *worldly ſubſtance*
to God. Nothing need hinder. You have no
increaſing family, you have no wife or children
to provide for, which might occaſion a thouſand
doubts (without any extraordinary meaſure of divine light) whether you had done either too
much or too little for them. You may *make yourſelf friends of* all *the mammon of unrighteouſneſs*
which God intruſts you with: having none that
has any right to complain, or to charge you
with unkindneſs for ſo doing. You may lay out
all your talents of every kind, entirely for the
glory of God: as you have none elſe to pleaſe,
none to regard, but him *that lived and died for
you.*

IX. I ſay, ſecondly, *Prize* the advantages you
enjoy: know the value of them. Eſteem them as
highly while you have them, as others do after
they have loſt them. Pray conſtantly and fervently

vently for this very thing, that God would teach you to fet a due value upon them. And let it be matter of daily thankfgiving to God, that he has made you a partaker of thefe benefits. Indeed the more full and explicit you are herein, the more fenfible you will be of the caufe you have to be thankful: the more lively conviction you will have, of the greatnefs of the blefling.

X. If you know and duly prize the advantages you enjoy, then 3. be careful to keep them. But this (as eafy as it may feem) it is impoffible you fhould do by your own ftrength: fo various, fo frequent and fo ftrong are the temptations which you will meet with to caft them away. Not only the children of the world, but the children of God will undoubtedly tempt you thereto: and that partly by the moft plaufible reafons, partly by the moft artful perfuafions. Mean time the old deceiver will not be wanting to give an edge to all thofe reafons, and perfuafions, and to recall the temptation again and again, and prefs it clofe upon you heart. You have need therefore to ufe every help. And the firft of thefe is earneft prayer. Let no day pafs without this, without praying for this very thing, that God would work what with men is impoffible: that he would vouchfafe to preferve his own gift, and that you may not fuffer any lofs this day, either by the fubtlety or power of devils or men, or the deceitfulnefs of your own heart.

XI. A fecond help may be, the converfing

frequently

frequently and freely with thofe of your own fex, who are like-minded. It may be of infinite fervice, to difclofe to thefe the very fecrets of your hearts: efpecially the weakneffes fpringing from our natural conftitution, or education, or long continued habit, and the temptations which from time to time moft eafily befet you. Advife with them on every circumftance that occurs; open your heart without referve. By this means a thoufand devices of Satan will be brought to nought. Innumerable fnares will be prevented; or you will pafs through them without being hurt. Yea, and if at fome time you fhould have fuffered a little, the wound will fpeedily be healed.

XII. I fay, *Of your own fex :* for in the third place, it will be highly expedient, to avoid all needlefs converfation, much more all intimacy with thofe of the other fex; fo expedient, that unlefs you obferve this, you will furely caft away the gift of God. Say not, " But they have " much grace and much underftanding." So much the greater is the danger. There would be lefs fear of your receiving hurt from them, if they had lefs grace or lefs underftanding. And whenever any of thefe are thrown in your way *make a covenant with your eyes,* your ears, your hands, that you do not indulge yourfelf in any that are called *innocent freedoms.* Above all, *Keep your heart with all diligence.* Check the firft rifings of defire. Watch againft every fally of imagination, particularly if it be pleafing.

If

If it is darted in whether you will or no, yea let no *vain thought lodge within you.* Cry out, " My " God and my all, I am thine, thine alone ! I " *will* be thine for ever ! O save me from setting " up an idol in my heart ! Save me from taking " any step toward it ! Still bring my *every thought* " *into captivity, to the obedience of Christ.*"

XIII. " But how shall I attain to, or how preserve this strength and firmness of spirit ?" In order so this, I advise you, fourthly (need I say, to avoid the sin of *Onan :* seeing Satan will not cast out Satan ? Or rather) Avoid with the utmost care, all *softness* and *effeminacy :* remembering the express denunciation of an inspired writer, οἱ μαλακοὶ, the *soft* or *effeminate*, whether poor, or rich (the apostle does not make any difference, upon that account) *shall not inherit the kingdom of God.* Avoid all delicacy, first in spirit, then in apparel, food, lodging, and a thousand nameless things : and this the more speedily and the more resolutely, if you have been long accustomed thereto. Avoid all needless *self-indulgence*, as well as *delicacy* and *softness.* All these tend to breed, or cherish those appetites and passions, which you have renounced for Christ's fake. They either create or increase those desires, which *for the kingdom of heaven's sake* you are determined not to gratify. Avoid all *sloth, inactivity, indolence.* Sleep no more than nature requires. Be never idle. And use as much bodily exercise, as your strength will

will allow. I dare not add Monfieur Pafcal's rule, avoid *all pleafure*. It is not poffible to avoid all pleafure even of fenfe, without deftroying the body. Neither doth God require it at our hands. It is not his will concerning us. On the contrary he *giveth us all things to enjoy*; fo we enjoy them to his glory. But I fay, avoid all *that* plea- fure, which any way hinders you from enjoying him : yea, all fuch pleafure as does not prepare you for taking pleafure in God. Add to this *con- ftant* and *continued* courfe of *univerfal* felf-denial, the *taking up your crofs daily*, the *enduring hard- fhip as a good foldier of Jefus Chrift*. Remember *the kingdom of heaven fuffers violence, and the vio- lent take it by force*. This is the way : walk therein : think not of a fmoother path. Add to your other exercifes conftant and prudent *fafting*, and the Lord will uphold you with his hand.

XIV. I advife you laftly, if you defire to keep them, ufe all the advantages you enjoy. In- deed without this, it is utterly impoffible to keep them ; for the mouth of the Lord hath fpoken (the word which cannot be broken, which muft be fulfilled, with regard to all the good gifts of God) *To him that hath*, ufes what he hath, *fhall be given : and he fhall have more abun- dantly : but from him that hath not*, ufes it not, *fhall be taken even that which he hath*. Would you therefore retain what you now have, what God hath already given ? If fo, *giving all diligence*, ufe it to the uttermoft. *Stand faft* in every inftanee

of

of the *liberty wherewith Chrift hath made you free.*
Be not *intangled* again in the *cares of this life,*
but *caft all your care on him that careth for you.*
Be *careful for nothing, but in every thing make*
your requefts known unto God with thankfgiving.

See that you *wait upon the Lord without dif-*
traction: let nothing move you from your center.
One thing is needful; to fee, love, follow Chrift,
in every thought, word and work.

Flee the *forrow of this world:* it *worketh death.*
Let not your heart be *troubled.* In all circumftances, let your *foul magnify the Lord,* and your
fpirit rejoice in God your Saviour. Preferve a
conftant ferenity of mind, an even chearfulnefs
of fpirit.

Keep at the utmoft diftance from *foolifh defires,*
from defiring any happinefs but in God. Still
let *all* your *defire be to him, and to the remember-*
ance of his name.

Make full ufe of all the *leifure* you have: never be unemployed: *never triflingly employed:* let
every hour turn to fome good account. Let
not a fcrap of *time* be fquandered away: *Gather*
up the fragments, that nothing be loft. Give *all*
your time to God: lay out *the whole,* as you
judge will be moft to his glory. In particular,
fee that you wafte *no part* of it in unprofitable
converfation: but let all your difcourfe *be fea-*
foned with falt, and meet to minifter grace to the
hearers.

Give *all your money* to God. You have no pretence for *laying up treasure upon earth.* While you " gain all you can," and " save all you can," " give all you can," that is all you have.

Lay out *all your talents* of every kind, in doing all good to all men; knowing that *every man shall receive his own reward, according to his own labour.*

XV. Upon the whole, without difputing, whether the *married or fingle life* be the more *perfect ftate* (an idle difpute; fince perfection does not confift in any *outward ftate* whatever, but in an *abfolute devotion* of *all* our heart and *all* our life to God) : we may fafely fay, bleffed are *they who have made themfelves eunuchs, for the kingdom of heaven's fake :* who abftain from things lawful in themfelves, in order to be more devoted to God. Let thefe never forget thofe remarkable words†, *Peter faid, Lo, we have left all and followed thee. And Jefus anfwered and faid, Verily I fay unto you* (a preface denoting both the certainty and importance of what is fpoken) *There is no man that hath left* (either by giving them up, or by not accepting them) *houfe, or brethren, of fifters, or father, or mother, or wife, or children, or lands, for my fake and the gofpel's; but he fhall receive an hundred fold—now, in this time; and, in the world to come, eternal life.*

† Mark x. 28, 30.

A LETTER

A

LETTER

TO A

FRIEND,

CONCERNING

TEA.

Newington, Dec. 10, 1748.

DEAR SIR,

1. I Have read your letter with attention, and much approve of the spirit with which it is wrote. You speak in love. I desire to do so too; and then no harm can be done on either side. You appear not to be wedded to your own opinion, but open to further conviction. I
would

would willingly be of the fame temper; not obftinately attached to either fide of the queftion. I am clearly fatisfied of the neceffity of this; a willingnefs to fee what as yet I fee not. For I know, an unwillingnefs to be convinced, would utterly blind either you or me: and that if we are *refolved* to retain our prefent opinion, reafon and argument fignify nothing.

2. I fhall not therefore think it is time or pains mifemployed, to give the whole caufe a fecond hearing: to recite the occafion of every ftep I have taken, and the motives inducing me fo to do: and then to confider, whatfoever either you or others have urged, on the contrary fide of the queftion.

3. Twenty-nine years fince, when I had fpent a few months at Oxford, having as I apprehended, an exceeding good conftitution, and being otherwife in health, I was a little furprized at fome fymptoms of a paralytic diforder. I could not imagine what fhould occafion the fhaking of my hand; till I obferved it was always worft after breakfaft, and that if I intermitted drinking tea for two or three days, it did not fhake at all. Upon enquiry, I found tea had the fame effect upon others alfo of my acquaintance; and therefore faw, that this was one of it's natural effects (as feveral phyficians have often remarked) efpecially, when it is largely and frequently drank; and moft of all on perfons of weak nerves. Upon this I leffened the quantity, drank

it weaker, and added more milk and fugar. But ftill for above fix and twenty years, I was more or lefs fubject to the fame diforder.

4. July was two years, I began to obferve, that abundance of the people in London, with whom I converfed, laboured under the fame, and many other paralytic diforders, and that in a much higher degree; infomuch that fome of their nerves were quite unftrung; their bodily ftrength quite decayed, and they could not go through their daily labour. I enquired, " Are you not an hard drinker?" And was anfwered, by one and another, and another, " No, indeed Sir, not I; I drink fcarce any thing but a little tea, morning and night." I immediately remembered my own cafe; and after weighing the matter throughly, eafily gathered from many concurring circumftances, that it was the fame cafe with them.

5. I confidered, " What an advantage would " it be to thefe poor enfeebled people, if they " would leave off what fo manifeftly impairs " their health, and thereby hurts their bufinefs " alfo? Is there nothing equally cheap which " they could ufe? Yes, furely: and cheaper too. " If they ufed Englifh herbs in its ftead, (which " would coft either nothing, or what is next to " nothing) with the fame bread, butter, and milk, " they would fave juft the price of the tea." " And hereby they might not only leffen their " pain, but in fome degree their poverty too. For

" they

" they would be able to work (as well as to save)
" considerably more than they can do now.
" And by this means, if they are in debt, they
" might be more just, paying away what they
" either earned or saved. If they are not in
" debt, they might be more merciful, giving it
" away to them that want."

6. I considered farther, " What an advantage
" might this be, particularly in such a body of
" men as those are, who are united together in
" these societies? Who are both so numerous
" and so poor? How much might be saved in so
" numerous a body, even in this single article of
" expence? And how greatly is all that can possi-
" bly be saved, in every article, wanted daily, by
" those who have not even food convenient for
" them ?"

7. I soon perceived, that this latter considera-
tion was of a more general nature than the former: and that it affected many of those, whom
the other did not so immediately concern: seeing
it was as needful for *all* to save needless expences,
as for some, to regain the health they had impaired. Especially, considered as members of a
society, the wants of which they could not be
unapprized of. They knew, of those to whom
they were so peculiarly united, some had not
food to sustain nature: some were destitute of
even necessary cloathing: some had not where
to lay their head. They knew, or might know,
that the little contributions made weekly, did in

no

no wife fuffice to remove thefe wants, being barely fufficient to relieve the fick: and even that in fo fcanty a manner, that I know not, if fome of them have not, with their allowance, pined away, and at length died for want. If you and I have not faved all we could to relieve thefe, how fhall we face them at the throne of God?

8. I reflected, "If one only would fave all " that he could, in this fingle inftance, he might " furely feed or cloath one of his brethren, and, " perhaps, fave one life. What then might be " done, if ten thoufand, or one thoufand, or only " five hundred would do it?" Yea, if half that number fhould fay, " I will compute this day " what I have expended in tea, weekly or yearly. " I will immediately enter on cheaper food. " And whatever is faved hereby, I will put into " that poor box weekly, to feed the hungry, and " to cloath the naked." I am miftaken, if any among us need want, either food or raiment from that hour.

9. I thought farther, " It is faid, nay, many " tell me to my face, I can perfuade this people " to any thing. I will make a fair trial. If I " cannot perfuade them, there may be fome good " effect. All who do not wilfully fhut their eyes " will fee, that I have no fuch influence as they " fuppofed. If I can perfuade any number; " many who are now weak or fick, will be re- " ftored to health and ftrength. Many will pay
" thofe

" thofe debts, which others, perhaps equally
" poor, can but ill afford to lofe. Many will
" be lefs ftraitened in their own families. Many
" by helping their neighbour, will lay up for
" themfelves treafures in heaven."

10. Immediately it ftruck into my mind, " But
" example muft go before precept. Therefore I
" muft not plead an exemption for myfelf. from
" a daily practice of twenty-feven years. I muft
" begin." I did fo. I left it off myfelf in Auguft, 1746. And I have now had fufficient time
to try the effects, which have fully anfwered my
expectation : my paralytic complaints are all
gone : my hand is fteady as it was at fifteen : although I muft expect that, or other weakneffes,
foon; as I decline into the vale of years. And
fo confiderable a difference do I find in my expence, that I can make it appear, from the accounts now in being, in only thofe four families
at London, Briftol, Kingfwood, and Newcaftle, I
fave upwards of fifty pounds a year.

11. The firft to whom I explained thefe things
at large, and whom I advifed to fet the fame example to their brethren, were, a few of thofe,
who rejoice to affift my brother and me, as our
fons in the gofpel. A week after I propofed it
to about forty of thofe whom I believed to be
ftrong in faith : and the next morning to about
fixty more, intreating them all to fpeak their
minds freely. They did fo : and in the end, faw
the good which might infue ; yielded to the force

M 3 of

of scripture and reason: and resolved all (but two or three) by the grace of God, to make the trial without delay.

12. In a short time, I proposed it, but with all the tenderness I could, first, to the body of those who are supposed to have living faith, and after staying a few days, (that I might judge the better how to speak) to the whole society. It soon appeared (as I doubted not but it would) how far these were from *calling me Rabbi*; from implicitly submitting to my judgment, or implicitly following my example. Objections rose in abundance from all sides. These I now proceed to consider: whether they are advanced by you, or by others, and whether pointed at the premisses, or directly at the conclusion.

13. I. Some objected, " Tea is not unwhole-
" some at all; not in any kind prejudicial to
" health."

To these I reply, first, You should not be so sure of this. Even that casual circumstance, related in Dr. Short's history of it, might incline you to doubt, viz. that " while the Chinese dry the
" leaves, and turn it with their hands upon the
" tin-plates, the moisture of them is so extremely
" corrosive, that it eats into the flesh, if not
" wiped off immediately." It is not probable then, that what remains in the leaves is quite friendly to the human body.

Secondly, Many eminent physicians have declared

clared their judgment, that it is prejudicial in feveral refpects: that it gives rife to numberlefs diforders, particularly thofe of the nervous kind: and that, if frequently ufed by thofe of weak nerves, it is no other than a flow poifon.

Thirdly, If all phyficians were filent in the cafe, yet plain fact is againft you. And this fpeaks loud enough. It *was* prejudicial to *my* health: it *is* fo to many at this day.

14. " But it is not fo to *me*," fays the objector, " why then fhould I leave it off?"

I anfwer, firft, to give an example to thofe to whom it is undeniably prejudicial.

Secondly, That you may have the more wherewith to give bread to the hungry, and raiment to the naked.

15. " But I cannot leave it off; for it helps " my health. Nothing elfe will agree with " me."

I anfwer, firft, will *nothing* elfe agree with you? I know not how to believe that. I fuppofe your body is much of the fame kind with that of your great grandmother. And do you think nothing elfe agreed with her? Or with any of her progenitors? What poor, puling, fickly things, muft all the Englifh then have been, till within thefe hundred years! But you know they were not fo. Other things agreed with them. And why not with you?

Secondly, If in fact nothing elfe will, if tea has already weakened your ftomach, and im-

paired

paired your digeſtion to ſuch a degree, it *has* hurt *you* more than you are aware; it has prejudiced *your* health extremely. *You* have need to abhor it as deadly poiſon, and to renounce it from this very hour.

So ſays a drinker of drams, " Nothing elſe " will agree with me. Nothing elſe will raiſe " my ſpirits. I can digeſt nothing without." Indeed! Is it ſo? Then touch no more, if you love your life.

Thirdly, Suppoſe nothing elſe agrees with you at firſt; yet in a while many things will. When I firſt left off tea, I was half aſleep all day long: my head ached from morning to night. I could not remember a queſtion aſked, even till I could return an anſwer. But in a week's time all theſe inconveniences were gone, and have never returned ſince.

Fourthly, I have not found one ſingle exception yet: not one perſon in all England, with whom after ſufficient trial made, *nothing elſe* would agree.

It is therefore well worth while for *you* to try again; if you have any true regard for your own health, or any compaſſion for thoſe who are periſhing all around you, for want of the common neceſſaries of life.

16. If you are ſincere in this plea; if you do not *talk* of your health, while the real objection is your inclination, make a fair trial thus, 1. Take half a pint of milk every morning, with a
little

little bread, not boiled, but warmed only; (a man
in tolerable health might double the quantity.) 2.
If this is too heavy, add as much water, and boil
it together with a fpoonful of oatmeal. 3. If this
agrees not, try half a pint, or a little more of
water-gruel, neither thick nor thin; not fweet-
ened, (for that may be apt to make him fick) but
with a very little butter, falt, and bread. 4. If
this difagrees, try fage, green balm, mint, or
penny-royal tea, infufing only fo much of the
herb as juft to change the colour of the water.
5. Try two or three of thefe mixed, in various
proportions. 6. Try ten or twelve other Englifh
herbs. 7. Try *felton*, a mixture of herbs to be had
at many grocers, far healthier as well as cheaper
than tea. 8. Try cocoa. If after having tried
each of thefe, for a week or ten days, you find
none of them will agree with your conftitution,
then ufe (weak green) tea again: but at the fame
time know, that your having ufed it fo long,
has brought you near the chambers of death.

17. II. " I do not know, fays another, but
" tea may hurt me. But there is nothing faved
" by leaving it off: for I am fure other things
" coft full as much." I pray, what other things?
Sack and fugar cofts more; and fo do ragouts,
or pheafants, or ortolans. But what is this to
the point? We do not fay, *all* things are
cheaper. But any of the things above-mentioned are; at leaft if prudently managed. There-

fore,

fore, if you really defire to fave what you can, you will drink tea no more.

18. " Well, I do not defign to buy any more " myfelf; but where others drink it, there is no- " thing faved by my abftaining." I anfwer, firft, Yes, fomething is faved, though but little; efpe- cially if you tell them before, I fhall not drink tea. And many a little, you know, put together, will make a great fum.

Secondly, If the whole faved were ever fo little, if it were but two mites, when you fave this for God and your brethren's fake, it is much.

Thirdly, Your example in faving a little now, may occafion the faving of more by and by.

Fourthly, It is not a little advantage which you may reap, even now, to your own foul: by habituating yourfelf not to be afhamed of be- ing fingular in a good thing : by taking up your crofs and denying yourfelf, even in fo fmall an inftance, and by accuftoming yourfelf, to act on rational grounds, whether in a little matter or a great.

19. " But what is faved, will be no better em- " ployed." Do you fay this with regard to your- felf, or others? If with regard to yourfelf, it will be *your* fault, if you do not employ it better. I do not fay you *will*, but I am fure you *may*. And if you *do* not, it is your own fin, and your own fhame.

If with regard to others, how do you know that

that it will not be employed better? I truſt it
will. It cannot be denied, that it often *has*, and
that it always *may* be. And it is highly probable
all who ſave any thing from the beſt motive,
will lay it out to the beſt purpoſe.

20. " As to example," you ſay, " I have
" lately been without hopes of doing any good
" by it." I ſuppoſe you mean, becauſe ſo exceeding few will follow either your example or
mine. I am ſorry for it. This only gives me a
freſh objection to this unwholſome, expenſive
food, viz. That it has too much hold on the
hearts of them that uſe it: that (to uſe a ſcriptural phraſe) they are *under the power of* this
trifle. If it be ſo, were there no other reaſon
than this, they ought to throw it away at once.
Elſe they no more regard St. Paul than they do
you or me: for his rule is home to the point.
*All things are lawful for me: but I will not be
brought under the power of any.* Away with it
then, however lawful, (that is, though it were
wholeſome as well as cheap) if you are already
brought *under the power of* it.

And the fewer they are who follow this rule,
the greater reaſon there is, that you ſhould add
one example more to thoſe few. Though,
bleſſed be God, they are not ſo few as you ſuppoſe. I have met with very many in London,
who uſe leſs of it, than they had done for many
years; and above an hundred, who have plucked

M 6   out.

out the right eye, and caſt it from them; who wholly abſtain from it.

21. You add, but I am " equally, yea abun-
" dantly more, concerned to ſet an example, in
" all Chriſtian behaviour." I grant it : this therefore *ought you to have done, and not to leave the
other undone.*

22. But " one day, (you add) I ſaw your bro-
" ther drink tea, which he ſaid was for fear of
" giving offence."

I anſwer, firſt, Learn from hence to follow neither his, nor my practice implicitly; but weigh the reaſon of each, and then follow rea-ſon, whereſoever it ſtands. But,

Secondly, Examine your heart, and beware inclination does not put on the ſhape of reaſon.

Thirdly, You ſee with your own eyes, I do not drink it at all, and yet I ſeldom give offence thereby. It is not then the bare abſtaining, but the manner of doing it, which uſually gives the offence.

Fourthly, There is therefore a *manner* where-in you may do it too, and yet give no more of-fence than I. For inſtance, If any aſk you; ſimply reply, " I do not drink tea, I never uſe it." If they ſay, " Why you *did* drink it?" Anſwer, " I did ſo; but I have left it off a con-
" ſiderable time." Thoſe who have either good-nature or good-manners will ſay no more. But if any ſhould impertinently add, " O, but why
" did you leave it off?" Anſwer mildly " Be-
cauſe

caufe I thought water-gruel (fuppofe was wholefomer, as well as cheaper." If they (with ftill greater ill-manners and impertinence) go on, " What! you do it becaufe Mr. Wefley bids you." Reply calmly, " True: I do it becaufe Mr. Wefley on good reafons advifes me fo to do." If they add the trite cant phrafe, " What, you *follow man!*" Reply, without any emotion, " Yes; I follow any man, you or him, or " any other, who gives me good reafons for fo " doing." If they perfift in cavilling, clofe the whole matter with, " I neither drink it, nor " difpute about it."

23. If you proceed in this manner, with mild-nefs and love, exceeding few will be offended. " But you ought, fay fome, to give up an indif- " ferent thing, rather than give an offence to " any. So St. Paul, *I will eat no flefh whilft the* " *world ftandeth, left I make my brother to offend.*" I reply, This is not an indifferent thing, if it af-fects the health either of myfelf or my brethren. Therefore that rule, relating wholly to things indif-ferent, is not applicable to this cafe. Would St. Paul have faid, I will drink drams while the world ftandeth, left I make my brother to offend? " But tea is not fo hurtful as drams." I do not believe it is. But it is hurtful. And that is enough. The queftion does not turn on the *degree* of hurtfulnefs. " However, it is but a *fmall* thing." Nay, nothing is fmall if it touches confcience. Much lefs is it a fmall thing, to

preferve

preferve my own or my brother's health, or to be a faithful fteward even of the mammon of unrighteoufnefs. O think it not a fmall thing, whether only one for whom Chrift died, be fed or hungry, cloathed or naked.

To conclude the head of offence. You muft at leaft allow, that all this is no plea at all for your drinking tea* at home. " Yes it is ; for my " hufband or parents are offended, if I do not " drink it." I anfwer, firft, Perhaps this, in fome rare cafes, may be a fufficient reafon, why a wife or a child fhould ufe this food, that is, with them ; but no where elfe. But, fecondly, Try, and not once or twice only, if you can't overcome that offence by reafon, foftnefs, love, patience, long-fuffering, joined with conftant and fervent prayer.

24. Your next objection is, " I can't bear to " give trouble: therefore I drink whatever " others drink where I come, elfe there is fo " much hurry about infignificant me." I an- fwer,

Firft, This is no plea at all, for your drinking- tea at home. Therefore touch it not there, what- ever you do abroad.

Secondly, Where is the trouble given even when you are abroad, if they drink tea, and you fill your cup with milk and water ?

Thirdly. Whatever trouble is taken, is not for " infignificant _me_," but for that poor man, who is half-ftarved with cold and hunger : for that miferable.

miferable woman, who while fhe is poifoning herfelf, wipes her mouth, and fays fhe does no evil; who will not believe the poifon will hurt her, becaufe it does not (fenfibly at leaft) hurt you. O throw it away! Let her have one plea lefs, for deftroying her body, (if not her foul) before the time!

25. You objeĉt farther, " It is my defire to be " unknown for any particularity, unlefs a pecu- " liar love to the fouls of thofe who are prefent." And I hope, to the fouls of the abfent too; yea, and to their bodies alfo in a due proportion, that they may be healthy, and fed, and cloathed, and warm, and may praife God for the confola- tion.

26. You fubjoin. " When I had left it off " for fome months, I was continually puzzled " with, Why, what, &c. And I have feen no " good effeĉis, but impertinent queftions and " anfwers, and unedifying converfation about " eating and drinking."

I anfwer, Firft, Thofe who were fo uneafy about it plainly fhewed, that you touched the apple of their eye. Confequently thefe, of all others, ought to leave it off; for they are evident- ly *brought under the power of it.*

Secondly, Thofe impertinent queftions might have been cut fhort, by a very little fteadinefs and common fenfe. You need only have taken the method mentioned above, and they would have dropped in the midft.

Thirdly, It is not ftrange you faw no good

effects of leaving it off, where it was not left off at all. But you saw very bad effects of not leaving it off, *viz.* The adding sin to sin : the joining much unedifying conversation to wasteful, unhealthy self-indulgence.

Fourthly, You need not go far to see many good effects of leaving it off; you may see them in me. I have recovered thereby that healthy state of the whole nervous system, which I had in a great degree, and I almost thought irrecoverably lost, for considerably more than twenty years. I have been enabled hereby to assist in one year above fifty poor with food or raiment, whom I must otherwise have left (for I had before begged for them all I could) as hungry and naked as I found them. You may see the good effects in above thirty poor people just now before you, who have been restored to health, thro' the medicines bought by that money which a single person has saved in this article. And a thousand more good effects you will not fail to see, when her example is more generally followed.

27. Neither is there any need that conversation should be unedifying, even when it turns upon eating and drinking. Nay, from such a conversation, if duly improved, numberless good effects may flow. For how few understand, *Whether ye eat or drink, or whatever ye do, do all to the glory of* God ? And how glad ought you to be of a fair occasion to observe, that though the kingdom of God does not consist in *meats and drinks,*

drinks, yet without exact temperance in thefe, we cannot have either *righteoufnefs, or peace, or joy in the* Holy Ghoft ?

It may therefore have a very happy effect, if whenever people introduce the fubject, you directly clofe in, and pufh it home, that they may underftand a little more of this important truth.

28. But " I find at prefent very little defire " to change either my thoughts or practice." Shall I fpeak plain ? I fear, by not ftanding your ground, by eafinefs, cowardice, and falfe fhame, you have grieved the Spirit of God, and thereby loft your conviction and defire at once.

Yet you add, " I advife every one to leave " off tea, if it hurts their health, or is inconfiftent " with frugality ; as I advife every one to avoid " dainties in meat, and vanity in drefs, from " the fame principle." Enough, enough ! Let this only be well purfued, and it will fecure all that I contend for. I advife no perfons living to leave it off, if it does not hurt the health either of them or their brethren : and if it is not incon-fiftent with the Chriftian frugality, of cutting off *every* needlefs expence.

29. But " to be fubject to the confequences of " leaving it off again ! This I cannot bear."

I anfwer, firft, It may be fo. You cannot eafily bear it. For by your giving up the point once, you have made it much harder to ftand

· your

your ground now, than it was at firft. Yet ftill
'tis worth all your courage and labour; fince the
reafons for it are as ftrong as at the beginning.

Secondly, As to the confequences you fear,
they are fhadowy all; they are a meer lion in
the ftreets. " Much trouble to others."—Abfolutely none at all, if you take the tea-kettle, and
fill your cup with water. " Much foolifh difcourfe."—Take the preceding advice, and it will
be juft the reverfe. " Nothing helpful toward
" the renewal of my foul in the image of Jefus
" Chrift."--What a deep miftake is this? Is it
not helpful to fpeak clofely of the nature of his
inward kingdom? To encourage one another in
cafting off every weight, in removing every
hindrance of it? To inure ourfelves to the bearing his crofs? To bring Chriftianity into common life? And accuftom ourfelves to conduct
even our minuteft actions by the great rules of
reafon and religion?

· 30. Is it " not of any importance" to do this?
I think, it is of vaft importance. However, " it
" is a very fmall circumftance in felf-denial." It
is well if you find it fo. I am fure I did not.
And I believe the cafe is the fame with many
others at this day. But you fay, " I have fo
" many other affaults of felf-indulgence, that this
" is nothing.—It is nothing," faid one to a young
woman, " to faft once or twice a week; to
" deny yourfelf a little food. Why do not you
" deny yourfelf as to anger and fretfulnefs, as to
                                    " peevifhnefs

" peevifhnefs and difcontent ?" She replied,
" That I want: fo I deny myfelf in little things
" firft, till I am able to do it in greater." Neither you nor I can mend her reply. Go thou and
do likewife.

31. I have done what I propofed, and indeed
in many more words than I at firft intended. I
have told you the occafions of every ftep I have
taken, and the motives inducing me thereto;
and have confidered what either you, or others,
have urged on the contrary fide of the queftion.

And now the advice I would give upon the
whole is this: firft, Pray earneftly to God for
clear light, for a full, piercing, and fteady conviction, that this is the more excellent way.
Pray for a fpirit of univerfal felf-denial, of chear-
ful temperance, of wife frugality: for bowels of
mercies, for a kind compaffionate fpirit, tenderly fenfible of the various wants of your brethren : and for firmnefs of mind, for a mild, even
courage, without fear, anger, or fhame. Then
you will once more, with all readinefs of heart,
make this little (or great) facrifice to God: and
withal prefent your foul and body a living facrifice, acceptable unto God through Jefus Chrift.

DESIDERATUM:

OR,

ELECTRICITY

Made PLAIN and USEFUL.

By a Lover of Mankind, and of Common Sense.

The PREFACE.

1. IN the following tract, I have endeavoured to comprize the sum of what has been hitherto published, on this curious and important subject, by Dr. Franklin, Dr. Hoadly, Mr. Wilson, Watson, Lovett, Freke, Martin, Watkins, and in the monthly magazines. But I am chiefly indebted to Dr. Franklin for the speculative part, and to Mr.

Lovett

Lovett for the practical: though I cannot in every thing subscribe to the sentiments either of one or the other.

2. Indeed I am not greatly concerned for the philosophical part, whether it stand or fall. Of the facts we are absolutely assured: although they are of so surprizing a nature, that a man could not have asserted them a few years ago, without quite giving up his reputation. But who can be assured of this or that hypothesis, by which he endeavours to account for those facts? Perhaps the utmost we have reason to expect here, is an high degree of probability.

3. I am much more concerned for the physical part, knowing of how great importance this is: how much sickness and pain may be prevented or removed, and how many lives saved by this unparallelled remedy. And yet with what vehemence has it been opposed? Sometimes by treating it with contempt, as if it were of little or no use: sometimes by arguments, such as they were; and sometimes by such cautions against its ill effects, as made thousands afraid to meddle with it.

4. But so it has fared with almost all the simple remedies, which have been offered to the world for many years. When Sir John Floyer published his excellent book on cold-bathing, many for a time used and profited by it. So did abundance of people by cold water, when it was publicly recommended by Dr. Hancock. The ingenious and benevolent bishop of Cloyne brought tar-water likewise into credit

dit for a season: and innumerable were the cures wrought thereby, even in the most desperate and deplorable cases. Nor was it a little good which was done by the use of sea-water, after Dr. Russel had published his tract concerning it. Indeed each of these did wonders in its turn. But alas! their reign was short. The vast party which were on the other side, soon raised the cry, and ran them down. In a few years they were out of fashion, out of use, and almost out of memory: and the foul, hard-named exotics took place again, to the utter confusion of common sense.

5. Must not Electricity then, whatever wonders it may now perform, expect soon to share the same fate? And yet it is absolutely certain, that in many, very many cases, it seldom or never fails. " I can truly say, (says Mr. Lovett,' I scarce ever knew any who made the trial and did not succeed. Not that all disorders will yield thereto. Neither in this any more than the common way, will the same treatment of the same disorder in different persons have always the same success." Indeed there cannot be in nature any such thing as an absolute panacea: a medicine that will cure every disease incident to the human body. If there could, electricity would bid fairer for it than any thing in the world: as it takes place in such a vast number of disorders, some of them so widely different from the others.

6. And yet there is something peculiarly unaccountable, with regard to its operation. In some cases, where there was no hope of help, it will succeed

ceed beyond all expectation. In others, where we had the greatest hope, it will have no effect at all. Again, in some experiments, it helps at the very first, and promises an entire cure: but presently the good effect ceases, and the patient is as he was before. On the contrary, in others it has no effect at first: it does no good; perhaps seems to do hurt. Yet all this time it is striking at the root of the disease, which in a while it totally removes. Frequent instances of the former we have in paralytic, of the latter in rheumatic cases.

7. But still one may upon the whole pronounce it the desideratum, the general and rarely failing remedy, in nervous cases of every kind (old palsies excepted); as well as in many others. Perhaps if the nerves are really perforated (as is now generally supposed) the electric ether is the only fluid in the universe, which is fine enough to move through them. And what if the nervous juice itself be a fluid of this kind? If so, it is no wonder that it has always eluded the search of the most accurate naturalists.

8. Be this as it may, Mr. Lovett is of opinion, " the electrical method of treating disorders, cannot be expected to arrive at any considerable degree of perfection, till administered and applied by the gentlemen of the faculty." Nay then, quanta de spe decidi! All my hopes are at an end. For when will it be administered and applied by them? Truly, ad Græcas Calendas. Not till the gentlemen of the faculty have more regard to the interest of their
neighbours

neighbours than their own. At least, not till there are no apothecaries in the land : or till physicians are independent of them.

9. *Therefore, without waiting for what probably never will be, and what indeed we have no reason to expect, let men of sense do the best they can for themselves, as well as for their poor, sick, helpless neighbours. How many may they relieve from racking pain or pining sickness by this unexpensive and speedy remedy ? Restoring them to ease, health, strength, generally in a few minutes, frequently in a moment ! And if a few of these lovers of mankind, who have some little knowledge of the animal œconomy, would only be diligent in making experiments, and setting down the more remarkable of them, in order to communicate them to one another, that each might profit by the other's labour : I doubt not, but more nervous disorders would be cured in one year, by this single remedy, than the whole English Materia Medica will cure, by the end of the century.*

10. *It is not impossible, but the Gentlemen Reviewers may bestow a compliment on me as well as on Mr. Lovett. If they are so kind, I would only beg them, not to plume themselves upon a discovery, which I have helped them to myself : namely, that "the following is little more than an extract from others :" I intended it so to be. I designed only to collect together the substance of the most celebrated writings on the subject ; and to place them in one connected view, for the use of those who have little time or money to spare. I only wish, some who*

who has more leifure and ability than me, would confider it more deeply, and write a full practical treatife on electricity, which might be a blessing to many generations.

Nov. 1, 1759.

I. 1. FROM a thoufand experiments it appears, that there is a fluid far more fubtle than air, which is every where diffufed through all fpace, which furrounds the earth, and pervades every part of it. And fuch is the extreme finenefs, velocity, and expanfivenefs of this active principle, that all other matter feems to be only the body, and this the foul of the univerfe. This we might term *elementary fire*; but that it is hard for us to feparate the ideas of *fire* and *burning :* although the latter is in reality but a preternatural and violent effect of the former.

2. It is highly probable this is the general inftrument of all the motion in the univerfe : from this *pure fire*, (which is properly fo called) the vulgar *culinary* fire is kindled. For in truth there is but one kind of fire in nature, which exifts in all places and in all bodies. And this is fubtle and active enough, not only to be, under the great Caufe, the fecondary caufe of

motion, but to produce and fuſtain life throughout all nature, as well in animals as in vegetables.

3. To this effect the learned Biſhop of Cloyne
obſerves, " The vital flame is ſuppoſed to be the
cauſe of all the motions in the body of man,
whether natural or voluntary. And has not fire
the ſame force to animate throughout, and actuate the whole ſyſtem of the world? Cheriſh-
ing, heating, fermenting, diſſolving, ſhining,
and operating in various manners, as various
ſubjects offer to employ, or to determine its
force? It is preſent in all parts of the earth and
firmament, though latent and unobſerved, till
ſome accident produces it into act, and renders
it viſible in its effects."

4. This great machine of the world requires
ſome ſuch conſtant, active and powerful principle,
conſtituted by its Creator, to keep the heavenly
bodies in their ſeveral courſes, and at the ſame
time give ſupport, life and increaſe to the various
inhabitants of the earth. Now as the heart of
every animal is the engine which circulates the
blood through the whole body, ſo the ſun, as the
heart of the world, circulates this fire through
the whole univerſe. And this element is not
capable of any eſſential alteration, increaſe or
diminution. It is a ſpecies by itſelf; and is of
a nature totally diſtinct from that of all other bodies.

5. That this is abſolutely neceſſary both to

Ized

feed common fire, and to suſtain the life of animals, it ſeems may be learned from an eaſy experiment. Place a cat, together with a lighted
candle, in a cold oven: then lute the door cloſe,
having fixt a glaſs in the middle of it: and if you
look through this, you may obſerve, at one and
the ſame inſtant, the candle goes out, and the
animal dies. A plain proof, that the ſame fire
is needful to ſuſtain both culinary fire and animal life: and a large quantity of it. Some
doubtleſs pervades the oven door; but not
enough to ſuſtain either flame or life. Indeed
every animal is a kind of fire-engine. As ſoon
as the lungs inſpire the air, the fire mingled with
it is inſtantly diſperſed through the pulmonary
veſſels into the blood: thence it is diffuſed
through every part of the body, even the moſt
minute arteries, veins and nerves. In the mean
time the lungs inſpire more air and fire, and ſo
provide a conſtant ſupply.

6. The air ſeems to be univerſally impregnated
with this fire, but ſo diluted, as not to hurt the
animal in reſpiration. So a ſmall quantity of a
liquor dropt in water, may be friendly to an human body, though a few drops of the ſame liquor, given by themſelves, would have occaſioned certain death. And yet you cannot conceive one particle of the water, without a particle
of the medicine. It is not impoſſible, this may
be one great uſe of air, by adhering ſo cloſely to
the elementary fire, to temper and render ſalutary

to

to the body, what would otherwise be fatal
to it.

7. To put it beyond difpute, that this fire is
largely mixt with the air, you may make the
following experiment. Take a round lump of
iron, and heat it to a degree called a *welding*
heat : take it out of the fire, and with a pair of
bellows blow cold air upon it. The iron will
then as effectually melt, as if it were in the hot-
teft fire. Now when taken out of the forge, it
had not fire enough in it to conquer the cohefion
of its parts : but when this fire is joined with
that which was mixt with the air, it is fufficient
to do it. On the fame principle we account for
the increafe of a coal or wood fire by blowing
it.

8. And let none wonder that fire fhould be fo
connected with air, as hardly to be feparated.
As fubtle as fire is, we may even by art attach it
to other bodies ; yea, and keep it prifoner for
many years : and that either in a folid or a fluid
form. An inftance of the firft we have in fteel :
which is made fuch, only by impacting a large
quantity of fire into bars of iron. In like manner
we impact a great quantity of fire into ftone, to
make lime. An inftance of the fecond kind we
have in fpirits, wherein fire is imprifoned in a
fluid form. Hence common fpirits will burn all
away. And if you throw into the air fpirits rec-
tified to the higheft degree, not one drop will

come

come down again, but the univerfal fire will take hold of and abforb it all.

9. That this fire fubfifts both in air, earth and water; that it is diffufed through all and every part of the univerfe, was *fufpected* by many of the antient naturalifts, and *believed* by the great Sir Ifaac Newton. But of late years it has been fully demonftrated: particularly, by Mr. Stephen Gray, a penfioner at the Charter-houfe; who fome years fince prefented to the Royal Society, an account of many experiments he had made, whereby this fubtle fluid became clearly percep- tible both to the fight and feeling. Becaufe the glafs tube, by means of which thofe experiments were made, was obferved when rubbed to attract ftraws and other light bodies (a known property of amber, called in *Latin Electrum*) *thofe* expe- riments were termed *electrical:* a word which was foon affixt to that fubtle fluid itfelf, and every thing pertaining to it. But improperly enough: feeing the attracting (or feeming to attract ftraws and feathers, is one of the moft inconfiderable of all the effects, wrought by this powerful and univerfal caufe.

10. It was afterwards found, that a glafs globe was on fome accounts preferable to a glafs tube: particularly, as it was lefs labour to turn the one for fome hours together, by means of a fmall wheel, in the mean time rubbing it with a dry hand, or a little cufhion, than to rub the tube for fo long a time. It was likewife obferved, that a

greater

greater quantity of ethereal fire might be *collected* by this means than by the other. I fay *collected*; for that fire is no more *created* by rubbing, than water is by pumping. The grand refervoir thereof is the earth, from which it is diffufed through all the other parts of common matter. Accordingly in thefe experiments, the globe rubbing againſt the cuſhion, collects fire from it. The cuſhion receives it from the frame of the machine; the frame of the machine from the floor. But if you cut off the communication with the floor, no fire can be *produced*, becaufe none can be *collected*.

11. In the year 1746. Mr. de Mufchenbroek, profeſſor of natural philofophy at Leyden, was led by a cafual experiment, into many new difcoveries. Thefe were chiefly made by means of a large but thin glafs phial. The beſt way to prepare which is, to coat it with thin lead; to line it on the infide with leaf gold, to within two inches of the top, and to faſten fome tinfel fringe to the bottom, (or to the end of the wire within the phial) fo as to touch the gold lining. By this wire going through the cork, the phial is hung on any metallic body, which communicates by a wire, with the globe or tube. This metallic body has been termed, *the prime conductor*, as it conducts or conveys the fire collected by the tube or globe, either into the phial, or into any other body communicating therewith.

12. But all bodies are not capable of receiving

it

it. There is in this refpect an amazing difference between them. The excrements of nature, as wax, filk, hair, will not receive the ethereal fire, neither convey it to other bodies: fo that whenever in circulating it comes to any of thefe, it is at a full flop. Air itfelf is a body of this kind; with great difficulty either receiving or conveying this fire to other bodies: fo are pitch and rofin (excrements, as it were, of trees.) To thefe we may add glafs, amber, brimftone, dry earth, and a few other bodies. Thefe have been frequently ftiled *electrics per fe*; as if they alone contained the *electric fire*: an eminently improper title, founded on a palpable miftake. From the fame miftake, all other bodies, which eafily receive and readily convey it, were termed *non-electrics*; on a fuppofition, that they contained no *electric fire*; the contrary of which is now allowed by all.

13. That this fire is inconceivably fubtle, appears from its permeating even the denfeft metals, and that with fuch eafe, as to receive no perceptible refiftance. If any one doubt, whether it pafs through the fubftance, or only along the furface of bodies, a ftrong fhock taken through his own body, will prevent his doubting any longer. It differs from all other matter in this, that the particles of it repel, not attract, each other. And hence is the manifeft divergency in a ftream of electrical effluvia. But though the particles of it repel

N 4

each

each other, yet are they attracted by all other matter. And from thefe three, the extreme fubtlety of this fire, the mutual repulfion of its parts, and the ftrong attraction of them by other matter, arifes this effect, that if a quantity of electric fire be applied to a mafs of common matter of any bignefs or length, (which has not already got its quantity) it is immediately diffufed through the whole.

14. It feems, this globe of earth and water, with its plants, animals, buildings, have diffufed through their whole fubftance, juft as much of this fire as they will contain. And this we may term their *natural quantity*. But this is not the fame in all kinds of matter : neither in the fame kind of matter in all circumftances. A folid foot of one kind of matter (as glafs) contains more of it than a folid foot of another kind. And a pound weight of the fame kind of matter, when rarefied, contains more than it did before.

15. We know that this fire is *in* common matter, becaufe we can pump it *out*, by the globe or tube : we know that common matter has near as much of it as it can contain, becaufe if we add a little more to any portion of it, the additional quantity does not enter, but forms a kind of atmofphere round it. On the other hand we know that common matter has not more of it that it can contain. Otherwife all loofe portions of it would repel each other; as they conftantly do, when they have fuch atmofpheres. Had the earth, for inftance, as much electric fire, in proportion,

as

as we can give to a globe of iron or wood, the particles of duſt and other light matter, would not only repel each other, but be continually repelled from the earth. Hence the air being conſtantly loaded therewith, would be unfit for reſpiration. Here we ſee another occaſion to adore that wiſdom, which has made all things by weight and meaſure.

16. The form of every electric atmoſphere, is that of the body which it ſurrounds: becauſe it is attracted by every part of the ſurface, though it cannot enter the ſubſtance, already replete. Without this attraction, it would not remain round the body, but diſſipate into the air.

17. The atmoſphere of an electrified ſphere, is not more eaſily drawn off, from any one part of it than from the other, becauſe it is equally attracted by every part. But it is not ſo with bodies of other figures. From a cube it is more eaſily drawn off at the corners than at the ſides: and ſo from the corners of bodies of any other form, and moſt eaſily from the ſharpeſt corners. For the force with which an electrified body retains its atmoſphere, is proportioned to the ſurface on which that atmoſphere reſts. So a ſurface four inches ſquare retains its atmoſphere, with ſixteen times the force that one of an inch ſquare does. And as in pulling the hairs from an horſe's tail, a force inſufficient to pull off an handful at once, could eaſily pull it off hair by hair: ſo though a blunt body cannot draw off all the atmoſphere at

once,

once, a pointed one can eafily draw it off, particle by particle.

18. If you would have a fenfible proof, how wonderfully pointed bodies draw off the electric fire, place an iron fhot of four inches diameter on the mouth of a dry bottle. Sufpend over it a a fmall cork-ball by a filken thread, juft fo as to reft againft the fide of the fhot. Electrify the fhot, and the ball will be repelled four or five inches from it. Then prefent to the fhot fix or eight inches off, the point of a fharp bodkin. The fire is inftantly drawn off; fo the repulfion ceafes, and the ball flies to the fhot. But a blunt body will not produce this effect, till it is brought within an inch of the fhot. If you prefent the point of the bodkin in the dark, you may fee fometimes at a foot diftance, a light gather upon it like a glow-worm, which is manifeftly the fire it extracts from the fhot. The lefs fharp the point is, the nearer it muft be brought before you can fee the light. And at whatever diftance you fee the light, you may draw off the electric fire.

19. To be convinced that pointed bodies *threw* off, as well as *draw* off the fire, you may lay a long fharp needle on the fhot. It cannot then be electrified, fo as to repel the ball, becaufe the fire thrown upon it, continually runs off at the point of the needle: from which in the dark you may fee fuch a ftream of light, as in the preceding inftance.

20. While the electric fire, which is in all

bodies,

bodies, is left to itfelf, undifturbed by any external violence, it is more or lefs denfe, according
to the nature of the body which it is in. In denfe
bodies it is more rare : in rare bodies it is
more denfe. Accordingly every body contains
fuch a quantity of it, rare or denfe, as is fuitable
to its nature. And there is fome refiftance to
every endeavour of altering its denfity, in the
whole of any body, or in any part of it. For
all bodies refift either the increafe or diminution
of their natural quantity. And on the other
hand, when it has been either increafed or diminifhed, there is a refiftance to its return to its
natural ftate.

21. With regard to the different refiftance
made by different bodies, in either of thefe cafes
it is an invariable rule, that glafs, wax, rofin,
brimftone, filk, hair, and fuch like bodies, refift
the moft ; and next to thefe, the air, provided
it be dry, and in a fufficient quantity ; that
this refiftance is leaft in metals, minerals, water,
quickfilver, animals and vegetables ; which we
may rank together becaufe the difference in their
refiftance is very inconfiderable : and that in
thefe bodies the refiftance is greater, when their
furfaces are polifhed, and extended in length, than
when their furfaces are rough and fhort, or end in
fharp points.

22. When a body has more electric fire forced into it, than it has naturally, it is faid to be
electrified *pofitively*. When part of the natural

quantity.

quantity is taken away, it is faid to be electrified *negatively*. Now when an iron bar is *negatively* electrified, the fire drawn out, does not go in again as foon as the experiment is over, but forms an atmofphere round it, becaufe of the refiftance it finds in its endeavour to dilate itfelf, either into the air or into the bar. And when it is electrified *pofitively*, the fame kind of atmofphere is formed, by the fire accumulated upon it. Whether therefore bodies are electrified negatively or pofitively, and remain fo when the experiment is over, there are fimilar atmofpheres furrounding them, which will produce fimilar effects.

23. But we can electrify no body beyond a certain degree ; becaufe when any is electrified to that point, it has an atmofphere round it fufficiently ftrong to ballance any power that endeavours to electrify it farther. Nor is the electric fire either from the tube or the globe, able to force its way thro' this.

24. And in the ordinary courfe of nature, this fubtle, active fluid, which not only furrounds every grofs body, but every component particle of each, where it is not in abfolute contact with its neighbouring particle, can never be idle, but is ever in action, tho' that action be imperceptible to our fenfes. It is ever varying its condition, tho' imperceptibly, in all parts of all bodies whatever: and electrifying them more or lefs, tho' not fo forcibly as to give fenfible

figns

figns of it. All bodies then, and all their component particles, when in their natural fituation, have round their furfaces, where they are not in abfolute contact with other furfaces, an imperceptible atmofphere fufficient to balance the fmaller force with which they are attacked, every way fimilar to the perceptible atmofphere of bodies forcibly electrified. In thefe imperceptible atmofpheres is placed the power which refifts their being electrified to an higher degree than they are naturally. And this power lies in the elafticity of the fubtle fluid, every where difperfed both round all bodies and in them.

25. Glafs is very difficulty electrified, which feems to prove it has a very denfe electric atmofphere. Metals are eafily electrified. Confequently they have rare and therefore weakly-refifting atmofpheres. But as heat rarefies all bodies, fo if glafs be heated to a certain degree, even below melting, it will give as free a paffage to the electric fire, as brafs or iron does: the atmofphere round it being then rendered as rare as that of metals. Nay when melted, it makes no more refiftance than water. But its refiftance increafes, as it cools. And when it is quite cold, it refifts as forcibly as ever. Smoothly-polifhed wax refifts as much as glafs. But even the fmall heat raifed by rubbing, will render its atmofphere as rare as that of metals, and fo intirely deftroys its refiftance. The fame is true of rofin and brimftone. Even the heat arifing from friction, de-

ftroys

ſtroys the reſiſtance which they naturally make to being electrified ; a ſtrong proof, that the reſiſtance of all bodies thereto, is exerted at their ſurfaces, and cauſed by an electric atmoſphere of different denſities, according to different circumſtances.

26. Moſt experiments will ſucceed as well with a globe of brimſtone, as with one of glaſs. Yet there is a conſiderable difference in their nature. What glaſs repells, brimſtone (as alſo roſin) attracts. Rubbed glaſs emits the electric fire ; rubbed brimſtone, roſin and wax receive it. Hence if a glaſs globe be turned at one end of a prime conductor, and a brimſtone one at the other, not a ſpark of fire can be obtained : one receiving it in, as faſt as it is given out by the other. Hence alſo if a phial be ſuſpended on the prime conductor, with a chain from its coating to the table, and only one globe turned, it will be electrified, (or *charged* as they term it) by twenty turns of the wheel ; after which it may be *diſcharged*, that is unelectrified, by twenty turns of the other wheel.

27. The difference between *non-electrics* (vulgarly ſpeaking) and *electrics per ſe*, is chiefly this. 1. A *non-electric* eaſily ſuffers a change, in the quantity of fire it contains. Its whole quantity may be leſſened by drawing out a part, which it will afterwards reſume. But you can only leſſen the quantity contained in one of the ſurfaces of an *electric :* and not that, but by adding at the ſame time

an

an equal quantity to the other furface. So that the whole glafs will always have the fame quantity in its two furfaces. And even this can only be done in glafs that is thin: beyond a certain thicknefs we know no power that can make this change. 2. The ethereal fire freely moves from place to place, in and through the fubftance of a *non-eleƈric*. But through the fubftance of an eleƈiric it will by no means pafs. It freely enters an iron-rod, and moves from one end to another, where the overplus is difcharged. But it will not enter, or move through a glafs-rod. Neither will the thinneft glafs which can be made, fuffer any particle of it entering one of its furfaces, to pafs through to the other.

28. Indeed it is only metals and liquids, that perfeƈly *conduƈ* (or tranfmit) this fire. Other bodies feem to conduƈ it, only fo far as they contain a mixture of thefe; accordingly, moift air will conduƈ it, in proportion to its moiftnefs. But dry air will not conduƈ it at all: on the contrary, it is the main inftrument, in confining any eleƈric atmofphere, to the body which it furrounds. Dry air prevents its diffipating (which it does prefently when *in vacuo*) or paffing from body to body, a clear bottle full of air, inftead of water, cannot be eleƈrified. But exhaufted of air, it is eleƈrified as effeƈually as if it was full of water. Yet an eleƈrical atmofphere and air, do not exclude one another.

For

For we breathe in it freely, and dry air will blow through it, without altering it at all.

29. When a glass phial is electrified, whatever quantity of fire is accumulated on the inner surface, an equal quantity is taken from the outer. Suppose, before the operation begins, the quantity of fire contained in each surface, is equal to twenty grains: suppose at every turn of the globe, one grain is thrown in: then after the first stroke there are twenty-one within, nineteen only without; after the second, the inner surface will have twenty-two, the outer but eighteen; and so on, till after twenty strokes, the inner will have forty, the outer none. And the operation ends; for no power or art of man can throw any more on the inner surface, when no more can be taken from the outer. If you attempt to throw more in, it is thrown back through the wire, or flies out in cracks through the sides of the phial. The equilibrium cannot be restored in this phial, but by a communication formed between the inner and outer surface, by something external, touching both the outer, and the wire which communicates with the inner surface. If you touch these by turns, it is restored by degrees; if both at once, it is restored instantly. But then there is a shock occasioned by the sudden passing of the fire through the body, in its way from the inner to the outer surface. For it moves from the wire to the finger, (not from the finger to the wire, as is com-

monly

monly fuppofed.) Thence it paffes through the body to the other hand, and fo to the outer furface.

30. The force with which this fhock may be given, is far greater than one would conceive. It will kill rats, hens, or even turkeys in a moment: others, that are not quite killed, it ftrikes blind. It will give polarity to a fine needle, making it point north and fouth, as if touched by a loadftone. It will invert the polarity of a compafs, and make the north point turn to the fouth. At the fame time the ends of the needles are finely blued like the fpring of a watch. It will melt off the heads and points of pins and needles; and fometimes the whole furface of the needle is run, and appears as it were bliftered, when examined by a magnifying glafs. It will melt thin gold or filver, when held tight between two panes of glafs, together with the furface of the glafs itfelf, and incorporate them in a fine enamel. Yea, a ftrong fpark from an electrified phial, makes a fair hole through a quire of paper doubled: which is thought good armour againft the pufh of a fword, or even a piftol bullet. And it is amazing to obferve in how fmall a portion of glafs, a great electrical force may be. A thin glafs bubble, about an inch diameter, being half filled with water, partly gilt on the outfide, when electrified, gives as ftrong a fhock as a man can well bear; allowing then that it contains no more fire after charging than before,

fore, how much fire muft there be in this fmall glafs! It feems to be a part of its very fubftance. Perhaps if that fire could be feparated from it, it would be no longer glafs. It might in lofing this, lofe its moft effential properties, its tranfparency, brittlenefs, and elafticity.

31. Some have not improperly fuppofed, that all *electric* bodies, fo called, are by their original conftitution, throughly faturated with electric fire : that it remains fixt in them, (unlefs while the texture of thofe bodies is quite altered by liquefaction) that fire fixt in a body conftitutes an *electric*, and all bodies where it is not fixt are *non-electrics*. Agreeably to which they fuppofe, that in all *non-electrics*, the original fire, loofely inhering, is eafily driven on by the new-collected fire, which then poffeffes its place : but that in *electrics*, the original fire being impacted into their fubftance, and therefore more firmly inhering, will not give way to, or be driven on by the new collected fire. Such is air in particular ; with the particles of which the original fire is clofely incorporated. Dry air feems to be fo fully faturated with it, that it is fcarce capable of receiving any more ; whereas all new-collected fire is continually endeavouring to return into the earth. Let wires be electrified ever fo ftrongly, yet the moment any part of them is touched by a perfon ftanding on the floor, they are electrified no longer ; all the fire efcaping through him into the earth.

32. Upon

32. Upon the principles of electricity, we may give a more rational account, of many appearances in nature, than has yet been done: of thunder and lightning in particular. In order to which we may obferve, all electrified bodies retain the fire thrown into them, till fóme non-electric approaches: to which it is then communicated with a fnap, and becomes equally divided. Electric fire is ftrongly attracted by water, and readily mixes with it. And water being electrified, the vapours arifing from it, are equally electrified. As thefe float in the air, they retain the additional fire, till they meet with clouds not fo much electrified. Then they communicate it with a fhock.

33. The ocean is compounded of water, and falt; one an electric, the other not. When there is a friction among the parts near its furface, the fire is collected from the parts below. It is then plainly vifible in the night, at the ftern of every failing veffel. It appears from every dafh of an oar: in ftorms the whole fea feems on fire. The particles of water then repelled from the electrified furface, continually carry off the fire as it is collected. They rife and form clouds which are highly electrified, and retain the fire till they have an opportunity of difcharging it.

34. Particles of water rifing in vapours, attach themfelves to particles of air. One particle of air may be furrounded by twelve particles

of

of water as large as itself, all touching it, and by
more added to them. Particles of air thus loaded
would be drawn nearer together by the mutual
attraction of the particles of water, did not the
fire, common or electric, included therein, affist
their mutual repulfion. Hence they continue fufpended. But if air thus loaded, be compreffed
by adverfe winds, or by being driven againft
mountains, or if it be condenfed by the lofs of
its fire, it will continue fufpenfed no longer,
but will defcend in dew. And if the water furrounding one particle of air comes into contact
with that furrounding another, they naturally
coalefce into a drop, and fo defcend in rain.

25. The fun fupplies common fire to all vapours rifing either from fea or land ; vapours,
having both this and electric fire, are better
fupported than thofe which have this only. For
when vapours rife into the coldeft region, the
common fire may fail. But the cold will not
diminifh the electric ; this is always the fame.
Hence clouds raifed from frefh waters, from
moift earth, or growing vegetables, more eafily
defcend and depofite their waters, as having but
little electric fire, to keep the particles feparate from each other. So that the greateft part
of the water raifed from the land, falls on the
land again. But clouds raifed from the fea, having both fires, and much of the electric, fupport
their water far more ftrongly, and being affifted
by winds, may bring it from the middle of the
wideft

wideſt ocean to the middle of the broadeſt con-
tinent. And yet a way is provided whereby theſe
alſo are readily brought to depoſite their water.
For whenever they are driven againſt mountains
by the winds, thoſe mountains take away their
electric fire; and being cold, the common alſo:
hence the particles immediately cloſe. If the
air was not much loaded, the water falls in dew
on the top and the ſides of the mountain. If it
was the electric fire being taken at once from the
whole cloud, it flaſhes brightly, and cracks
loudly. And the particles inſtantly coaleſcing
for want of that fire, fall in an heavy ſhower.

36. When a ridge of mountains ſtops the clouds,
and draws the electric fire from the cloud firſt
approaching it, the next when it comes near
the firſt, now deprived of its fire, flaſhes into it,
and depoſits its own water. The third cloud
approaching, and all that ſucceed, act in the ſame
manner; as far back as they extend, which may
be for ſeveral hundred miles. Hence the continual ſtorms of thunder, lightning and rain, on
the eaſt ſide of thoſe vaſt mountains, the Andes,
which running north and ſouth, intercept all the
clouds brought againſt them from the Atlantic
ocean. In a plain country, there are other means
to make them drop their water. For if an electrified cloud coming from the ſea, meets in the
air a cloud coming from the land, and therefore
not electrified, the firſt will give its flaſh into the
latter, and thereby both will be made to depoſit

their

their water. The concuffion of the air contri-
butes alfo to fhake down the water, not only
from thofe two clouds, but from others near
them. When the fea and land clouds would
pafs at too great a diftance from each other, they
are mutually attracted till within the diftance.
For the fphere of electrical attraction is far beyond the flafhing diftance. And yet where a
cloud contains much fire, it may ftrike at a confiderable diftance. When a conductor has but
little fire in it, you muft approach very near before you can draw a fpark. Throw into it a
greater quantity of fire, and it will give a fpark
at a greater diftance. But if a gun barrel, when
electrified, will ftrike and make a noife, at the
diftance of an inch, at what a diftance, and with
how great a noife, may ten thoufand acres of electrified cloud ftrike? No wonder that this fhould
melt metals (which our artificial flafh does in
fome degree) though perhaps not fo properly by
its heat, as by infinuating into the pores, and
creating a violent repulfion between the particles
of the metal it paffes through. This overcomes
the attraction whereby they cohere, and fo melts
the metallic body. And this accounts for its
melting a fword in the fcabbard, or gold in the
pocket, without burning either.

37. But thunder-clouds do not always contain
more than their natural quantity of electric fire.
Very frequently they contain lefs. And when
this is the cafe, when they are negatively electrified,

fied, although the effects and appearances are nearly the same, yet the manner of operation is different. For in this cafe, it is really the fire from the mountains, or other parts of the earth which ſtrikes into the cloud; and not, as we imagine, fire from the cloud which ſtrikes into the earth. And we may eaſily conceive, how a cloud may be negatively electrified. When a portion of water is rarefied into a thin vapour, the fire it contains is rarefied too. Conſequently it has then leſs than its natural quantity of fire. Such a cloud therefore coming within a due diſtance of the earth, will receive from it a flaſh of electric fire; which flaſh, to fupply a great extent of cloud, muſt often contain a great quantity of fire. Such a cloud alſo paſſing over woods of tall trees, may ſilently receive ſome ſupply, either from the points of the boughs, or from the ſharp ends and edges of the leaves. The cloud thus fupplied, flaſhes into other clouds that have not been ſo ſupplied; and thoſe into others, till an equilibrium is produced, among all that are within a ſtriking diſtance of each other. And hence are repeated ſtrokes and flaſhes, till they defcend in ſhowers to the earth, their original. Rain, eſpecially when in large drops, generally brings down the electric fire: falling ſnow often; ſummer hail, always, though ſilently. Conſequently, any of theſe may prevent thunder and lightning; or at leaſt, abate its violence. Rain is helpful in another reſpect likewiſe. By wet-

ting

ting men or beasts, it saves many lives. For if your cloathes are throughly wet, and a flash of lightning strikes the top of your head, it will run in the water over the surface of your body into the ground : whereas if your cloaths were not wet, it would go through your body. Hence a wet chicken cannot be killed by a stroke from the phial : whereas a dry one is killed in an instant. See here also the wisdom and goodness of him, *who sendeth forth lightnings with the rain!* It should likewise be observed, that wherever electrified clouds pass, spires, towers, chimneys, and high trees, as so many points, draw the electric fire, and the whole cloud frequently discharges there. Therefore it is highly dangerous in such a storm, to take shelter under a tree.

38. Common fire (if it be any thing more, than a different modification of the same element) is more or less in all bodies, as well as electrical. If there be a sufficient quantity of either in any body, it is inflamed. But when the quantity of common fire therein is small, there needs more electric fire to inflame it. Where the quantity of common fire is greater, less of the electric will suffice. So if spirits are heated, a small spark inflames them. If they are not, the spark must be greater. Sulphureous vapours, whether rising from the earth, or from stacks of moist hay or corn, or any other heated and reeking vegetable, contain abundance of
common

common fire. A small addition of electric then will inflame them. Therefore they are easily kindled by lightning.

39. Any who would be clearly convinced of the nature of lightning, may make the following experiment. Make a small cross of two thin strips of wood, the arms being just so long, as to reach the four corners of a large, thin silk handkerchief when extended. Tie the corners of this to the extremities of the cross: and so you have the body of a kite: add to this a proper tail, loop and string, and it will rise in the air like one made with paper: but this is fitter to bear the wind and wet in a storm without tearing. To the top of the cross fix a sharp-pointed wire, rising a foot above it. Tie a silk ribbon to the end of the twine next the hand: and where the silk and twine join, fasten a key. Raise this kite when a thunder-storm is coming on: but he that holds the string must stand in a porch, or under some other covering, that the ribbon may not be wet. He must likewise take particular care, that the twine do not touch the top or side of the porch. As soon as the thunder-cloud comes over the kite, the pointed wire draws the electric fire from it. The kite and all the twine are then electrified, as plainly appears by this, that the loose filaments of the twine stand out every way, and are attracted by an approaching finger. And when the kite and twine being wet, conduct the fire freely, it will stream from the key, on the

approach

approach of the knuckle. By this key the phial may be charged, and all other experiments made, as by the globe. And this is a demonstration, that the electric fire thereby obtained, is the very same with that of lightning.

40. May not the knowledge of this power in pointed bodies, of drawing off the fire contained in these clouds, suggest to us a very probable method of preserving houses, churches, ships from the stroke of lightning? Might we not fix on the highest part of them, upright rods of iron made sharp as needles, and gilt, to prevent rusting, which otherwise would hinder their free conveyance of the electric fire? From the foot of those rods (which need not be above half a inch diameter) a wire may pass down the outside of the building into the ground; or down round one of the shrouds of a ship, and down her side, till it reaches the water. Would not these rods silently draw off the electric fire, before the cloud was nigh enough to strike? And thereby in a good measure secure us from that most sudden and terrible mischief! Let it not be objected, that the using this probable means of preventing a threatning danger, would imply any denial of, or distrust in Divine Providence. Not at all: we know the Creator of the universe, is likewise the governor of all things therein. But we know likewise, that he governs by second causes: and that accordingly it is his will, we should use all the probable means he has given us to attain

every

every lawful end. It is therefore no more an impeachment of his providence, when we fore-see a ftorm of lightning and rain, to fhelter our houfe (as far as we are able) from the one, than to fhelter ourfelves in that houfe from the other. Is it not juft as innocent (if it be poffible) to keep our rooms tight from lightning, as from wind and water?

41. It may not be improper to add one or two obfervations, before we proceed to what is of more importance. Scarce any phenomenon in nature has been efteemed more difficult to be accounted for, than thofe luminous appearances in the fky, termed *Aurora Borealis*, or *Northern Lights*. But thefe alfo may be rationally ex-plained, upon the principles of electricity. We often fee clouds at different heights, paffing different ways, north and fouth at the fame time. This manifeftly proves different currents of air, one of them under the other. Now as the air between the tropics is rarefied by the fun, it rifes; the denfer air preffing into its place. The air fo raifed, moves north and fouth, and if it has no opportunity before, muft defcend in the polar regions. When this air with its vapours defcends into contact with the vapours arifing there, the electric fire which it brought begins to be communicated, and is feen in clear nights; being firft vifible where it is firft in motion, namely in the moft northern parts. But from

O 2   thence

thence the ftreams of light feem to fhoot foutherly, even to the zenith of northern countries.

42. Another phenomenon of a totally different kind, may be accounted for on the fame principles, although Mr. Prior fuppofes Solomon himfelf to afk, as a queftion which he could not anfwer,

" Whence does it happen, that the plant which well
We name the *fenfitive*, fhould move and feel ?
Whence know her leaves to anfwer her command,
And with quick horror fly the neighb'ring hand ?"

Allowing for poetical amplification, the plain fact is this. The fenfitive plant, as it were, fhrinks away as foon as your hand approaches it. And from a turgid and vivid appearance, inftantly droops and hangs its leaves. Now fuppofe this plant to contain more electric fire than any other plant or animal, it muft of courfe communicate that fire to any other that touches it. And if fo, its leaves and branches muft be in a languid ftate, till they have recovered their natural quantity. To illuftrate this, fet any fmall tree in a pot on a cake of brimftone. Electrify it and it grows extremely turgid, fo as to erect its leaves. But the moment you touch one of them, the whole tree droops, and hangs all its leaves and branches.

To

To throw all the light I can on the subject, I subjoin a few extracts from several other writers.

An extract from Dr. Watson's experiments and observations.

1. When two plates, the one electrified, the other not, were brought near each other, the flashes of *bright flame* were so large, that in a dark room, I could distinctly see the faces of 13 persons. P. 6.

2. A piece of large blunt wire was hung to the conductor. To the end of this, when electrified, a black surface not electrified being brought near, (though not near enough to cause a snap) a brush of *blue flame*, quite different from the former, issued of more than an inch long, and an inch thick. P. 7.

3. If a person strongly electrified lays his hand on the cloaths of one that is not, especially if they are thin woollen or silk, they both feel as it were *many pins pricking* them, as long as the globe is in motion.

4. If oil of turpentine be set on fire in a vessel held by one electrified, *the smoke* arising therefrom, received against a plate held at a foot distance from the flame, by one standing on rosin, will enable him to fire warm spirits of wine. The electric strokes have been likewise felt upon touching the second man, when the plate he

held

held in the fmoke has been between feven and eight feet above the flame. P. 8.

5. Take burning fpirits of wine inftead of oil of turpentine ; and if the fecond man hold the end of an iron rod at the top of the *flame*, he may kindle other warm fpirits held near his finger. Hence we find that either fmoke or flame conducts the electric fire, and does not perceptibly diminifh its force. P. 9.

6. If the wire of the phial be not touched, the electrified water or fteel duft will retain its force many hours, may be conveyed feveral miles, and will afterward exert its force upon touching the wire. P. 16.

7. If an egg is hung on the conductor, and a perfon grafping the electrified phial with one hand, brings the palm of his other near the bottom of the egg, he receives a fmart ftroke on the hand, as with a ferula, and his hand feems full of a more red fire than is ufually obferved. P. 24.

8. Any number of perfons communicating with each other, the firft of whom grafps the phial, and the laft touches the conductor, receives the fame fhock as if it was one only. P. 25.

9. The electric force always defcribes a circuit, and moves in the ftraiteft line it can, between the conductor and phial. P. 26.

10. To prove this, while the machine ftood on wax, I ftood upon the floor; and putting one hand on the machine, touched the gun bar-

rel

rel with the other. Upon this fire iffued, and the fnapping continued as long as I held my hand on the machine, but no longer. This fhewed at once, that the electric fire paffed from the floor through my body to the machine. P. 36.

1 . If the electric fire is not ftopt, no fign of i efence is obfervable in the bodies fufpended to the globe. Though it throws ever fo much of this fire upon them, it paffes from them to the floor whence it came. But if it is ftopt, it is then accumulated in or upon thefe bodies; although this can be done only to a certain degree, after which it continually difperfes. If when it is accumulated, a man ftanding on the floor touches thofe bodies, the fnap is felt, and the fire is feen. But this fnapping is not, when the fire paffes off continually, as from a piece of blunt wire hung to the barrel, and a hand brought near it. Then it appears like a blue cone of flame, with its point towards the wire. When the hand is held at a proper diftance, there is a blaft therefrom, as of cold air. If you do not determine the electric fire to a point, it is difperfed from all parts of the electrified body: but if you do, by thus holding your hand near the fire, you fee how it paffes to the floor, and fo into the earth. The globe therefore only circulates this fire, which is collected by its friction againft the hand or cufhion, and which is conftantly fupplied to thefe from the earth. And accordingly the ingrefs of it, as well as the egrefs is vifible. For, if while any une-

lectrified

ieĉtrified body touches the barrel, you bring your finger near the wood-work of the machine, you will fee the brufh of blue flame fet in from it to the wood-work. And this flame paffes diverging into the machine, and continues as long as the barrel is touched. P. 44.

12. That the electric atmofphere which furrounds all electrified bodies, extends to a confiderable diftance, appears from their attracting a fine thread, at the diftance of fome feet. If no unelectrified body is near, this atmofphere feems to be equally fpread over that which is electrified. But if one unelectrified is brought near, the greateft part of it is determined that way : whence the attraction of the other parts of the electrified body is confiderably diminifhed. This is the caufe of electric repulfion, which does not operate, till the electric ether is fufficiently accumulated. This repulfion is ftrongeft in thofe parts of the electrified body, where unelectrified bodies are brought near it. For by thefe the electric blaft, which otherwife is general, is particularly determined. P. 46.

13. When the machine is placed upon rofin, if a man ftanding likewife on rofin, touches the barrel while the globe is turning, he will receive a fnap or two, and no more. But if he touch the wood-work of the machine with one hand, and the barrel with the other, he receives fnaps again, which continue as long as he touches the machine, and no longer. Here the man by
touching

touching the machine with one hand, becomes
a part thereof; and by turning the globe, part of
the electric fire inherent in his body, is transmit-
ted to the barrel: but it is restored to him, on
his touching the barrel with his other hand. If
instead of touching the machine or barrel, he
holds his finger near either, or both, you see
the fire go out and return. P. 64.

14. May we not gather from the preceding
experiments, 1. That the attraction and repul-
sion of electrified bodies, is owing to the flux of
electric ether? 2. That this ether is no other
than pure fire? 3. That this fire appears in different forms, according to its different modifica-
tions? When brought towards a point is it not a
lambent flame? When nearer still, may we not
both hear and feel it? And does not its lighting
up spirits demonstrate, that it is real fire? 4.
That this fire is intimately connected with all
bodies, though least of all with pure, dry air?
We have extracted it from water, flame, smoke,
red-hot iron; and from a mixture 30 degrees
colder than the freezing point. 5. That it is
extremely subtle and highly elastic? 6. That the
electric machine may as properly be termed a
fire-pump, as Mr. Boyle's machine, an *air-pump?*
And lastly, that fire is not mechanically produ-
cible from other bodies, but is an original, diftinct principle?

An

An extract from Mr. Wilson's *dissertation on* electricity.

Prop. 1. When two bodies equally replete with electric matter approach each other, no flame or snap will ensue. P. 5.

Prop. 2. Two bodies equally electrified repel each other. P. 6.

Prop. 3. An electric body interposed between a person and the earth, prevents his exciting electricity in another body by friction. P. 11.

Prop. 4. If there is originally a certain quantity of electric matter in a body of a given magnitude and density ; and that matter be equally distributed therein, by its elastic force, according to the density of the parts ; upon increasing the quantity of matter by adding other bodies of the same kind, the quantity of electric matter will be increased in the same proportion. P. 14.

Prop. 5. As electric bodies act on light bodies that are not electrified, so unelectrified bodies act on the electric matter contained in electrified bodies. P. 16.

Let a wire be electrified in the dark, and if you hold any unelectrified body 7 or 8 inches from the end of it, a stream of fire will issue from it, which will diverge to that body. But the divergency will lessen as it approaches it, till the rays become parallel. If the body be held not directly before the end of the wire, but wide

of

of it at about two inches diſtance, the fire will de-
ſcribe curvilinear rays towards that body. P. 17.

Hence it appears, that uneleĉtrified bodies
aĉt in like manner with eleĉtrified; only the
aĉting force of the one, being increaſed by friction, is greater than that of the other.

Prop. 6. When two equally electric atmoſ-
pheres are brought ſo near as to touch, they repel each other with a force equal to their denſities. P. 19.

Prop. 7. If while a fluid ſurrounds a globe
which is eleĉtrified and turned round an axis paſſing thro' its center, an uneleĉtrified body be held
near the equator of it, the fluid will riſe ſucceſ-
ſively towards that body, as it turns round, in
like manner as the ſea is affeĉted by the moon.
P. 23.

The ſhock given by the phial is in proportion
to the ſize of it, the thinneſs of the glaſs, and
the number of points in contaĉt with its ſurface.
P. 25.

*An Extraĉt from Mr. Martin's Eſſay on Elec-
tricity.*

1. The eleĉtric *matter* is emitted from ſome
ſort of bodies when rubbed, which are called
eleĉtrics. P. 9.

2. By other ſorts of bodies, therefore termed
non-eleĉtrics, it is not emitted.

3. It will run off to all *non-eleĉtrics,* but is re-
ſtrained by all eleĉtrics.

4. It ſhines like a *flame,* and is emitted with

a ſnap;

a *snap* ; if towards a *non-electric*, the fire is condenſed leſs or more, and ſo appears of a bluiſh, purple, yellow, or white colour.

When the electric fire is not ſo much condenſed as to explode, as in thunder and lightning, it goes off in a dilated ſtream of purple flame, greatly reſembling that part of the *Aurora Borealis*, which appears in ſtreams of light.

When it is little condenſed, it appears *bluiſh*, as all other faint lights do : when a little denſer, it appears *purple* : when denſer ſtill, it looks *yellow*, like candle-light : when highly condenſed, it is clear and *white* like the light of the ſun. So the white lightning is of all others moſt fierce. So phoſphorus rubbed a little, ſpends itſelf in an harmleſs blue flame; but upon a greater attrition kindles into a white flame, and burns with an outrageous and unquenchable fire. P. 17.

And as lightning pervades ſoft ſubſtances unhurt, but diſſolves hard and compact bodies, ſo electric fire pervades the ſoft muſcular parts of the body, but violently ſtrikes the bones and tendons. Again, as thoſe denſer parts of lightning which we call thunder-bolts, ſtriking againſt hard bodies, glance by reflection to different parts, ſo this fire ſtriking againſt the elbow, is reflected from thence acroſs the breaſt, to the other elbow. P. 18.

Indeed different perſons are affected thereby in a very different manner. Some are extremely

capable

capable of it, some not: and some are not susceptible of it at all; a person, for instance, who has the small-pox, cannot be electrified by any means whatever. P. 20.

Experiment 1. On the axis, in the center of my globe, is fixt a circular string of threads. When the globe is at rest, they all hang down; when it is in motion, they all extend themselves from the center, strait toward the inner surface of the globe (like the spokes of a coach-wheel) which they nearly touch. Thus they continue till the electric virtue ceases, and then gradually fall down, as at first. P. 22.

Exp. 2. While they are extended, if you move your hand toward the surface of the globe, they move every way toward the hand. Hence we see the amazing subtlety of this fire, which pervades glass as readily as if nothing were in the way.

Exp. 3. Place a hoop of fine threads round the globe in motion, and all of them will stand perpendicular to the surface. Hence we learn that the electric power acts equally, both within and without the globe, and in directions perpendicular to its surface.

Exp. 4. If the room be then darkened, the ends of the threads on the outside, will be all tipt with fire. But those within are not, which shews that this power acts only *ab intra* outwardly. P. 23.

Exp. 5. An iron rod being hung on silken strings,

strings, with one end about ¼ of an inch from the globe, will at the other end (which terminates in a conical point) emit a purple flame diverging every way. Hold your finger within ¼ of an inch, and the fire will issue more largely. P. 24.

Exp. 6. Hold your finger still nearer, and the rays will be so condensed as to run to it in a stream of yellow flame ; which is also sensible to the feeling, as a gentle wind, and smells like the fire of phosphorus.

Exp. 7. If you put your finger on the-rod, the flame instantly disappears, the fire all runing off upon the finger. But take it off, and the flame appears again.

Exp. 8. Apply your finger near a tin tube so suspended, and you may see the fire, and both hear and feel the snap. P. 25.

Exp. 14. Under an electrified plate, put some leaf-gold or other light substances on another plate unelectrified : and it will be attracted and repelled alternately, between the two plates. For, each time it touches the lower plate, it discharges the electric fire, and so becomes again attractable. P. 28.

Exp. 18. If to a gun barrel you adapt a small tin cup, and pour in water ; a person holding his finger perpendicular over the water, within ¼ of an inch of its surface, will find the water rise in form of a cone to meet his finger, and from

the

the top of it, a ſtream of fire will iſſue to the finger and ſnap as uſual. P. 30.

Exp. 19. A dry ſpunge is an *electric*. But if it be dipt in water, and then hung on the barrel, put your finger near it, and the fire iſſues out, and the drops which before fell very ſlowly, will now fall very faſt. If the room be darkened, they will appear as drops of fire. P. 31.

Exp. 20. A ſyphon hung on the cup, drops very gently till it is electrified; but then the water runs in a ſtream, which in the dark is like a ſtream of fire.

Exp. 21. Open a vein in a perſon ſtanding on the roſin, and the blood will fly out to a certain diſtance. But let him be electrified, and it will ſpin out with a much greater force, and to a far greater diſtance.

Exp. 24. If mercury be put for water, the electric force is ſomething greater, but in no proportion to its denſity.

Exp. 25. When the mercury is ſaturated, the electric ſtreams will iſſue thro' the wire more copiouſly than from the phial of water, and will ſnap of themſelves, which the ſtreams iſſuing from the water ever do.

Exp. 27. The electrified phial will not retain the fire very long; but if you hold it up in a dark room, it will be ſeen to go off from the point of the wire, in a ſmall white flame. P. 34.

Exp. 30. A cup of water held by an electrified

fied perfon will emit fire more forcibly than
his body. P. 35.

Exp. 32. A perfon ftanding on the ground,
cannot eafily kifs an electrified perfon ftanding
on the rofin. P. 36.

Exp. 38. If a fquare piece of leaf-gold be placed between two plates, about two inches afunder, one of them electrified, the other not, at
firft it will be attracted, and repelled alternately,
till in a while it will lofe its motion, and remain
fufpended between them. P. 39.

Exp. 42. If the globe be exhaufted of air,
and then turned, the electric fire will act wholly
within the globe, where it will appear (in a dark
room) as a reddifh or purple flame, filling the
whole globe. But this, as the air is re-admitted
into it, will gradually difappear. In this cafe,
the electric fire is confined within, by the elaftic
air on the outfide. P. 40.

*An extract from Mr. Watkins's account of electrical
experiments.*

When the machine is to be ufed, the globe
fhould be wiped clean, with a clean, dry, warm
flannel, its pivots oiled, and the cufhion and
phial warmed. In damp weather there fhould
be a fire in the room. P. 4.

Exp. 4. Let an unelectrified plate, with fcour-
ing fand upon it, be held 5 or 6 inches under
an electrified plate, and the fand will be fo attracted

tracted and repelled, as to resemble a stormy shower. P. 16.

Exp. 7. If a glafs ball, of 4 or 5 inches diameter, be hung by a wire to the gun-barrel, and a ball of ¼ of an inch diameter, exceeding thin, placed on a fmooth plate, be brought near it, this will not only be attracted by the large ball, but will perform continual revolutions round it, exactly as the planets do round the fun. P. 22.

Exp. 9. Hang a loadftone on the barrel, and a key on the armature of it : and if you bring your finger near the key, it will fnap and emit fire. A plain proof that the electric and magnetic power no way hinder each other. P. 25.

Exp. 35. A fparrow killed by the electri fhock, was found livid without, as if killed with a flafh of lightning, and moft of the blood veffels within were burft. Animals fhocked on the head, if not killed, are commonly ftruck blind. P. 55.

Exp. 41. Ice held by an electrified perfon, will fire warm fpirits of wine. P. 61.

Exp. 43. Mr. Watfon put an ounce of oil of vitriol, an ounce of iron filings and four ounces of water, into a flafk. An ebullition enfued. An electrify'd perfon applied his finger to the mouth of the flafk. The vapour took fire, and burnt out of the neck a long time. P. 63.

From an experiment made by Mr. Watfon, and others, it appeared, that the electric fire circu-

lated

lated, without interruption, from the Surry fide of the Thames over Weftminfter-bridge, to the Weftminfter fide, and thence through the river to the Surry fide again, which is upwards of 800 yards. Spirits of wine alfo were fired at the fame diftance.

From this, and feveral other experiments, it appeared, that diftance, fimply confidered, did little, if at all, impair the force of the electric fhock.

They afterwards conveyed this fhock through a circuit of four miles, and found the motion of the electric fire to be nearly, if not quite inftantaneous.

II. I have been hitherto endeavouring to make electricity plain : I fhall endeavour in the fecond place, to make it ufeful.

1. This ethereal fire, in its unmixt ftate, feems too violent an agent for the human body to bear. Therefore the wife author of nature has provided the air to temper and adapt it to our ufe. So tempered, it is the grand inftrument of life : " it gives and preferves," fays bifhop Berkeley, " a proper tone to the veffels. It promotes all fecretions, keeping every part in motion : it pervades the whole animal fyftem, producing great variety of effects, various vibrations in the folids, and ferments in the fluids." Indeed from many, experiments we know, it communicates activity and motion to fluids in general, and particularly accelerates the motion of the blood in an human body.

body. This is quickened three or four pulses in half a minute, by a person only standing on glass, and being electrified. And it is certain many bodily disorders may be removed, even by this safe and easy operation.

2. But because plain matters of fact weigh more than nice speculative reasoning with all who do not obstinately steel themselves against conviction, I shall, first, briefly specify several disorders wherein electrification has been found eminently useful, and then subjoin a few particular instances.

3. The disorders in which it has been of unquestionable use, are,

Agues,   Gravel,
St. Anthony's fire,   Head-Ach,
Blindness, even from a   Hysterics,
   Gutta Serena,   Inflammations,
Blood extravasated,   King's Evil,
Bronchocele,   Knots in the flesh,
Chlorosis,   Lameness, Leprosy,
Coldness in the feet,   Mortification,
Consumption,   Pain in the Back, in the
Contractions of limbs.   Stomach,
Cramp,   Palpitation of the heart,
Deafness, Dropsy,   Palsy, Pleurisy,
Epilepsy,   Rheumatism,
Feet violently disorder'd, Ringworms,
Felons,   Shingles,
Fistula Lacrymalis,   Sprain,
Fits, Ganglions, Gout,   Sciatica,

                                      Surfeit,

Surfeit,	Toe hurt,
Swellings of all kinds,	Tooth-ach,
Throat-fore,	Wen.

It will be eafily obferved, that a great part of thefe are of the nervous kind; and perhaps there is no nervous diftemper whatever, which would not yield to a fteady ufe of this remedy. It feems therefore to be the grand *defideratum* in phyfic, from which we may expect relief when all other remedies fail, even in many of the moft painful and ftubborn diforders to which the human frame is liable.

I have fcarce known an inftance wherein a few fhocks all over the body, have failed to cure either a *quotidian* or *tertian ague*.

Anne Heathcote, daughter of Mr. Heathcote, brazier, in Long-Alley, near Moorfields, was feized, in May laft, with what is commonly called an *ague in the head*, having a violent pain in her head, face, and teeth. After trying abundance of remedies to no purpofe, fhe was, in Auguft, electrified through the head. Immediately the pain fixed in her teeth. She was electrified four times more, and has felt nothing of it fince.

4. " Having obferved," fays Mr. Lovet, " the great efficacy of electrical ether, in foon relieving moft kinds of *inflammations*, I was inclined to think the fame efficacy would appear when it was applied to *St. Anthony's fire*. But when a cafe offered, the inflammation was fo great, that

at

at firft I almoft defpaired of fuccefs. About noon I made the firft trial, by drawing off fparks while the perfon was electrified, on the rofin. Before night, the angry fwelling was much appeafed, and in a few days quite cured."

5. A boy about feven years old (fays Mr. Floyer, a furgeon in Dorchefter) was taken blind fuddenly in both his eyes, without any previous pain or fever. Three or four days after, he was brought to me. He was as blind as if his eyes had been cut out. Taking the cafe to be a perfect *gutta ferena* in both eyes, I told his parents, it was my opinion he would never fee again. However I determined to try the electric fhock: and the next morning, faftening a wire coming from the phial to his legs, and another round his head, I brought the latter near the conductor, and gave him four fhocks fucceffively. That day he was put to bed and continued there, fweating profufely, till the next morning, when he agreeably alarmed his father by crying out, he could fee the window. When he was brought to me the fecond time, he could fee when I put my hand between his eyes and the light of the fun. This gave me encouragement to repeat what we had done the day before. The next day he could a little contract and dilate his eyes; the third day he could diftinguifh objects; the fourth, colours. The fifth day, after repeating the experiment, his fight was perfectly reftored, and the eyes, in every refpect,

as

as well as if no diforder had happened to them.

6. From a gentleman in Newcaftle-upon-Tyne, I have the following account. Laft week a poor man in Sandgate, that had been blind twenty-four years, was led to the machine. I fet him upon the electrical board, and drew fparks for about twenty minutes from the pupil of his eye. After he had refted himfelf a little, and was able to look up, he told us he could fee Sidgate, which he had not feen for many years before. He could alfo diftinguifh objects in the room, and was able to walk home without a guide. He came a fecond time, and was fo much better, that I imagine he did not think it neceffary to come any more.

7. He adds, about the time I wrote laft, a young woman was cured of a fourteen years blindnefs. She was able, before fhe went home, to diftinguifh one letter from another.

8. From the fame perfon, a few days after-wards, I received the following lines.

" The cure of the blind man of Newcaftle, has fpread through all the country ; in confe-quence of which, I am, much againft my will, become an oculift.

" I have had feveral in hand, and among the reft a girl, about feventeen, has been with me about three weeks. Her cafe is owing to a film, or fkin, grown over her eyes. It came by the fmall-pox about twelve years ago. Her friends have

have had all the advice, and ufed all the means in their power, but to no purpofe; except that fhe has loft her left eye irrecoverably, by one of the perfons they applied to.

"When fhe came to me, the *iris* of the right eye alfo was very near covered with a very thick fkin, fo that fhe could do very little more than diftinguifh day from night. It was grown much worfe this winter, and was fo blood-fhot and angry, that I told her mother I could do nothing for her. However fhe made fuch a lamentable complaint, that I confented to try.

"The method I have taken, is drawing fparks from her eye, and fometimes giving fhocks from her head or neck, down her arm, to carry off the frequent complaints of pain and dizzinefs in her head; which never fails of fucceeding in about ten minutes. We have electrified her about half an hour twice every day. The fkin waftes gradually, and grows thinner and lefs every day; fo that now the colour of the eye appears through it, except in the middle, and towards the nofe, where the film at firft feemed twice as thick as the reft. The other day, as I had her under hand, fhe faw the buttons of my fhirt fleeve, and of my coat; and yefterday faw the teeth of one of her companions that was laughing at her. But her eye is fo weak, that I advifed her to make very little ufe of it yet."

"A perfon having a dark lived fpot under his eye from a blow three days before, it was, in
lefs

lefs than a quarter of an hour, quite taken away, by drawing the fparks from the parts." Mr. L.

Here *extravafated blood* was manifeftly diffolved and reforbed into the veffels. I have lately known an inftance of this kind. One, whofe eyes were almoft beat out, as they term it, by the fame operation, loft all the fwelling, and the blacknefs too, in twelve minutes.

10. " A woman troubled with a *bronchocele*, the moft obftinate of all fwellings, whofe neck was eighteen inches and one half about, is already fo far relieved, that the largeft part of her neck is but fifteen inches and an half about, the fmalleft not thirteen. And the fwelling now waftes fo faft, that there is hopes of a perfect cure." Mr. L.

" She applies the wire from the phial to one fide of the fwelling, and laying one end of another wire to the other fide of it, then guides the other end of that wire to the electrical apparatus."

11. William Jones, a plaifterer, living at Mr. Frazer's, in King-ftreet, Seven Dials, fell from a fcaffold on Thurfday, Feb. 15 laft. He was grievoufly *bruifed*, both outwardly and inwardly, and lay in violent pain, utterly helplefs, till Saturday in the afternoon, when he was brought (carried) by two men to be electrified. After a few minutes he walked home alone, and on Monday went to work.

Mary Ofgathorp had her foot *bruifed* by a
ftone

ſtone falling on it, which occaſioned a running
fore. It continued, though frequently healed
for a time, upwards of eight years: but was entirely healed a month ago by electrifying, and
has never broke out ſince.

12. A number of moderate ſhocks daily repeated for ſome time, effectually cure *coldneſs in
the feet*. It does not fail.

13. Angus M'Innon, of Lincoln's-inn-fields,
was afflicted with a violent cough, till his
ſtrength was waſted away, and he had all the
ſymptoms of a true *conſumption*. He was electrified three times about eighteen months ago,
and reſtored to perfect health.

Elizabeth Collis, a child of twelve years old,
living with Mrs. Wragg, in Windmill-ſtreet, was
ſo far gone in a genuine *conſumption*, that ſhe was
judged to be quite paſt recovery. This ſummer
ſhe was electrified four times, and has been
quite well ever ſince.

14. A man at Upſal in Sweden, whoſe knee-
joint had been *contracted* above five years, (originally from an ill-cured rheumatiſm) was quite
reſtored by drawing off ſparks daily for a few
weeks.

15. " Mrs. M—— D——, of Worceſter,
was long afflicted with a moſt violent *cramp* in
her legs. This diſorder ſeized her before ſhe
was twenty years of age, and continued till ſhe
was upwards of ſeventy. It was moſt violent
when ſhe was in bed; at which time ſhe was

forced to tumble out on the floor, sometimes twice or thrice in the same night. It was attended with exquisite pain, bursting the small blood-vessels, which afterwards appeared of a livid hue for a considerable time.

" She was intirely cured in a few days, by being electrified once a day, thus. Having taken off her shoes, she put one foot on the end of the chain, which came from the charged phial, putting the lower end of a wire to the other foot; so that this being touched, both legs might receive the shock at once." Mr. L. I never once knew it fail in this disorder.

16. *Deafness* rising from hardened wax, or following a fever, is cured by only drawing off sparks. This was frequently tried at Upsal. At Stockholm, a gentleman of distinction, who had been almost *deaf* a considerable time with a singing in his ears, was perfectly cured in three or four minutes.

A young man, who had almost lost his *hearing* for six months, by violent vomitings, which forced blood out of his ears, was perfectly cured in a few minutes.

Samuel Jones, gardener, at Lambeth-Marsh, in the year of the great frost, leaped into the Thames to save a man from drowning. Hereby he became so deaf of both ears, that he could not hear any sound at all, were it ever so near, or ever so loud. In February last, after being once electrified, he could hear the noise of a

coach

coach at some diftance. After the third time, he could hear the found of the machine. He came no more; fo it is fuppofed he is well.

A man, fifty-feven years old, who had been deaf for thirty-two years, was fo far relieved in a few days, as to hear tolerably well.

A girl of feven, born deaf, (who confequently could not fpeak) began prefently to hear words which were fpoken very loud in her ear, and could repeat fome of them in a few days.

I have known hearing hereby given to a man born deaf.

17. "In May 1738, came to me one Mary Smargins, born in the ifland of Nevis, in the Weft-Indies, 28 years old. She had been fo *deaf* (from a cold at firft) for feventeen years, as not to hear any one, unlefs they were very near and fpoke loud. Her deafnefs had no intervals. She always heard the leaft with the left ear. On Saturday, May 28, the phial being electri- fied by two turns of the wheel only, I applied one wire to the left temple, juft above the ear, the other to the oppofite temple. She felt a fmall warmth in her head, chiefly from ear to ear. I repeated it four times, a little ftronger each time. The warmth increafed at each fhock, and though I ftruck her at each ear alternately, fhe always felt moft warmth at the deafeft ear. At laft fhe complained of fmall twitchings in her ears, chiefly in that ear, and crofs her head. No other part of her body felt the fhocks. The

warmth

warmth increased all day with twitchings at intervals. The next morning I repeated the experiment, which then affected her arms and body also. The twitchings were more violent; the warmth greater round the ears, chiefly the deafer ear. These effects continued all the day, and she heard confiderably better. But toward evening, by fitting in an open window, she catched cold: on which the warmth left her, and she felt very chill all over her body. On Monday she was extremely ill, with pains all over her. On Tuesday she was much better, and felt the fame kind of warmth round each ear again. On Wednesday the noife and beating in her head, which she had had from the firft of her deafness, much abated. In the evening a violent shooting went a-crofs her head, from the left to the right ear. On Thurfday I repeated the experiment. Some minutes after, blowing her nofe, there issued corrupted matter with a finall quantity of clotted blood. From this time she had little noife or beating in her head, and heard perfectly well.

She had a great cold, and her eyes were much inflamed, when I began the experiment. But after the firft day's experiment, the inflammation decreafed, and after the fecond, was wholly removed.

I was able at firft to bear the ftrongeft fhocks. But after repeating them fome weeks, I could hardly bear a finall fhock: and a ftrong one occafioned eafioned a violent convulfion of the mufcles of my arm and body.

Upon rubbing with my hand a globe, while turning, I have feveral times felt a violent head-ach. But it always went off upon difcontinuing the rubbing. I have known many perfons, who found an unufual pain for fome days after receiving the fhock." Thus far Mr. Wilfon.

I am furprized at this. For I never yet knew any perfon, man, woman, or child, fick or well, who found any fuch inconvenience. Only I have known rheumatic pains increafe on the firft or fecond trial, which were afterwards perfectly cured.

Mary Baker, chairwoman, aged 27, living at Mrs. Hunt's, in Neal's-yard, near the Seven Dials, having been long ill of a *dropfy*, was admitted laft year into St. George's hofpital. But on November 28, fhe was difcharged out of it as incurable, as fhe was alfo from the Weft-minfter infirmary. In fpring laft fhe was electrified, and foon after parted with feveral gallons of water. After being twice more electrified fhe was well, and able again to earn her living.

18. It is of great ufe in the *epilepfy* or *falling ficknefs*; unlefs it be hereditary, and then it does at leaft no harm.

The following cafe feems to have been of the *epileptic* kind. E—— T——, of Worcefter, was troubled with a very uncommon diforder, for ten or eleven years. The contraction ufually

P 3 began

began under her left breaſt, and darted thence to her right, and back again to her left breaſt and ſhoulder. It then ſtruck down to her elbow, wriſt and fingers, which were inſtantly ſo contracted, that if ſhe had not time to catch up ſomething in her hand, the nail of the forefinger would ſo wound the thumb, as to make the blood run down. The contraction likewiſe twiſted and drew her hand behind her, turning it up again to the ſhoulder. The intervals of this terrible diſorder were uncertain : ſometimes ſhe had eaſe for a month; ſometimes ſhe was taken twice in a day. It would yield to no medicine, but was by this method entirely cured in a few weeks. She ſtood on the wire, coming from the phial, and then touched the apparatus with a finger of the hand affected. By this means the fire circulated the neareſt way, through the body to the arm and fingers. This was ſeveral times repeated to each finger. Mr. L.

19. Sarah Betteſworth, aged 22, then living in Cow-Lane, was ſome years ſince ſeized with ſuch violent fits, that five or ſix men were ſcarce able to hold her. In autumn 1756, while ſhe was in one of them, the apothecary being aſked by her maſter if he ſhould electrify her ? Made light of it. However he did ſo, applying the bottle to one ſhoulder as ſhe lay on the ground, and the wire to the other. On the firſt ſhock her ſtruggling ceaſed, and ſhe lay ſtill. At the ſecond her ſenſes returned. After two or three
more‘

more, she rose in good health. Some months after she relapsed, and was electrified again, and again entirely cured. Last Easter she fell into a fit again, through a fright, but by a few shocks was cured and restored to health.

William Matthews, schoolmaster, aged thirty-two, living at the Foundery, near Moorfields, had epileptic fits (supposed to be hereditary) from his birth, till he was six years old. Thence he was free till thirteen. They then returned on occasion of a fright, and continued so to do twice or thrice in a year, till he was seventeen. From that time, they came almost every month, till the year 1753; since then they usually returned about once in ten or eleven weeks. In the middle of March last he began to be electrified, both through the head, and from head to foot. April 4, he had a slight fit, but from that time to this, Nov. 1, has had none at all. Can all England afford such a cure as this, wrought by a course of medicines?

20. " John Webb of Worcester, seventy years of age, was much *disordered in his feet* for ten or twelve years. The pain resembled that of the gout : and such a coldness attended it as was scarce supportable. If he warmed them by the fire, they raged still more, as also when they began to be warm in bed. The nails of his toes very frequently dropt off : the toes in general appeared livid ; and frequently large black or bluish spots were formed at the end of

them,

them, or on the top and fides of his feet. Thefe when they firft came, were exceedingly painful; but after a time grew dry and hard. His heels likewife were generally puffed up like blown bladders.

" All thefe complaints gardually decreafed, till they totally went away, by his being electrified once a day for fome time, and afterwards twice a week. At firft only fparks were drawn. Afterwards the chain was brought from the phial to the part affected of one foot; then one end of a wire was laid to the part affected of the other foot, and the other end of it brought to the conductor." Mr. L.

21. Felons are fpeedily cured by drawing fparks. If any diforder be fuperficial, this operation fuffices: but if it lie deeper, then the giving of fhocks is found to be more effectual.

22. " Ann T—— had a *fiftula* near the inner corner of her eye, which healed and broke again feven times. The laft time it healed, it continued well for fome time. After which it began with a fmall fwelling, till it was as big as a filbert. Form the time fhe was electrified, by drawing off fparks, it gradually decreafed, till it was entirely diffipated." Mr. L.

Eliz. Johnfon, daughter of Mr. Johnfon, gunmaker in the Tower, was taken on New-year's-day laft, with fharp pains in her bowels, which foon threw her into *convulfion fits.* Thefe returned

ed five or six times a day, for ten or eleven
days. She was electrified all over, and had no fit
for eight months. She was then frighted into a
fit. She was again electrified, and continues
well.

23. " A young lady had been affected with
fits near seven years, which seized her without
any warning, and threw her flat on her face,
quite insensible. These frequently returned twice
in a day. This was attended with almost a continual coldness in her feet. Her stomach also was
much affected. She stood upon a wire coming
from the coat of the phial, and to complete the
circuit, another wire was laid upon her head,
by which means the fire was conveyed to that
part. By this means both the fits and coldness
were gradually removed, and a complete cure
effected." Mr. L.

24. " Elizabeth B——, near the Old Hills,
a few miles from Worcester, had for fifty years
been afflicted with severe fits. They threw
her down to the ground, quite insensible, sometimes twice or thrice a day. She had tried many
remedies, but to no purpose. From the latter
end of the year 1752, she received several
shocks. An inveterate head-ach, which attended
her, quickly decreased, and in some months
her fits too totally ceased." Mr. L.

25. Electricity was tried at Upsal in three
cases of a *Ganglion*, which it perfectly dif-
persed.

26. Slight

26. Slight attacks of the *gout* are suddenly and effectually removed, by drawing sparks from the part affected.

" A person, who within the space of two or three years had several attacks of the *gout*, since the first of which, he had always a stiffness and pain in the joint of óne of his great toes, and for a considerable time in both, was quite cured, by setting him on rosin, while one on the floor drew sparks from the diseased parts." Mr. L.

William Sinnock, cabinet-maker, in Lombard-Court, Seven Dials, was in Feb. 1758, seized with sharp pains in his feet, which continued three months, and for six weeks disabled him from doing any work. They returned in February last. He was electrified twice, and has felt no pain since.

Thomas Willis, chairmaker, aged 44, was for many years afflicted with the *gravel* in the kidneys. In July last he was electrified twice. After the second time he parted with a large quantity of gravel. He was electrified twice more, and has not found the least complaint since.

27. In very bad fits of the *head-ach*, I have often, says Mr. L. used this remedy with surprizing success.

" A man of Bromsgrove, afflicted for near a fortnight with a violent and constant *head-ach*, was twice electrified by a few light shocks, with half an hour's interval, and entirely cured." Mr. L.

A——

A——— T——— of White-chappel had a violent head-ach, which continued for feven or eight weeks. After fhe was electrified the pain increafed for three hours. It then gradually decreafed, till fhe was quite well. This proves that it may remove even a diforder, which at firft it feems to increafe.

28. Samuel Rennee, aged feven, the fon of Richard Rennee, weaver, living in York-ftreet, by taking cold, was feized with a violent *head-ach*, which continued with fhort intermiffions for above a year. Tuefday, March 8, 1757, he was moderately electrified all over. The pain left him from that hour.

29. " A man who had a fixed pain juft above his eye-brow for feveral days, was by little fhocks at the part, cured in a few minutes; fo was Mr. Higgins, of Worcefter, of a *periodical head-ach*, which commonly began at five or fix in the evening, and affected him from the top of his right temple to his ear, till he went to bed. This was cured only by drawing fparks." Mr. L.

" M———t D———s was afflicted with an almoft conftant, as well as violent pain in the *hinder part* of her *head* for near three quarters of a year; efpecially when fhe lay down in bed, being then fo intolerable, fhe could not forbear fhrieking. Having ufed many other means with no effect, fhe was electrified once a day. This prefently relieved (fometimes by fparks, fometimes light

P. 6   fhocks)

fhocks) and in fome weeks perfectly cured her."
Mr. L.

" E—— T—— wss troubled for eleven years
with a fevere *head-ach*, which baffled all the efforts of medicine. By moderate fhocks applied
to her head, fhe was cured in a few weeks."
Mr. L.

30. Abigail Brown, aged 22, then living in
Red-Crofs-ftreet, was from a child frequently
afflicted with a violent *head-ach*. In October
1757, fhe was electrified five days fucceffively,
having one wire applied to the fore part, another
to the hinder part of the head, and receiving
feven or eight fhocks each time. Hereby fhe
was entirely cured, nor has found any pain in
her head fince, unlefs occafionally for want of
fleep.

Sarah Webb, wife of Mr. Webb, Tallow-
chandler in Grub-ftreet, aged 46, was from 20
years old, fubject to a violent pain on the top of
her *head*. This frequently obliged her to keep her
bed, nor could any remedy for it be found. In
December laft fhe received gentle fhocks from
temple to temple, and from the forehead to the
back of the head. This was done three days fucceffively, and fhe was entirely cured.

31. Richard Outen, rope-maker, aged 23,
living in Bunhill-row, was troubled with a violent *head-ach* over the eyes, before he was ten
years old, arifing from a blow on the head. He
was fcarce free from it a month together for above

12

12 years. It uſed to throb and ſhoot through the head, ſo that often he was almoſt diſtracted. In December 1756, he was electrified once, receiving three ſhocks, by one wire applied to the forehead, and another to the back of the head. He was worſe than ever for ſome hours, till he went to bed, but awaked in the morning perfectly well: and has continued ſo ever ſince.

32. In deep *hyſterical* caſes, the perſon ought to ſit on the roſin at leaſt half an hour every morning and evening. At firſt ſparks may be drawn off; and afterwards ſhocks given, more or leſs, as the diſorder requires. This would ſeldom fail of the deſired effect, as may well be ſuppoſed from the following inſtances.

" A young gentlewoman, about ten miles from Worceſter, ſometime after ſhe recovered from a fever, was ſeized with violent *hyſterics*, which ſoon deprived her both of memory and underſtanding. The fire was conducted through her head by ſparks and ſhocks ſeveral times a day, during the week ſhe ſtayed at Worceſter: in which time not only her memory, but her underſtanding was perfectly reſtored.

" Mrs. Higgins, of Worceſter, was troubled for above ten years with an *hyſterical* diſorder, and a *coldneſs in her feet*. From thence that coldneſs moved gradually up to her head, in half a minute's time, which then ſeemed a palſy in the head. Soon after her teeth would chatter as in a violent ague. Thence the ſhaking proceeded

ed

ed to her arms, and whole body, and was fo violent, (as hyfterics mimic moft diftempers) as to
refemble St. Vitus's Dance.

" Sometimes fparks were drawn, fometimes
fhocks were given ; and fhe ftood near half an
hour daily on the rofin. In lefs than a fortnight the fits went entirely off ; and in a while
after, the coldnefs of her feet " Mr. L.

33. A perfon had rigid *knots* in the thigh like
what appear in violent cramps, but not fo hard or.
painful. Thefe were entirely diffipated in a
minute or two, only by drawing fparks.

34. One at Upfal who had *loft the ufe of his
limbs* from cold, for feveral years, was in fome
weeks quite reftored.

One at Stockholm, who had ufed crutches for
feven years, could walk without them in thirteen
days.

Eliz. Buttle, nurfe, aged 31, living in Fether-
ftone-ftreet, in May laft, felt fuch a pain round
her ankle-bone, that fhe could fcarce fet her foot
to the ground. This grew worfe and worfe
for about a month. In June fhe was electrified
feven times round the ankle and thrice upon the
knee. Immediatly her *lamenefs* ceafed, with the
pain that occafioned it.

35. Mary Lallo, aged 25, then living in St.
Thomas the Apoftle's, when fhe was a child,
was taken with a pain in the bone of the left leg
from the knee to the bottom of the foot, which
then felt as if a great weight had been faftened

to

to it. This continued by intervals for many years. Frequently she could not walk without holding some one, and then in great agony. In February 1757, she received several small shocks on the knee, within four or five minutes. The pain instantly ceased. She walked home quite well, and has continued so ever since.

A girl also of 13, who after the small pox had been *lame* from four years old, having been electrified about twenty times walked without a staff.

" A young lady from a strain in the knee-joint, or rather the crural ligament, was quite disabled from walking. About three quarters of a year after, when she came to me, the muscular part of the leg was much fallen away, and a continual coldness attended the foot.

" I ordered her to sit on the rosin at least half an hour daily, and to receive several shocks thro' the disordered part of the knee. The first month there was little effect. In the next there was a visible alteration for the better ; the third she could walk a few steps without any crutch or staff. In the following month, she seemed quite well, and left off electrifying : but after a time relapsed. After the relapse, the progress of the cure was more tedious, and it was four or five months before she could leave her remedy quite off." She was then totally cured. Mr. L.

36. " A young woman drinking at a cold spring when very hot, was seized with a kind of
fever

fever for a quarter of a year. Many red spots then appeared on her arms, and soon after a thin dry crusty substance, which appeared rather as scales than scabs, from her elbows down to her fingers. This *leprous* disorder (which many call a *surfeit*) continued near three years. Indeed it lessened the first and second winter; but the third was the same as in summer.

"By drawing sparks once a day from the parts affected, in three weeks or a month, all the scales disappeared." Mr. L.

37. "A gentleman in Worcester had a *mortification*, which began in his toe, and in spite of all the means used, gradually increased. He was *shocked*, and the mortification stopped: but on his neglecting this, it began again; and increased so far that the case seemed desperate. Yet on his being *shocked* again through the mortified part, such a change appeared as astonished the surgeon, who owned it had done more good in two days than had been done in six weeks before." Mr. L.

38. A clergyman near London had from a child almost a constant *pain* in the lower part of his left side. He was once electrified by standing with his left foot on the chain, and has never felt the pain since.

James Kitely, of Lambeth, had a sharp *pain* in his left side about three years. After being electrified three or four times, the pain left him, and came no more.

Mary

Mary Burgis, living at the Tun in Knaves-Acre, had a *pain in her side* for seven years. In May last, she was entirely cured the first time of electrifying.

Michael Hayes, of King-street, Westminster, aged 86, had a violent *pain* in his left ankle for near four years. This sometimes disabled him from walking, which otherwise he could do without any difficulty. He was electrified through the part, and perfectly cured before he left the room.

39. Eleanor Story, living in Clerkenwell Church-yard, catching cold, was seized with *pain* and *weakness* in the small of her *back*, as if it had been broke. By following the prescriptions of Dr. L. the pain after a fortnight settled in her shoulder. There it continued so violent, that often she had scarce any use of her arm. She afterward used abundance of remedies for above two years, but all to no effect. On Tuesday March 21, 1757, she received two strong shocks on each shoulder, which made the skin red and sore. That night she was in more pain than usual, trembled all over, and could get little sleep. The next morning she received several shocks all over, and so on Thursday morning and evening. After the second time her pain was gone, and she had the full use of both her arms.

John Reed, cabinet-maker, in Warder-street, was for six years afflicted with violent *pains* in the back of his neck. In spring 1758, he was

elec-

electrified about thrice a week for a month, and quite cured.

40. Jofeph Jones was taken about March 12, 1757, with a violent *pain in the flomach*. He received the fame day a few gentle fhocks. The pain went off, and returned no more.

Mary Peltecree, warper, living in Primrofe-ftreet, was troubled fix months with a *pain in her flomach and back*, accompanied with extreme weaknefs and faintnefs, which made her incapable of her work. By the advice of a phyfician, fhe took many medicines, but with no effect. Five weeks ago fhe was electrified, receiving the fhock through the ftomach. This was done for five days fucceffively. She has been perfectly well ever fince.

H—— W——, throwfter, aged 23, living in Fleet-ftreet, Bethnal-green, not being regular, was taken a year ago with a violent *pain in her flomach*. She had the advice of a phyfician, and took many medicines, but to no purpofe. At length fhe was electrified, nine or ten days, and is in perfect health.

Ann Wild, of Round-Court, by taking cold in childbirth, contracted a violent *pain in her flomach*. After it had continued four years, fhe was perfectly cured by twice electrifying.

Mrs. Edwards, living in Nottingham-Court, Short's-Gardens, was ill of a *pain in her flomach* for eight years. It often took away her reft,

as

as well as appetite, and brought her to the gates of death. By once electrifying she was cured.

Eleanor Taylor, mantua-maker, aged 48, living in King-street, Oldstreet-square, was taken in September 1758, with a violent *disorder in her stomach*, which felt as if it were ready to burst, and often made her sweat to her fingers ends. This continued for upwards of four months, and gave her little rest day or night. In February following she was seized with the rheumatism, throughout the left side. For this, having quite lost the use of her left arm, she came to be electrified. She felt the shock chiefly in her stomach; and her disorder there was cured. After three days she was electrified again, and cured of the rheumatism also.

A gentlewoman in London had an almost continual *pain in her stomach*, more or less for eight years. She received one shock on her stomach, and was well from that moment.

41. Silas Told, schoolmaster, aged 48, living in Christopher's-Alley, Moorfields, in the year 1741, had a pleuretic pain, for which he lost an unusually large quantity of blood. Immediately he was seized with a strong *palpitation of the heart*, which continued, more or less, without the intermission of one day, for more than sixteen years. In February 1757, while I was electrifying for a *pain in my stomach* (which was wholly removed by one shock) he came in and said, " My heart is very bad, and I think I will

try

try it too." He did fo, receiving a fhock through the breaft, and has been ever fince perfectly well.

42. A citizen of Upfal, who was thoroughly *paralytic*, was perfectly cured only by drawing fparks.

April 18th, 1756, a remarkable cafe happened at Edinburgh. Robert Moubray, in the beginning of January was ftruck with a *palfy of the tongue*, and foon after entirely loft the ufe of his fpeech. Laft week he began being electrified, and by Saturday he was able to put out his tongue, which before was dead and motionlefs. On Monday he could fpeak a little, and on Tuefday he could fpeak as well as ever.

Thomas Dobfon, leatherpipe-maker, aged 27, living in Barnaby-ftreet, was feized with a *palfy in the tongue*, on July 24th laft. It grew worfe and worfe till Saturday 28, and then quite deprived him of his fpeech. He was electrified for five days, by drawing fparks from the tongue, and fhocking him all over. And hereby not only his palfy was cured, but convulfions alfo, which he had had for four years.

" Mr. P. had a year or two ago a flight touch of a *palfy*. On a fudden his arm dropped down, quite without ftrength; and though after chafing it well, he recovered the ufe of the upper and middle joint, yet the lower part was ftill fo weak, that he could by no means write his name. But

by

by a few fhocks in the arm he was effectually relieved.

" The fame perfon had lately a much worfe
ftroke. All his right fide was fo affected, that he
could not walk without two to fupport him. After he had been electrified three times, he could
walk with the fupport of one only, and in a
fhort time he was perfectly well. He ufed
to ftand on the chain with the right foot, and
touch the apparatus with his right hand."
Mr. L.

I have not yet known any inftance of this
kind. Many *paralytics* have been helped: but,
I think, fcarce any *palfy* of a year ftanding has
been thoroughly cured.

43. A gentlewoman in London, who for feveral years was never long together without
fharp pains in her knee, which feemed chiefly
rheumatical, was freed from them in a moment
by one fingle fhock.

John Ramfay, cabinet-maker, living in the
Strand, by being very wet, catched a violent
cold, in the latter end of June 1756. This occafioned a *rheumatic pain*, which fixed in his
left knee. From this he was feldom free for a
week together till November. He was then very
ill till February, being feldom able to do above
half a day's work, femetimes none for a week
together. He was for ten weeks an out-patient
of St. George's Hofpital; but received no benefit. On Monday the 21ft of March he was
elec-

electrified through the knee, and four times more within seven days. The pain was removed, and his sleep, which had been long lost, returned, as before he was first taken.

Ann Walter, servant, aged 22, then living in Brick-Lane, Spittlefields, was cured entirely of a violent *rheumatism* in her left arm, by being electrified five times.

A stone cutter at Stockholm, whose knees and joints of his toes had been rendered stiff, and his fingers crooked by a mixture of *gout* and *rheumatism*, after being electrified a few days, was able to go to work. It has been found to remove or greatly abate all *rheumatic* pains.

Ann Cambell, living in Queen-street, Seven Dials, had a severe *rheumatism* fourteen weeks. For nine weeks she could not dress herself, nor get out of bed without help. She had the advice of several physicians, but in vain. In spring, 1758, she was electrified five times, and thereby restored to full health.

William Tyler, living at the Sun in Long-lane, Smithfield, was on March the 9th last, about three in the morning, seized with *rheumatic pains*, chiefly on his right side, so violently, that he was as helpless as an infant, and was frequently constrained to shriek out, like a woman in labour. I came before nine. After the second shock he felt some change: after the third he was able to raise himself a little. After two

more

more he rofe and walked about the room, and before noon he was quite eafy and well.

Sarah Guildford, aged 37, living on Saffron-hill, was for upwards of feven years fo afflicted with the *rheumatifm* in her right fide, that the knee and ankle were wafted exceedingly. January the 2d laft fhe was electrified, and perfectly cured in one day. But it threw her into a profufe fweat, particularly from thofe parts which had been moft affected.

Ann Cardiff, fervant, at the Golden Head, Iflington, aged 40, about fixteen years ago, was taken with a violent *rheumatifm*, by catching cold in lying-in. It returned every year, and the laft winter took away the ufe of her limbs. She followed the advice of feveral phyficians, till they pronounced her incurable. October the 15th laft fhe was electrified, firft by general fhocks, then through the parts moft affected. The firft and the fecond time it made her extremely weak and faint. The third time fhe was better, and after nine times all her weaknefs and pains were gone.

Margaret Virgin, filk-winder, aged 39, living in White Horfe-yard, Seethin-lane, was troubled with the *rheumatifm* before fhe was ten years old, and more and more till when fhe was about twelve fhe was confined to her bed for near twenty-one weeks. From that time fhe was feldom free from it, fo that many times fhe was quite incapable of bufinefs. Laft winter fhe was

fo

fo ill as to be forced to quit her work, not being able to lift an arm to her head. In January fhe was electrified twice: the firft time all over: the fecond time through the left arm. The ufe of her arm was immediately reftored. Her pains entirely left her, ever fince fhe has been more capable of any kind of work than fhe had been for twenty years.

Mary Trumble, of White Crofs-ftreet, aged 49, began to be afflicted with the *rheumatifm* before fhe was 30 years of age. It returned in her fhoulders or head every winter: and for the three winters laft paft fo increafed, that fhe could by no means turn either arm behind her, and was extremely pained. Laft winter it was worfe than ever. A little before Chriftmas fhe received five or fix fmall fhocks. Immediately, fhe was eafy, recovered the full ufe of both arms, and has retained it ever fince.

William G. of the Little Minories, London, had been violently afflicted with the *rheumatifm* many years. For feveral winters he was not able to work. But after having received a few fhocks, in a quarter of an hour all his complaints vanifhed away, and he was afterward as well in winter as in fummer.

44. Almoft all kinds of *inflammations, ring-worms, tetters, fhingles*, as well as moft kinds of *fwellings*, may be totally cured by drawing fparks only.

45. A lad at Stockholm, who had a fevere
fciatica

sciatica in the right hip, so as not to bear being touched, was cured in a few days.

John Ellison, then an officer of excise, living in Hunt-street, Spittlefields, was, upon catching cold, seized with a violent *sciatica*, which held him several months without intermission, and frequently almost took away the use of his limb. In August 1754, he was electrified, receiving two shocks. His pain raged the more for four or five hours; but afterwards entirely ceased. And from that time to this he has been perfectly well, without the least relapse.

" Mr. R—— S—— of Worcester, troubled with a *sciatica* for some years, was cured at once by shocks conveyed to the parts affected." Mr. L.

Mary Butler, aged 86. living in Eagle-street, Red Lion-square, having been afflicted with the *sciatica* for more than twenty years, was last month electrified ten or twelve times, and has been easy ever since.

It seems the electric fire in cases of this and of many other kinds, dilates the minute vessels, and capillary-passages, as well as separates the clogging particles of the stagnating fluids. By accelerating likewise the motion of the blood, it removes many obstructions.

46. Thomas Nevil, weaver, aged 26, living at the bottom of Vine-Court, Spittlefields; when about 16 years of age, *sprained* his loins so violently, that from that time he found a continual

weaknefs, frequent pains and an inability to do any hard work. On Thurfday, March 10th, 1757, he was electrified, receiving five or fix fhocks thro' the parts affected. When he went home he felt no pain, but much forenefs on the part, on which a red fpot appeared, like a fmall pin's head. But the next morning he was perfectly well, and has been ever fince ftronger than before the firft hurt.

Francis Halfpenny, Taylor, aged 30, living in Redcrofs-ftreet, Southwark, when about 18 years old, had a fall from a tree. By this he received fuch a fprain, that he could not walk twenty yards, unlefs exceeding flow, without a gnawing, aking pain down his thigh. About the middle of September laft he was electrified thro' the upper part of the thigh. This was repeated at five or fix different times. The firft fhock removed the pain down to the knee. At the third electrifying it went quite away. And fince that time he has been full as well as he was before his fall.

47. " E—— H——, of Tedny, had a very painful *fwelling* in the ball of her great toe for fome years. Having made ufe of many other means in vain, fhe was at length electrified. After the firft operation (by drawing fparks) the pain was much abated : and in a fhort time the fwelling difappeared and the pain left her."

" Mr. Jofhua W—, of Perfhore, was troubled for feven or eight years with a pain in his
second

fecond toe. Tho' nothing was to be feen, it was as tender as a boil, and the pain was fo great, particularly in walking, that he at length determined to have it cut off. By drawing fparks he was cured in an hour."

"A gentleman of Worcefter, ran a bodkin into the fide of his hand, near the fore and middle fingers. The wound was no more than a prick of a large pin, yet in three or four days a *fwelling* came both in the palm and on the back of the hand.

"The fifth day a furgeon was called, who for three months dreffed both the infide and the outfide of the hand to no purpofe. A cauftic was then applied; but with no more fuccefs than all the other means.

"Finding no alteration, nor likelihood of any, he was electrified twice (by drawing off fparks) on the infide of his hand, at the bottom of the middle finger. In four days it broke, and in about three weeks healed." Mr. L.

Jane Davifon, quilter, aged 26, living in Quaker-ftreet, had about fix years ago a violent tooth-ach, which occafioned a *fwelling* in her right cheek. This continued gradually increafing on the infide of the cheek, till it grew into an hard flefhy lump. Defpairing of any help, fhe let it alone, till laft month fhe was perfuaded to be electrified. She received feveral ftrong fhocks thro' the part. After this was done the firft time the fwelling not only increafed exceedingly,

but

but was violently painful. The next day, the
other cheek likewife fwelled, and that fwelling
fpread thro' the upper lip, acrofs the mouth.
Neverthelefs fhe was electrified again. Two
or three days after it broke, and for two days
together, difcharged abundance of purulent
matter mixt with blood. But in a few days
the wound was entirely healed, and all the fwelling gone.

48. " E-----T------, taking cold, was feized
with a *fore throat*, which grew worfe and worfe
for fix days. She then could not fwallow even
a bit of bread foaked in tea. The fame morning
fhe was electrified, fo as to direct the fhock in
a right line thro' the part affected. By the time
fhe got home fhe could eat any thing. Two
fhocks more made a perfect cure."

49. " The *tooth-ach*, if proceeding from a
fcoibutic habit, from hollow teeth, or from a
defluxion of rheum, is prefently affuaged or totally removed by this remedy.

" This may frequently be done by drawing
fparks from the tooth or cheek: in more flub-
born cafes, by moderate fhocks. The fooner
you touch the phial, the weaker the fhock; fo
that you may leffen or increafe it at pleafure.

" In giving the fhock, the moft effectual way,
is, to bring one wire under the chin and tooth,
(if it be on the under-fide) and lay the end of
the other wire on the top of the tooth. If it be
on the upper-fide, bring one wire to the top of
the

the head over the tooth, and apply the other to the bottom of it." Mr. L.

Sarah Ellifon, the wife of John Ellifon, above-mentioned, catched cold in lying in, which fixed a fharp pain in her teeth, and the fide of her face. She ufed all manner of means to remove this for upwards of fix years. Among many others, fhe had at feveral times, three teeth drawn, and was fourteen times bliftered, but without effect. In July 1754, fhe received fix fhocks through her head. The pain ceafed immediately, and returned no more.

50. " A perfon had a fwelling, fuppofed to be a _wen_, between the neck and the fhoulder-blade, as big as an egg, and nearly as hard, which had been growing to that fize for feveral years. She had not been electrified many times (by drawing fparks for five or fix minutes every day) before it began to foften. Soon after it difcharged a thin humour through a fmall orifice, and continued difcharging and foftening more and more, till it was entirely diffipated." Mr. L.

51. Whoever defires to fee a more circum-ftantial account of many of the preceding cafes, with the names of moft of the patients and their places of abode, may confult Mr. Lovett's trea-tife. It is wrote not only with admirable judg-ment, but with an excellent fpirit. A principle of benevolence to human kind may be eafily ob-ferved to breathe through the whole: nor can any lightly condemn it, but thofe whofe intereft

Q 3

naturally

naturally leads them to decry whatever would leffen their own gain.

52. After relating thefe cures. Mr. L. himfelf adds, " I cannot deny but I was almoft aftonifh-ed, at feeing fuch mighty things performed by electricity. But after having attentively confi-dered the nature of electric ether, its great fubtil-ty and power, its active and enlivening qualities, and its mighty tendency to accelerate the mo-tion of the fluids in general, and of the blood in particular :" (I would add, and to pervade the fineft arteries and nerves, to dilate their obftruct-ed or contracted orifices; as well as to reftore the tone of any mufcle or fibre, which is either impaired or deftroyed :) " I concluded that all thofe furprizing effects were no more than the neceffary confequences of fo powerful an agent, when thus determined, and directed. And the helping us in our bodily infirmities, was one great end it was ordained to ferve," (probably the great end) " after it had been thus fully and plainly difcovered to us."

53. It were greatly to be wifhed, that the gen-tlemen of the faculty would ftrictly examine the nature, properties, and effects of this fovereign remedy. For fuch it unqueftionably is, parti-cularly in nervous cafes; even in thofe cafes, which the common *Materia Medica* will in no wife reach. But it is not to be expected. They muft not difoblige their good friends the apothe-caries. Neither can it confift with their own
intereft,

intereſt, to make (although not every man) yet ſo many men their own phyſicians, which would be the unavoidable conſequence, if a regular ſyſtem of practical rules were formed from a proceſs of experiments, whereby a ſenſible man might judge in what caſes it would cure, and in what not : and in what manner it might be moſt effectually applied in any caſe wherein it was proper.

In order to prevent any ill effect, theſe two cautions ſhould always be remembered. Firſt, let not the ſhock be too violent ; rather let ſeveral ſmall ſhocks be given. Secondly, do not give a ſhock to the whole body, when only a particular part is affected. If it be given to the part affected only, little harm can follow even from a violent ſhock.

For inſtance. In a *paiſy of the tongue*, the ſhock may he given to the tongue only by applying one wire to the hinder part of the neck, and another to the tongue. And if in any caſe there be danger of too great a ſhock, it may eaſily be prevented.

It is highly probable, a timely uſe of this means might prevent before they were thoroughly formed, and frequently even then remove ſome of the moſt painful and dangerous diſtempers : *cancers* and *ſcrophulous tumours* in particular, though they will yield to no other medicine yet diſcovered. It is certain, nothing is ſo likely, by accelerating the contained fluids, to dilate

and

and open the paffages, as well as divide the coagulate! particles of the blood, that fo the circulation may be again performed. And it is a doubt, whether it would not be of more ufe, even in *mortifications*, than either the bark or any other medicine.

Before I conclude, I would beg one thing (if it be not too great a favour) from the gentlemen of the faculty, and indeed from all who defire health and freedom from pain, either for themfelves or their neighbours. It is, that none of them would condemn they know not what; that they would hear the caufe, before they pafs fentence; that they would not peremptorily pronounce againft electricity, while they know little or nothing about. Rather let every candid man take a little pains, to underftand the queftion before he determines it. Let him for two or three weeks (at leaft) try it himfelf in the above-named diforders. And then his own fenfes will fhew him, whether it is a mere play-thing, or the nobleft medicine yet known in the world.

THE
CONTENTS
Of the *Twenty-fourth* VOLUME.